Mail Superiority

How to Run a Profitable Annual Direct Mail Fundraising Program

Mail Superiority

How to Run a Profitable Annual Direct Mail Fundraising Program

Alan Sharpe

Andrew
Spencer
Publishing

Published by Andrew Spencer Publishing

38 Wethered Street
London, Ontario, N5Y 1G9

Library of Congress Cataloging-in-Publication Data

Sharpe, Alan.

Mail Superiority: How to Run a Profitable Annual Direct Mail Fundraising Program
/ Alan Sharpe.
p. cm.— (The Hands-On Fundraising Series)

Includes index.

1. Direct-mail fund raising. 2. Nonprofit organizations—Finance I. Title. II Series.

ISBN 978-0-9784053-6-6

First edition

First printing

Manufactured in Canada

9 8 7 6 5 4 3 2 1

Contents

INTRODUCTION xiii

PART ONE **Why Direct Mail Fundraising is So Powerful** 4

1. Why You Must Master Direct Mail Fundraising **4**
Eighty percent of your income comes from individuals 4
Most individual donors start with a small gift 5
Direct mail is expensive 5
Direct mail is difficult 5

2. Three Goals of Direct Mail Fundraising **6**
Goal #1: Acquire new donors each year 6
Goal #2: Renew your donors each year 7
Goal #3: Upgrade your donors 9

3. How a Direct Mail Fundraising Program Works **10**
Direct mail fundraising is a program, not a series of mailings 10
Runs for 12 months 12
Repeats every 12 Months 14
Is characterized by incremental improvements through testing 15
Direct mail fundraising works by building a broad base of support 16

4. What You Need to Succeed in Direct Mail Fundraising **18**
You need a case for support with broad appeal 18
You need new donors you can reach cost-effectively 19
You need dedicated fundraising software 20
You need an obsession with your data 21
You need a dedicated team 22
You need a commitment to donor-centered fundraising 23
You need a commitment to brand differentiation 26
You need a commitment to segmentation 27
You need frequency and volume 27
You need a commitment that lasts for decades 28

5. Fourteen Reasons Strangers Respond to DM Acquisition Letters **31**
Reason # 1: They hunt for meaning in life 31
Reason # 2: They want to meet an immediate need 31
Reason # 3: They want to receive a personal benefit 31
Reason # 4: They want to join others in a worthy cause 32
Reason # 5: They want to achieve status 32
Reason # 6: They are angry 32
Reason # 7: They are altruistic 32
Reason # 8: They are idealistic 32
Reason # 9: They give for religious reasons 33
Reason # 10: They give to solve a problem 33
Reason # 11: They give to save on taxes 33
Reason # 12: They give to achieve immortality 33
Reason # 13: They give to reduce guilt 34
Reason # 14: They give because they're fearful 34

PART TWO **How to Acquire New Donors with Direct Mail** 36

6. How Direct Mail Donor Acquisition Works **37**
Direct mail donor acquisition loses money initially 37
Direct mail donor acquisition needs a popular cause to succeed 39
Direct mail donor acquisition needs volume to succeed 40
Direct mail donor acquisition needs other mailings to succeed 40
Four tests to see if direct mail donor acquisition is right for you 41

7. Eight Steps for Acquiring Donors with Direct Mail **44**
Step #1: Develop your case for support 44
Step #2: Clone your best donors 45
Step #3: Find the names of potential donors 47
Step #4: Create a package 52
Step #5: Test the package against your lists 53
Step #6: Rollout 56
Step #7: Follow up with new donors 56
Step #8: Measure your results 58

8. How to Get the Most from Direct Mail Donor Acquisition **60**
Mistakes to avoid 61
Why donors stop responding to direct mail appeals 62
How donor acquisition integrates with your annual campaign 63
Easy ways to reduce donor attrition rates 63
Save money on direct mail acquisition mailings through testing 64

9. How Donor Acquisition Mailings Differ from Donor Renewal Mailings **66**

PART THREE **Anatomy of a Donor Acquisition Package** 70

10. Anatomy of a Donor Acquisition Package **70**
Outer envelope 72
Letter 75
Brochure 89
Reply device 97
Survey 103
Reply envelope 105

11. Why Donor Acquisition Letters are Longer **107**

PART FOUR **How to Renew Your Donors with Direct Mail** 110

12. Why You Must Renew Your Donors **112**
Avoid donors who never renew 115
Donors demand three things before they give again 117

13. Thank-you Letters, Cards and Notes **118**
Four reasons you must mail thank-you letters, cards and notes 118
Thank your donors using the four P's 120
Anatomy of an effective thank-you letter 126

14. Before You Ask Again, W-I-N Them **129**
Welcome your donors 129
Involve your donors 132

Give your donors News 133

15. Use Newsletters to Boost Donor Loyalty **136**
Nine common donor newsletter mistakes to avoid 137

16. How to Craft Fundraising Letters that Renew Donors **141**
Four goals of renewal letters 143
Mail a series of renewal appeals 145
Think friends, not funds 146
Treat donor groups differently 147
Treat high, medium and low donors differently 147
Spend time and money on your most promising donors 147
Think recency, frequency and monetary value 147

PART FIVE **Testing, Tracking and Analyzing with Confidence** 170

17. Your Data Never Lies (but it Misleads if You Let it) **152**

18. Testing Your Donor Acquisition Package **156**
Goal #1: Test as many lists as possible 156
Goal #2: Acquire as many donors as possible 156
Goal #3: Recover your costs 157
Goal #4: Discover which acquisition package performs best 157
Goal #5: Discover if direct mail is a cost effective way for your organization to acquire donors 157
Create your test package 157
Choose lists to test 158
How to budget for a typical mailing 160

19. Tracking Your Results **163**
Rule #1: Test things that are significant 165
Rule #2: Test things you can control 165
Rule #3: Make your test large enough to be significant 165
Rule #4: Test one thing at a time 165
Rule #5: Don't let large gifts skew your results 166
Rule #6: Acquire loyal donors in greatest numbers at lowest cost 166
Rule #7: If starting out, acquire as many donors as possible 166
Rule #8: Test every time you mail 166
Test prospect lists 167
Test the size of the initial gift in your ask string 167
Test premiums, front and back end 167
Test involvement devices 167
Test outer envelopes 168
Test personalization 168
Test the length of your letters 168
Test new packages 168
Avoid these mistakes 169

20. Analyzing with Confidence **170**
#1: Cost per thousand 170
#2: Cost per piece 170
#3: Response count 171
#4: Response rate 172
#5: Gross income 173

#6: Net Income 174
#7: Average gift 174
#8: Average cost per gift 175
#9: Return on your investment 175
#10: Cost to raise a dollar 176
#11: Cost to acquire a donor 177
#12: Net income per thousand pieces 178
#13: Renewal rate 178
#14: Attrition rate 179
#15: Donor loyalty 181
Direct Mail Fundraising Return On Investment 182

21. Response Rates to Expect in Direct Mail Fundraising 185

PART SIX **Planning Your Year** 188

22. Ask Early, Ask Of ten, Ask the Right Way 190

23. What Should You Mail? 196
Acquisition letters 196
Newsletters 198
Renewal letters 201
Major donor letters 204
Lapsed donor recovery letters 205
Special appeals 207

24. How to Plan a Typical Mailing 208
Working backwards from your drop date 208

PART SEVEN **Keys to Your Success** 212

25. Divide and Conquer 214
Segmentation 214
Concentrate on your best donors 216

26. Build Your List Three Ways 218
Method #1: Build Your List Yourself 218
Method #2: Rent A List From Someone Else 218
Method #3: Use A List Broker To Create A Custom List 219

27. How List Brokers Can Help Your Appeal 220
A typical list rental transaction 220

28. How to Upgrade Your Donors Over Time 222

29. Increase Your Average Fundraising Gift By Segmenting Your File 224

30. Improve Donor Tenure and You'll Boost Revenue 226
Learn from the for-profit world 226

31. Answers to Common Questions 228
Q. How many times a year should I mail my donors? 228
Q. When should we drop people them from our mailing list? 228
Q. How can we save money with donors who rarely give? 229

32. 41 Things You Can Mail to Your Donors 231

33. A Helpful List of DM Fundraising List Brokers and Managers 235

Glossary of Direct Mail Fundraising Terms 237

Index 251

About the author 257

Introduction

A couple of years ago the executive director of a non-profit organization phoned my office. His non-profit was in trouble. For the first time ever they were running a deficit. He had to turn the organization around. One area he decided to work on was his direct mail program.

They had been running a program for many, many years, and the executive director was suddenly anxious because his direct mail program was suddenly losing money. He asked me to audit his direct mail program.

He hired me to look at his database and look at his mailings and look at his schedule of mailings. Basically he asked me to look at his direct mail fundraising program from start to finish, and make some intelligent observations about what he was doing right that he should keep doing, what he was doing wrong that he should stop doing, and what he was not doing that he should start doing. Those are the three things I try to help people with when they hire me as a consultant.

So I looked at his mailings for the last five years. I looked at what he had mailed throughout the year, the appeals, the newsletters, the thank-you letters. I looked at the time of year that he mailed them. I looked at the content of each package. I looked at how much money he asked people for. I looked at his database. How many new donors he'd acquired each year, how much it cost to raise a dollar, how much it cost to raise a donor, and so on.

Basically, I did all the things in an audit that we're going to look at in this book. And then I presented my findings. I tried to be gracious.

First of all, I told him what he was doing right that he should keep on doing. I said, "You have a direct mail donor acquisition program, and that is good. Unlike some organizations, you're consistently using direct mail to acquire new donors. Congratulations!"

I also said, "In your acquisition program, you've been mailing letters every year for five years, and you've been acquiring new donors. Well done!" I also congratulated him that he had the courage to lose money initially on donor acquisition, while acquiring new donors, which is a good sign because you rarely break even on donor acquisition. It takes some intestinal fortitude to lose money with a view to making money later on.

But then I had some bad news. I had to say, "This is something you're doing now that you need to stop." And the bad news was that this executive director's donor acquisition program had not made any money for five years. It had acquired donors but those donors had not given enough money in five years to even pay for the cost of their acquisition mailing.

So the fundraising flow of money was actually going the wrong way. Instead of money coming from the donors to the organization, the organization was spending money to keep in contact with these donors—which is obviously a losing proposition. It makes no sense to acquire donors every year if after a few years it costs you money to keep them on board as donors rather than those donors paying for themselves and giving you some net revenue.

So he was shocked.

He knew that his program was in trouble and he knew that he needed a little bit of help, but he was absolutely astounded to discover that for five years he had been mailing packages to strangers with a view to acquiring them as donors, and that some of those donors had come on board, he'd managed to acquire them, but not a single one of them had paid for himself or herself. In all those five years.

Not only that, but he had never looked at his direct mail fundraising program in terms of return on investment. What we discovered was that five years previously, before I conducted my audit, his return on investment for his renewal mailings (letters mailed to existing donors) had been around 1,500 percent.

And for every year since that up until the day that I did my audit he had been losing money, and his return on investment had been dropping and dropping and dropping. It was now only 600 percent. So his return on investment was less than half of what it was five years previously.

He was startled. But, as a result of this audit, he was able to take some constructive steps to do something about this problem he faced. I don't know if he's been able to turn his direct mail fundraising program around. He resigned, and someone else took his place, and I haven't been in touch with them for a while.

All of this is my way of introducing you to the cold reality of direct mail fundraising. You need to know what you're doing or you can lose money and you can lose donors. Easily.

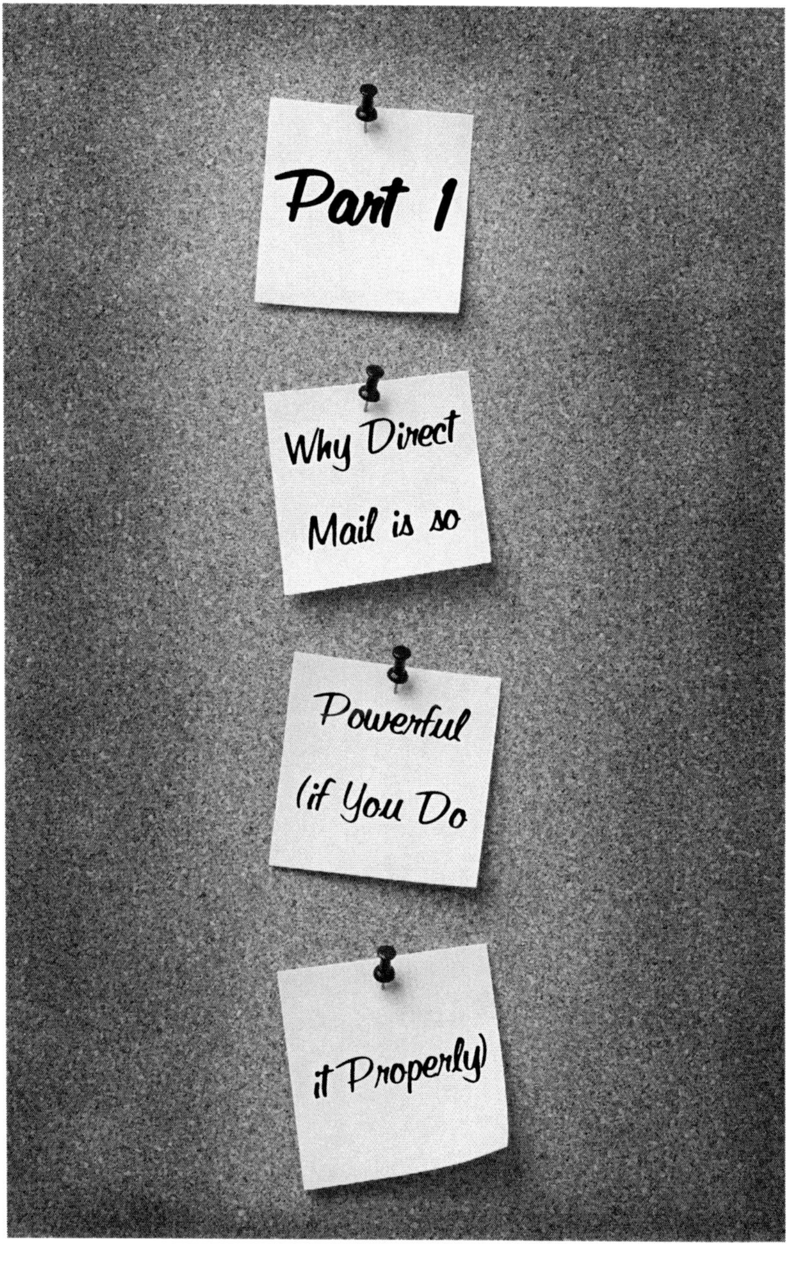
Part 1
Why Direct
Mail is so
Powerful
(if You Do
it Properly)

1

Why You Must Master Direct Mail Fundraising

If you ask your database administrator what percentage of your income you get from foundations and from government and from businesses, maybe even churches or religious organizations, and how much you get from individuals, you will likely find that you get 80 percent of your income from individual donors.

Not foundations.

Not businesses.

Not government.

But ordinary individuals.

Eighty percent of your income comes from individuals

And if you look at your average direct mail gift you'll probably discover that it's around $35, $45, maybe $50. The average is about $35. So you can see that if you get 80 percent of your income from individuals and if the majority of those individuals give to you by direct mail, and if the average gift is around $35, then you need many, many, many individual donors in order for you to run a profitable direct mail fundraising program.

In other words, you need a broad base of individual support for your existence. You certainly want to attract money from foundations and businesses and government, but for the long-term survival of your non-profit, you need to build a large following of individuals, individual supporters who send you a small gift at least once a year.

The most cost-effective way to build that broad base of support is a comprehensive, well-planned, well-executed, annual fundraising letter program. I'll just repeat that. The most cost-effective way to build a broad base of support is to run a comprehensive, well-planned, well-executed annual fundraising letter program. This is what this book is all about.

Most individual donors start with a small gift

Another reason that you should master direct mail fundraising is that most individual donors begin their support with a small gift of around $35. And so if you're hoping to get any kind of donor to stay with you for some length of time, you have to remember that most donors start small. And direct mail fundraising is an effective way to get a small gift from somebody.

If you go through your database again and look at the people who give you large amounts of money over time, and even people that give monthly, you'll discover that many of them began as direct mail donors.

They might have come to your organization through a walk-a-thon or a telethon or a special event, but the chances are pretty good that the majority of them that give in a major way today, or that have given you a bequest in their will or taken out a planned giving instrument, started as direct mail donors.

Direct mail is expensive

Another reason you must master direct mail fundraising with a comprehensive program is that direct mail is expensive. It costs money to put direct mail fundraising packages in the mail. Sometimes it will cost you $1 a package.

So if each package costs you a dollar and if you have 10,000 donors then that's a $10,000 mailing. And if it doesn't produce very well for you, you can lose money. It's not that hard to lose money in direct mail fundraising. So you need to be efficient. And you need to be effective.

Direct mail is difficult

It's not that hard to lose donors every year. Or to lose money every year. Or both. That executive director that I mentioned was going about his program the way that he had done for years and he hadn't changed much. His letters stayed much the same. His newsletter stayed much the same.

But the marketplace changed—and he didn't notice. And so he began to lose donors and he began to lose money. And before he knew it, he was in trouble. Direct mail is difficult and direct mail is expensive. And that's why you need to master it.

2

Three Goals of Direct Mail Fundraising

If your organization is typical as a non-profit, you lose around 15 percent of your donors each year. They simply stop responding to your appeals. In many cases it won't be your fault. Some of them die. Some of them move. Some of them lose their jobs. Some of them retire. And you don't have a great deal of control over those things.

It could be that you neglect your donors or you don't thank them enough or often enough or show them enough gratitude, so they drift away and go elsewhere. You do have some control over that, which we'll discuss later.

This process of losing around 15 percent of your donors each year is called "donor attrition," and a great deal of the time it's through no fault of their own. Now, 15 percent is an average. And it might not sound like that much but it's a terrifying percentage all the same.

Just imagine that you have 10,000 active donors today. If you lose 15 percent of them this year then you will lose 1,500 donors. So how many years would have to go by before you had no donors left? It wouldn't be that long, just through basic donor attrition. This goes on every year.

Goal #1: Acquire new donors each year

So because you lose around 15 percent of your donors every year, it's important that you create and manage a well-planned annual donor acquisition program.

In other words, you must have a program in place so that you annually acquire or make friends with new donors, new supporters, new members, to replace the ones you lose.

"Donor acquisition" sounds a little clinical. Another way to put it is simply that you try to make new friends every year.

You can see that if you lose 15 percent of your donors every year, then you obviously can't afford to simply mail to your existing donors only—because you'll be mailing to a smaller and smaller group every year. You need to replace the donors who never renew. In other words, if you have a donor that gives one year and then gives in the next year and then doesn't give in the third year, you have to replace that donor just to stay where you are.

Without a steady influx of new donors you'll be moving backwards every year. Not forward. So you need a direct mail donor acquisition program that acquires enough donors just to replace the ones that fall away— roughly 15 percent of your active donors. And if that's all you did then you would just keep your donor file at the same number that it is today.

But I imagine you want to grow your file and grow your revenue, so you need an acquisition program that goes beyond merely replacing those donors who fall away, and we'll soon look at how you do that. So Goal 1 of your direct mail fundraising program is to acquire new donors. You can't just tread water in the same place and hope you'll do all right—because you won't.

Goal #2: Renew your donors each year

Goal 2 of your direct mail fundraising program is to renew your donors each year. Or another way to put this is that you retain your friends. You keep your friends. You don't acquire them one year and lose them the next year.

On the west coast of the U.S., in California, there's a direct mail fundraising agency called Mal Warwick and Associates. Their president is Stephen Hitchcock. And he wrote a book on direct mail fundraising, a very good book, called *Open Immediately! Straight Talk on Direct Mail Fundraising*. And if you read that book you'll discover that about 65 percent of donors that are acquired by direct mail give one gift and never give again.

That's another scary statistic. Let me just repeat that. Sixty-five percent of donors that come on board or join your organization through direct mail, because you mailed them a direct mail letter, will give you one gift and then they'll fall away and never give again.

In other words, only 35 percent of donors acquired by direct mail ever renew their support. What this means is that the most important gift in direct mail fundraising is not the first gift but the second one. You don't want your direct mail fundraising program to always be in acquisition mode, where you're acquiring donors in large numbers who then fall away the next year and never give you a second gift.

You'll remember my friend, the executive director. He was acquiring donors every year, yes, but they were falling away and never giving him enough money over time to even pay for themselves, never mind bring in any net revenue.

So the most important gift in direct mail fundraising is not the first one but the second and the third. You're looking for repeat gifts in the same way that you're looking for friends that stay with you over time. What's vital over the long term isn't the first mailing that acquires your donor, although that's obviously important. That's obviously a vital letter that you mail. You need to acquire donors in the first place.

But what's more important than that is your second mailing, or even your third and your fourth mailing to that donor, the mailing that keeps the donor. A healthy annual direct mail fundraising program includes a series of mailings. They're called "renewal mailings" on the smug assumption that fundraisers have that our donors should renew their support every year.

If you subscribe to Time magazine, Newsweek, Harpers, People magazine—any magazine—your subscription lasts for a year. And as your subscription begins to run out, they send you reminder notices to let you know that your subscription is about to lapse, and that you need to renew your subscription.

Member-based organizations like Greenpeace and Amnesty International, where you actually are a member of the organization and not simply a donor, have membership programs where you're expected to renew your membership. So it's kind of natural that you get a membership renewal letter from these member-based non-profits.

Well, it helps you in direct mail fundraising to look at your overall program as one that requires you to renew your supporters every year. The idea is that every donor gives you at least one gift a year and in that way renews her support. That's what you should be aiming for in direct mail fundraising.

Goal #3: Upgrade your donors

You have a third goal in direct mail fundraising, and that is to upgrade your donors over time. First you acquire them. Then you renew them. Then you build a lasting friendship with your donors.

Remember that most people start supporting a non-profit organization by making a small donation. It might be a gift of $25, $30, $40. Often, they send that gift through the mail in response to a direct mail appeal, or maybe in response to a telethon that they see, or to an event that they're pointed to on the Internet. But in one way or another they send in their first gift.

You likely have major donors and people who leave you a large bequest in their will. You'll find that all of them likely started with a small gift, somewhere, sometime, to your organization. People don't start supporting you with a large gift and continue at that level.

So there's a necessity that you have as an organization to not only acquire donors, to not only get them to renew their support every year, but to cultivate your direct mail donors over time, year after year, month after month. You must nurture them so that they increase their commitment, or increase their loyalty to your organization, by increasing the size of their gift or by boosting the frequency of their giving.

3

How a Direct Mail Fund-raising Program Works

If you think carefully about direct mail fundraising, you'll discover that it's not so much about funds. Direct mail fundraising is really direct mail friend raising. That sounds really corny to put it that way. But you're really not in the business of simply acquiring money from people. You want their friendship and their loyalty over time. You want more than just their money. You want more than just their donations. Really, you want the donor behind the donation.

Your direct mail program is primarily about finding new friends. That's acquisition. It's also about keeping those friends, which is what we call donor renewal. And your program is also about building lasting relationships with those friends, which we call donor cultivation. So it's really about making new friends, keeping those friends, and building lasting friendships with those friends.

If you manage all three of those aspects of your direct mail fundraising program, if you get all those things right year after year, then the results will eventually start showing on your bottom line, on your income statement. You'll generate net revenue every year. And you'll feel more fulfilled as a fundraiser because you have a program in place.

Let's just look at a couple of ways that direct mail fundraising works. It's important to understand that direct mail fundraising isn't just about writing a letter and putting it in an envelope and putting a stamp on it and dropping it in the mail. There's far more to a program than that.

Direct mail fundraising is a program, not a series of mailings

The first thing that you need to know about direct mail fundraising and how it works as a program is that it is a planned program and not a series of mailings. Each letter that professional fundraisers drop in the mail is not simply a one-off campaign or a mailing. It's part of a larger, year-long program, usually one that starts on January 1 and ends on December 31.

Raising money through the mail is complicated. It's expensive. It's time consuming. I'm not saying that it's not cost-effective, but that it costs money and in that way it's expensive. That's why professional fundraisers plan their mailings at least 12 months in advance. I'm not saying that they know what they are going to say in 12 months, or what their package will look like, but that they know that in 12 months' time they're going to do a mailing that is part of a program.

Direct mail fundraisers know that their direct mail fundraising program integrates with their whole annual campaign. It integrates with their annual fund, their special events, their website fundraising, their newsletters, their public relations, their major giving, their planned giving, their telephone fundraising. Direct mail integrates with the overall plan and the overall campaign.

The reason that you need to have a program and not simply drop a bunch of letters in the mail every year is that there are a couple of really bad disadvantages to just waiting until you have the money or waiting until you have the time or waiting until it's the time of year to put something in the mail.

If you mail letters that are unrelated to each other during the year and if you don't plan and run a coordinated annual program, here's what will happen . . .

Things will get overlooked. You'll drop your pieces in the mail and you'll forget things. There'll be parts of the package that don't go in or there'll be letters that get mailed to the wrong people or there'll be certain things you should have said that you didn't because you ran out of time and you didn't plan your mailings more carefully.

Deadlines get missed. Organizations that don't have a planned program and instead simply mail something whenever they get around to it discover that their mailings are often rushed and put together at the last minute. There's the tyranny of the urgent. These organizations put out fires all year or all month or all quarter until finally the time comes when they have to put something in the mail and so they rush and put it together at the last minute. That's a big disadvantage to not having a planned program.

Appeals sound shrill. Organizations that don't plan their mailings often have other problems, such as running a deficit or running really close to the bone as far as finances are concerned. And so their appeals tend to sound more shrill. An organization that has a planned program will know that the first mailing of the year will cover a certain topic and the second mailing of the year will cover another topic and so on. But an organization that doesn't have a program and doesn't plan will tend to think, "Oh, we have to raise money! We have to raise money!" And so the letter they compose and mail will simply be a begging letter that has lots of exclamation marks in it and is shrill in its tone. The appeal was not planned, so it sounds just like a begging letter.

Appeals stress a need for immediate funds. The final disadvantage of not having a planned program is that appeals tend to stress the need for immediate funds, to cover the shortfall that lack of planning produced. They stress the need for money to bail the organization out of trouble, to get the organization back in the black because they're in the red. That type of messaging is not the way to build a following of loyal donors.

A direct mail fundraising program runs for 12 months

You may discover that one of your greatest obstacles in operating a successful annual fund is thinking of it as an annual fund. We tend to call it an annual fund because it runs for 12 months. But you don't call it an annual fund because you're supposed to solicit gifts just one time a year.

But there are some organizations that are particularly notorious for this. They think that "annual fund" means you approach your donors for a gift once a year, usually at Christmas time.

But direct mail fundraising and the annual fund is not called an annual program because you're supposed to solicit gifts once a year or annually. In direct mail fundraising, the most important gift is not the first gift but the second one. And the majority of people who respond to a direct mail appeal give once and never again. So your goal is to convert those people from one-time donors into repeat donors. And you can't do that if you just mail them once and then don't mail them again for another 12 months.

If you mail them one letter and they respond and give you a one-time gift, and then you wait 12 months before writing to them again, you don't really have an annual fund. You have an expense fund. You'll discover pretty quickly that those mailings are going to cost you a great deal of money. All you're going to do is lose money.

There's a direct mail fundraiser I know that does a lot of direct mail fundraising for hospitals, and he says this is his greatest challenge, persuading the management of non-profit organizations to abandon what he calls this "annual fund mentality" where they think they just have to mail one letter a year. He says it's the greatest obstacle to ever getting a second gift. And I agree.

If you only mail one appeal letter a year you're likely to see your donors fall away at rates of 60 percent, 70 percent or higher. You need to solicit your donors more than once a year for a number of vital reasons. In other words, your direct mail fundraising program needs to run for 12 months. Here's why.

Donors give for many reasons. Some donors give because they're altruistic. Some give because of compassion. Some give because of guilt. Some give because of tax advantages. Some give because their Holy Scriptures dictate that they should give. But the main reason that people give and respond to direct mail appeals is that someone asked them for a gift. And as Mal Warwick has pointed out in his book, *Revolution in the Mailbox*, the majority of direct mail donors give out of discretionary funds. In other words, when your appeal arrives on their kitchen table and they go through it, they will give a gift with money that comes from readily available funds.

They don't borrow to give to you. And the majority of donors don't plan exactly how much money they're going to give to every organization and then just wait for the appeal letter to arrive. Your letter catches most people off guard. They read your appeal, and if they're going to respond, they're going to respond with money that they have on hand. In their bank account. Right now.

And so if you only mail them once a year, and if your letter arrives at the wrong time, then you've missed your shot for the next 12 months. But if you mail them a couple of times during the year, then the chances are much greater that, one of those times your letter appears in their mailbox, they'll have some funds available—and they will respond with a gift.

Another reason that your direct mail fundraising program lasts for 12 months and isn't just a one-time mailing is that friends stay in touch. You'll remember that your goal in direct mail fundraising is not to raise a dollar as much as it is to retain a donor—a donor who gives you a dollar, obviously, but your emphasis should be on keeping the donor rather than on getting the money from the person.

So you're after their friendship first, and *then* their finances. And you can't expect to raise money from people that only hear from you once a year. You need to mail more often than that.

Finally, you can't remember what you were doing on this day 12 months ago and neither can I. Neither can your donors. The way to stay in their memory is to stay in their mailbox.

Three characteristics of all direct mail fundraising programs that are run well:

1. Donors are solicited many times during the year.
2. The program relies heavily on past donors to repeat their gifts.
3. New donors are identified and acquired each year.

A direct mail fundraising program repeats every 12 months

Direct mail fundraising is a program that runs for 12 months and repeats every year. It's designed to be repeated year after year. What you're hoping for is that both the number and the monetary value of the gifts increase each time. Remember this as you sit down to put together your plan. You're only looking at 12 months. Next year you're going to repeat the system again.

Not all fundraising methods repeat every 12 months. Consider capital campaigns. They tend to run for a year or two. Maybe three. And they raise a great deal of money, usually in the millions.

But you don't have capital campaigns every year. Or at least you shouldn't. Your constituents will run out of energy if you do (and money). Capital campaigns come and go. You may think that you're forever in capital campaign mode, but you're not. Capital campaigns come years apart.

A direct mail fundraising program is characterized by incremental improvements through testing

In a successful direct mail fundraising program, the results of each mailing are compared with others for the same year. You take each mailing that you do and you compare it with the results of other mailings during the same year and you also compare each mailing with the same mailing that you made in the previous year.

In other words, let's say you take your year-end appeal, the one you do around Christmas. You can compare that mailing with the others that you do during that year and see how it is different. It likely raises more money. And you can also compare it with the previous year's Christmas and the previous year's Christmas and so on. What you're looking for are trends, and to discover where improvements are needed. You can usually spot trends when you compare a mailing with another mailing, and compare it with yet another mailing, and so on.

Now one of the nice things about direct mail is that you can measure your results. And because you can measure your results you can also test your mailings. You can take a package that you mail at the end of the year and you can look at the previous year's mailing and you can look at this year and what you're going to mail and you can change the letter. You can change the postage. You can change the envelope. You can change what goes inside the package. You can even change your timing.

And you can test. You can test one package against another. You can test one mailing list against another. You can test one ask against another. For example, you could ask for $30 year after year or, one year, you could conduct a test. Half of the letters you mail ask for $30 and the other half of the letters ask for $40. You test to see which of those two gift amounts generates the most revenue or the highest response rate.

So you can spend your dollars where they're most effective without relying on guesswork and without relying on hunches. That's the nice thing about testing.

Direct mail is one of the best mediums for measuring the return on your investment. All you have to do is code the reply device that your donors mail back to you. You count how many of those you get back in the mail with a gift. They tell you immediately and exactly how effective your mailing was. Those direct mail numbers never lie.

One of the nice things about direct mail fundraising is that you can calculate how well you're doing. You can measure:

- Your response count—the total number of donors who responded to your mailing
- Your response rate—the percentage of people that responded to your mailing. For example, if you mail 100 letters and you get a response count of one, that's a 1 percent response rate
- Your average gift—the size of the average gift
- Your gross income—the total amount of money you raised before you subtracted your expenses
- Your net income—what's left over after you've subtracted expenses. This is the most important number in direct mail fundraising. The money you have left after paying your expenses is the only money you can use for your mission
- Your cost to raise a dollar—how much money you must spend to raise one dollar

Direct mail fundraising works by building a broad base of support

In the city where I live, there's a non-profit that looks after women who have been physically and emotionally abused by their partners. Most of their clients are homeless. Many of them have children. Many of them suffer from mental illnesses. Some of them have drug problems.

This is an excellent charity that takes care of these women and their children. But one unfortunate thing is that this charity does not have a robust fundraising program. They rely for their existence on one grant from the federal government. It is around $250,000 annually.

Recently, they used all of that government funding to run their program and pay their staff and keep their doors open. Then the federal government said, "We're not going to give you that funding anymore." This charity was put into a crisis. They almost closed their doors because their one source of funding ended.

Since then they have started a grassroots fundraising effort. They're getting donations now from individual donors and businesses. You don't want to copy their mistake. You don't want to have your funding coming from just one or a few sources. You don't want to be getting most of your funding from a few foundation grants, for example, or from a few government grants, or from a few businesses. You need a broad base of support. And what I mean by a broad base is a pyramid with a large base.

Look at the picture below. That person at the top of the pyramid represents the donors who have made the greatest contributions to your charity, usually with many large, leaderships gifts for many years. Those two people beneath her represent major donors and others who have made significant gifts. The three beneath represent those who have been less generous than those above them but more generous than those beneath them, but have shown their increased commitment (such as monthly donors). Those on the bottom are the individuals who give smaller gifts over time.

Remember, the average gift sent through direct mail is $35. Your results may differ. But if you get $35 from one person it's not much. You need more than just a couple of individual donors giving at that level. The way direct mail fundraising works is that it builds this broad base of support at the bottom of the giving pyramid.

The most cost-effective way to build and sustain this broad base of support is to run a comprehensive, well-planned, well-executed annual direct mail fundraising program.

4

What You Need to Succeed in Direct Mail Fundraising

I suggest you need to do quite a few things well to do well in the mail. One of them is create a case for support that has broad appeal.

You need a case for support with broad appeal

If you want to attract new donors with fundraising letters, then your organization needs to have a compelling case for support.

The case for support is simply the case that you make for why a donor should give you a gift. But many non-profit organizations serve a constituency or champion a cause that is too small or too obscure to appeal to many donors. Let me give you an example.

Here in Canada you can get a list of all the charities in Canada sorted alphabetically. Run your finger down the list and you'll discover a non-profit in Saskatchewan called the Moose Jaw Amateur Radio Club. I'm sure it's a fine organization. And I'm sure they do great work and that everyone enjoys being part of this charitable organization. Should they use direct mail to attract new members? They have a charitable number. They issue income tax receipts. But they are an amateur radio club—they do not meet a pressing need, not even in Moose Jaw.

Heart disease is a pressing need. Climate change is a pressing need. Drunk driving, diabetes, battered women and poverty are all pressing needs. But the Moose Jaw Amateur Radio Club does not meet a pressing need. If you want to succeed at direct mail donor acquisition, then you need to have a case for support that meets a basic—preferably urgent—human need.

Let me give you another example.

I got a phone call a couple years ago from a non-profit in California. They wanted to use direct mail to start raising funds. This organization provides temporary shelter for lost reptiles. I'm not making this up. If a boa constrictor or a lizard or another exotic pet gets lost or sneaks out of the apartment and doesn't return, when somebody finds that pet they can hand it in to this charity that provides temporary shelter for lost reptiles until the owner is found.

That's this particular organization's case for support. I think you'll agree that this organization doesn't champion a cause that has broad appeal. Most people are horrified by snakes and repelled by lizards. Therefore, while this organization can certainly raise some money, they can't expect to raise money using direct mail.

If you want to succeed at direct mail, you need a case with broad support. One of the ways to determine whether you have broad appeal is to ask yourself how well known you are to how many people.

The average response rate for direct mail donor acquisition is one percent. In other words, if you want to acquire one donor you need to mail 100 letters. If you want to acquire 100 donors you need to mail 10,000 letters. That's basic direct mail fundraising math. It's unavoidable.

So direct mail is not the best donor acquisition tool for you if you are living in a small town or operating with a small pool of potential donors—people that are excited about reptiles, for example, or people that are interested in amateur radio. That's a very small pool of people.

If your organization is unknown, direct mail is probably not the right way for you to be acquiring donors. To have a broad base of support with broad appeal, you need to have broad name recognition. Lots of people need to get your letter and think, "I know these people."

If your organization is not well-known and you are starting from scratch, then you at least need to have a founder who has broad name recognition—someone like Hillary Clinton or Barack Obama or Nelson Mandela or Bono. You need to have some kind of broad name recognition in order to have broad appeal. That's number one in successful direct mail fundraising.

You need new donors you can reach cost-effectively

Secondly, you need to have new donors that you can reach cost-effectively. Let me give you an example. My wife and I adopted two boys from an evangelical adoption agency in Mississauga, Ontario, called Jewels for Jesus. It's a wonderful ministry that places babies for adoption in evangelical homes. However, due to their narrow base of support, Jewels for Jesus does not use direct mail fundraising to acquire new donors. It's not cost-effective for them to do so.

There are lots of Christians that would be excited about funding a charity that places babies in Christian homes, but they're not all found in Mississauga, Ontario. They are all over Canada. They are all over the world. And it's not cost-effective for this charity to use direct mail to try to reach these people nationally or globally. It would be far too expensive. Instead, they rely on word of mouth. They rely on special events. They rely on relationship building. But they do not use direct mail for donor acquisition.

To succeed at direct mail donor acquisition, your organization needs to have what one fundraiser calls a *natural constituency*—a large enough natural fan base that you can reach them cost-effectively through the mail. The most common way to reach those potential donors cost-effectively is to rent a list of names.

You need dedicated fundraising software

There's a third thing you need to do right if you're to succeed at direct mail fundraising—you need to have dedicated fundraising software. This is not optional. There's no way that you can succeed in direct mail fundraising by using a Microsoft® Access® database or an Excel® spreadsheet.

You need a software program that helps you record gifts, track the performance of your mailings, report on your progress and manage your database. Ideally your software should do more than just manage your direct mail program. It should be an integrated suite that also helps you manage special events, grant proposals, pledges for capital campaigns and planned giving. It should also integrate with your website if and when you need it to do that.

There are a variety of software programs than you can use. Some of the most expensive software is produced by Blackbaud. Their flagship product is called The Raiser's Edge.

Sage and eTapestry are each a little less expensive. And there are some software programs that are free. I recommend that you download the fundraising software comparison chart from the Grass Roots Fundraising Journal, which you will find at www.grassrootsfundraising.org/howto/software.html.

And there's also an excellent article called, "Selecting Fundraising Software," published by Tech Soup, at http://techsoup.com/learningcenter/software/page4829.cfm. With any program you choose, you need to have a dedicated fundraising software program. You can't wing it with an Excel spreadsheet or anything like that.

....

You need a software program that helps you record gifts, track performance, report on your progress and manage your database. The software should manage more than direct mail (special events, grants, pledges and planned giving). Ideally, it should integrate with your website, or be able to be integrated if needed.

Blackbaud	The Raiser's Edge	www.blackbaud.com
Cascade Data Solutions	Donation Director	www.donationdirector.com
Custom Management Software	The Silent Partner	www.silentpartner.com
DonorPerfect Fundraising Software	DonorPerfect	www.donorperfect.com
Compass Technology	Compass CRM for Fundraisers	www.compass.net
Donor2	Donor2	www.donor2.com
eBase	eBase	www.ebase.org
eTapestry	eTapestry	www.etapestry.com
Fundraiser Software	FundRaiser Basic	www.fundraiser-software.com
GiftMaker	GiftMaker	www.campagne.com
Kintera	Kintera Sphere	www.kintera.com
Sage Software	Sage Fundraising 50	www.sagenonprofit.com
Serenic DonorVision	Serenic DonorVision	www.serenic.com
Softrek Corporation	PledgeMaker	www.softrek.com
Telosa Software	Telosa	www.telosa.com
TowerCare Technologies	DonorPro	www.donorpro.com

....

You need an obsession with your data

To succeed at direct mail fundraising, you need to be obsessed about your numbers. First of all, you need to know how long your newly acquired donors take to break even. In other words, how many months does it take before a newly acquired donor pays for herself with another gift?

Other questions you could ask include:

- What percentage of donors give a second gift?

- Is this percentage increasing or decreasing?
- How much is your core donor group worth this year compared to last?
- What percentage of multi-year donors gave again this year?
- Do your renewal rates depend on the type of donor that you have? In other words, do your monthly donors renew better than your one-time donors?
- Do your older donors renew more quickly and faithfully than your younger donors?
- Do the donors that give to a particular program renew more successfully than those that give to other programs?
- Which segments of your donor file promise to be most profitable if you pay them more attention? Is it your major donors? Is it your young donors? Is it your newly acquired donors? Is it your women donors, your male donors? Is it your Hispanic donors? Is it your Republican donors?

You can answer these kinds of questions if you're obsessed with your data.

You need a dedicated team

Another thing you need to succeed in direct mail fundraising is a dedicated team. I don't mean that you need to have a lot of staff, because you can outsource a great deal of this. But you need to have a dedicated team that takes care of a number of things for you.

You need someone on your team in charge of direction. This is someone who decides how many appeals you'll mail during the year, someone who decides what your brand is. Not just your visual brand on paper, your logo, but what it is you stand for.

Apple Computer has a brand image in the marketplace and it's not just their logo. Steve Jobs, the iPod, iTunes, all have a brand image among consumers, and they are all part of the Apple brand.

The Red Cross has a brand image. Mothers Against Drunk Driving has a brand. Someone in your organization needs to set the direction. Someone on your team needs to set direction for how your direct mail integrates with online and offline fundraising methods and decides what you will say in each of your packages. This is essential.

Obviously, you need to have someone on your team who writes your letters. This can be someone on your staff or it can be a freelancer. You need someone to design your packages for you, make them look beautiful and make them effective. You need someone to print your letters and packages, and give you good advice on how to get all your pieces onto one sheet so they can save you money on printing. Four color, full color, black only—you need a printer to give you good advice on things like that.

You need a letter shop or a mailing house that will handle your packages for you—put your letters inside your envelopes, seal them, sort them, apply the postage, get them to the post office.

You need someone to process your gifts—open the envelopes and take the checks out and take them to the bank.

You need someone to manage the database. Donors come and go. They change their names. They get married. They change their mailing addresses. You need someone that can manage these changes in your database for you.

You need a commitment to donor-centered fundraising

What else do you need to succeed in direct mail fundraising? Well, you need a commitment to donor-centered fundraising. This is an expression that I got from Penelope Burk. She's written a book called *Donor Centered Fundraising.*

And I suggest that if you want to succeed in direct mail fundraising, then you need to be committed as an organization to putting the donor first. The reason for this is that it comes with the territory that in direct mail fundraising we tend to think of our donors as numbers and not as people. Every donor has a code or a donor number that identifies them in the database as a unique donor. It's usually a number or a string of numbers.

When we examine a donor's giving history and we see how much money they've given us, how often they've given to us and how recently they gave to us, we tend to think of donors in terms of their frequency, their recency and their monetary value. We think of our donors in terms of years, months and dollars.

And we tend to lump our donors into categories and give them impersonal labels. We'll call them a major donor or a lapsed donor. Or we may even refer to some of our donors as LYBUNTs (which stands for Last Year But Unfortunately Not This Year). That's not a very charitable designation.

Now, if you're also the person in your organization that goes face to face with donors, you'll know that you don't think of your donors this way. When you meet with Mrs. Carruthers for a cup of tea and talk about her cats, you don't think of her as a LYBUNT. You don't think of her a number. You know her by name.

You know your donors by name. And you're probably acquainted with their families, their spouses, their business, their hobbies, their interests and their style of dress. You know all about your donors and you don't think of them as numbers.

But the temptation when we're raising funds with appeal letters is to think of your donors in terms of what they can do for the organization monetarily. And yet donors who feel treated this way don't remain donors for very long. Today's donors give to charitable organizations for specific reasons, not simply because they have money to give away. They're not sitting at home waiting for your appeal to arrive.

So the secret to building long-term, profitable, mutually beneficial relationships with donors is to think the way your donors think. You need to learn to think like your donors.

If you arrive at the hospital pregnant they take you to obstetrics. If you arrive with a broken leg they take you to orthopedics. A hospital treats its patients according to the needs of the patient, not the needs of the hospital.

A healthy direct mail fundraising program works in the same way. It solicits and respects the goals, desires and wishes of its donors. In other words, it treats the donors according to the donors' needs, not the organization's needs. So, if you have donors in your file that want to give you a gift every month, you need to treat them accordingly. You need to segment your database so that you recognize that group of donors and allow them to give monthly.

If they want an annual receipt, they don't want you to give them an income tax receipt every time they mail you a gift. They just want one. And they tell you so. You need to segment your database, your file, so that you treat those donors the way they want to be treated and let them have just an annual receipt.

If you have donors in your file that tell you they want to receive updates on the work you're doing in Darfur or the work you're doing in the inner city or any area where you're working, and they say they want to receive those updates by email and not by mail, then you need to flag those donors so that you give them their updates on Darfur by email and not by mail.

You may have other supporters that have designated a gift of $2,000 recently for a particular initiative. Those donors need to know that you are delighted that they gave you that gift for that particular initiative. The appeal letters you send them over time need to acknowledge the donor support of that particular need.

They need to speak to these particular donors as partners and not as a paycheck. These donors need to know that you know that they support this particular initiative and you need to recognize that. That's why you segment your file.

Donors have their radio tuned to WIIFM all day. What's In It For Me? W-I-I-F-M. All of us give for selfish reasons. Your motivation may be to get an income tax receipt or to have your name engraved on the marble wall in the foyer of the hospital. It may be to get that "free" canvas tote bag the charity offered in exchange for a donation. It may be to make yourself feel better and not feel guilty.

When we mail a gift to our local museum or to the university from which we graduated or to the local women's shelter, there's likely some altruism in there as well as a wish to change the world, to make a difference. But we're also motivated by desire. Sometimes it's very, very small, but we want to feel good about ourselves. We want to feel good, so we give to feel good.

Some of us give until it hurts. But we don't give *because* it hurts. We give because giving feels good. And successful direct mail fundraisers use this trait, this kind of "what's in it for me" attitude that donors have. They use it to their advantage by giving donors what donors want.

A savvy organization will use direct mail not to ask for money that the organization needs, but to invite donors to accomplish their goals by making the world a better place. And obviously that involves writing a cheque, mailing it in and responding to the appeal.

You need a commitment to brand differentiation

Another thing that you need to succeed in direct mail fundraising is a commitment to differentiation. This is a very fancy word. It comes from the marketing area where companies know that if they're to get any kind of recognition in a consumer's mind they need to be different from competing products. So Coca-Cola has to be different from Pepsi. And BMW has to be different from Chevrolet. Businesses know that they need to be different in the minds of their buyers, their consumers. And non-profit organizations need to do the same.

Let me give you an example. In New York City there's an organization called The Cancer Research and Treatment Fund. In Virginia there's an organization called The Cancer Research and Prevention Foundation. In Maryland there's an organization called The National Foundation for Cancer Research.

Let's just look at those three in a column:

Cancer Research and Treatment Fund
Cancer Research and Prevention Foundation
National Foundation for Cancer Research

They are three distinct organizations. But are they different? I'm sure they are, but their names don't tell you that they are. And if they are not distinct in the minds of donors, the donors will be confused and not give.

Let me just give you a for instance. If a prospective donor received an appeal letter from each of those charities on the same day, would he know which one to support? One letter comes from the Cancer Research and Treatment Fund, another from the Cancer Research and Prevention Foundation, and a third from the National Foundation for Cancer Research. Would that donor know which organization to support, and why?

If you have a competitor either locally or nationally, in your city, in your region, or across the country, you need to tell potential donors in the mail, in your letters and in your newsletters how you are unique. How are you different from other charities like yours? Otherwise you won't raise many funds. And you won't keep many donors, and you won't last.

Your donors need to think of you as different. Sufficiently different that you occupy a different place in their mind when they think of your particular organization and the work that you do.

You need a commitment to segmentation

There are many, many times when you should not mail the same letter to everybody in your database. You may have a time of year when everybody gets a letter. It might be your Christmas appeal, for example, and it might be your first renewal mailing of the year. Everybody gets a letter, but not everybody should get the same letter.

You have people in your file, for example, that have not given you a gift for a year or two, and if they did give you a gift, they might have given only $20. They should not get the same letter as a more recent donor who gives you a couple of gifts a year and each one of those gifts is $500. They should not get the same appeal. They may get a letter at the same time of the year, but they should not get the same letter, and that's what I mean by segmenting your database.

You need to look at all your donors in your database and carve them up into meaningful segments so that you treat each segment differently based on the relationship you have with them and based on their value to you as an organization.

You need frequency and volume

Another thing you need to succeed in direct mail fundraising is frequency and volume. Your results may differ but direct mail fundraising usually works only when you mail at least eight times a year. Four of those mailings can be appeal letters and four can be newsletters. The appeals ask for money and the newsletters inform.

If you do not have enough money in your bank account to mail at least four appeals and four newsletters a year, direct mail is probably not right for your organization. Not yet. You need frequency to be successful.

Direct mail fundraising also works when you mail in volume. You're not likely to operate a successful program if you only have a few hundred supporters. They may be very faithful. They may be steadfast. They may be loyal. They may have a high response rate and give you a high average gift, but you're not going to have a successful direct mail fundraising program if you just have a few hundred supporters.

For one thing, if you're only mailing a few hundred pieces you're not going to qualify for discounts on postage, which usually kick in when you mail 1,000 pieces or more. So you're going to be mailing first class all the time if you only have a few hundred supporters.

And for another thing, the cost of hiring a professional writer or a professional designer or a fundraising consultant will be prohibitive if you only mail a few hundred pieces at a time. The cost per package would be too great.

Just imagine that you're mailing 100 pieces of mail and the direct mail fundraising consultant charges you $5,000. Well, that adds $5 to each package right away. That's a lot of groceries.

But if you're mailing 100,000 pieces and the direct mail fundraising consultant charges you that same $5,000, then your cost is going to go way down. It might only be five cents per package instead of $5. So your costs will be prohibitively high if you're just mailing to a few.

Direct mail fundraising needs volume to be successful. You need to be mailing in the tens of thousands or even the hundreds of thousands over time, and asking for small donations. That's the secret of successful direct mail fundraising.

You need a commitment that lasts for decades

Finally, in order to succeed in direct mail fundraising, you need a commitment that lasts decades. Raising money with the mail is a long -term commitment that you make to your organization and donors.

I could write a direct mail fundraising package that was an absolute tearjerker and induced plenty of guilt and manipulated donors into parting with large sums of money, but the kind of person that I would manipulate and reduce to tears wouldn't give over time in any sustainable way. Guilt is a short-term motivator.

The secret to success in direct mail fundraising is to plan your program and stick with it. Not to wait for a crisis to arise and write a shrill, guilt-inducing appeal.

You need to mail the best appeal that you can. You need to craft the most compelling donor newsletter stories that you can. You need to watch your numbers. You need to cut costs wherever possible. You need to avoid gimmicks and fads.

You need to acquire new donors each year. You need to build relationships with your supporters and members. You need to stick with your program. And month after month, year after year you'll gradually build a strong, broad base of loyal supporters who care about you, and who look forward to seeing your letters coming to their mailboxes.

It's hard to believe, but there are plenty of donors who actually look forward to receiving mail from non-profit organizations because those non-profit organizations have a long-term view. They're invested in their donors in a long-term way.

Capital campaigns and banquets are an excellent way to raise awareness. And they're an effective way to raise money. But they are also costly and time consuming. It tends to cost you money to raise funds. You can expect to spend 10 to 15 cents to raise a dollar. So if you're raising $1 million you're going to have to spend maybe $100,000, $150,000. Those are your costs.

And these special events are time consuming. Banquets are time consuming. Capital campaigns are time consuming. You can't run those things every month. And you can't afford to rely on them. You can't rely on them to strengthen the relationships that you have with your supporters because these events come and go. There's too much time in between.

But fundraising letters and donor communications such as newsletters, bulletins and email newsletters are a cost-effective way to build credibility. They're a cost-effective way to increase trust. They're a cost-effective way to inform your donors and to build relationships with your donors over time.

The concept that you need to keep in mind to be successful in direct mail fundraising is the lifetime value of each donor to your organization. You need to think of how long each donor will stay with your organization and how much they will give to your organization, and look at that lifetime value when you're looking at each donor.

In other words, you need to take a long-term view of your donors and you need to have a commitment that lasts decades.

Conclusion

I once worked for a non-profit organization as their director of development. At Christmas time they used to put a fundraising appeal in the mail, but before they mailed their fundraising appeal they always sent out a newsletter weeks before.

The newsletter used to arrive in the mailbox at the end of

October or beginning of November. And it would be followed by the appeal letter before Christmas.

About a year or two before they hired me, they got to the end of their year and, well, you know, various things happened and the deadline for the newsletter slipped. The staff procrastinated. They were putting out fires in various departments and, before they knew it, the deadline for the newsletter had come and gone.

They got so far behind in their drop date for their newsletter that by the time they found time to put it in the mail, they were within a few weeks of Christmas. And so they thought, "Well, we don't want to mail our newsletter and then a week or two later mail our appeal letter. Why don't we just mail both at the same time?" And they couldn't put a newsletter and an appeal letter together unless they put them in some kind of an outer envelope, so they decided to use a plastic bag.

So that's what arrived at Christmastime, this plastic see-through bag with an address stuck label on it. Inside was the newsletter, and inside the newsletter was the appeal letter. And that mailing "tanked," as people say. It should have been their most successful direct mail appeal of the whole year. Christmas always was—they raised more money at Christmas than at any time of the year. But it ended up being their worst mailing ever.

What they think happened was that Christmas was coming and donors got this plastic envelope in the mail, and they looked inside and they thought was just a newsletter. They thought, "Oh, this is a newsletter. Well, I'm busy." So they laid it aside. Instead of opening it and discovering the appeal letter giving their money to the organization, they left the house and went to Wal-Mart and bought Tickle-Me-Elmo dolls instead. They didn't know that there was an appeal letter inside that newsletter.

And the reason for that mistake was that this organization did not have a well-run, well-planned, integrated direct mail fundraising program. They did things *ad hoc*. They mailed when they had time and when they thought about it, or when they ran out of time.

I'm telling you this by way of warning. Direct mail fundraising is not about mailings. Direct mail fundraising is not about campaigns. It's a program. It's a direct mail fundraising program.

5

Fourteen Reasons Strangers Respond to Direct Mail Acquisition Letters

Imagine you're about to write a fundraising letter and mail it to people who have not given you a gift before. What should you write? How can you motivate them? Why should they respond to your letter with a gift?

Before you put your pen to paper, or your fingers to your keyboard, you need to understand what motivates people to respond to fundraising letters in general. There are at least 14 motivators.

Reason # 1: They hunt for meaning in life

One reason people respond to fundraising letters is that they want to find meaning in life. Giving to charity gives their life meaning. Some people are simply not happy unless they're making other people happy. To make others happy gives them meaning. And they'll support your organization for that reason.

Reason # 2: They want to meet an immediate need

Others give because they wish to meet an immediate need such as a flood, hurricane or drought. These types of people are moved to act when the need is great and when the crisis is of catastrophic proportions. They like to respond to emergencies.

Reason # 3: They want to receive a personal benefit

Another reason that people give is that they wish to receive a personal benefit. Some people give out of selfish reasons. They'll give you a gift because you've promised them a coffee table book or a backpack or a video. Some people will give you a donation because you're running a lottery or a sweepstakes. They want a chance to win something. They give to receive a personal benefit.

Reason # 4: They want to join others in a worthy cause

A fourth reason that people give is that they want to join others in a worthy cause. An example would be the People for the Ethical Treatment of Animals, PETA. They attract a certain kind of young person who wants to join forces with other people and sign petitions and campaign in the streets and protest and carry placards and walk naked through the city to protect animal rights. There's a certain type of donor that wants to join with others in a worthy cause and they'll donate to your organization and respond to your acquisition letter if you give them that opportunity.

Reason # 5: They want to achieve status

Others give because they want to achieve status. They'll give you a gift, usually a large gift, because they want you to acknowledge them in your annual report. They want to see their photo in the newspaper. They want to see their name engraved in marble over the archway of the library. And so they'll give to achieve status.

Reason # 6: They are angry

Other donors are angry, and they'll give to assuage their anger in some way. They wish to vent their anger. They might be angry at drunk drivers. They might be angry at government waste. They might be angry at political corruption. And so, because they're furious they want to do something about it.

And if you give them the chance through a fundraising letter to give a gift to your organization and help them give money that will make a difference, and reduce government corruption or reduce drunk driving, then their anger will gradually subside and they'll feel better.

Reason # 7: They are altruistic

I've met a couple of people in my life that were like this. My mother-in-law is like this. She gives because she cares. She doesn't give because she gets a personal benefit or achieves status or finds meaning in life. She's a sweetheart, and she gives because she's altruistic. She thinks of the other person and likes to help them. If you can get donors like this, they're gold. And you should hang on to as many as you can.

Reason # 8: They are idealistic

An eighth reason that people give to non-profits in response to a direct mail acquisition appeal is that they're idealistic. For example, it happens every year that I'll hear a knock on my front door and I'll open it find an adorable Girl Guide selling cookies. It is very, very hard to turn away a Girl Guide selling cookies! They are idealistic. They're young and they're sweet and they have great dreams for the world and nothing's impossible in their mind. Some donors are like that as well. They're idealistic. And if you present a case for support that is compelling (but nevertheless realistic) some donors who are idealistic and want the world to be a better place will support your organization.

Reason # 9: They give for religious reasons

Some people give because their holy book—maybe it's the Koran, the Torah, or the Bible—tells them that they should give to the poor or the needy, or that they should tithe 10 percent of their income. So they give out of religious practice. If you're a religious organization, people may respond to your appeal for that reason.

Reason # 10: They give to solve a problem

Some people give to solve a problem: battered women, abandoned pets, the polluted Great Lakes. Some donors are motivated to give because they see a problem in the world and they will give money to do something about it. Tom Ahern, who wrote the book *Raising More Money With Newsletters Than You Ever Thought Possible*, says, "People don't give to your organization. They give through your organization to change the world." They see a problem. They want to fix it. And if you give them that opportunity, they'll give you that donation.

Reason # 11: They give to save on taxes

Some tax laws in some countries allow donors to save money by giving gifts to charity. Some donors give for that reason. It's not the best motivator but it is a motivator.

Reason # 12: They give to achieve immortality

Some people believe that by giving to the hospital and having their family name appear in brass in the lobby or endowing a chair to their *alma mater*, the university they graduated from, they'll be remembered after their deaths. Their legacy will go on. They'll continue. And so they feel that they get some kind of immortality from their donation.

Reason # 13: They give to reduce guilt

It's no surprise that in the West, North America, the Western world, we feel guilty because we have so much and so many people in the world have so little. And so some people, if you send them a fundraising letter that shows a picture of a starving child or an AIDS orphan or poverty elsewhere in the world, you'll move them to give a donation because they feel guilty. They'll give because of guilt.

Donors who give out of guilt rarely give for very long. And you can't appeal to them on the basis of guilt, guilt, guilt in a long-term kind of way. It's a short-term motivator, but it is a reason that some people give.

Reason # 14: They give because they're fearful

Some people are afraid that their Social Security will run out by the time they reach retirement. Or they're terrified of violence, hand gun violence, gangs or drugs in their city. And so if you offer them a chance to make a difference and make Social Security more secure or make their streets safer, then they will respond. Fear is a strong motivator but it's a little bit like guilt. It's a short-term motivator. Donors are not likely to give out of fear unless you make them afraid, so avoid fear as a motivator in your fundraising letters.

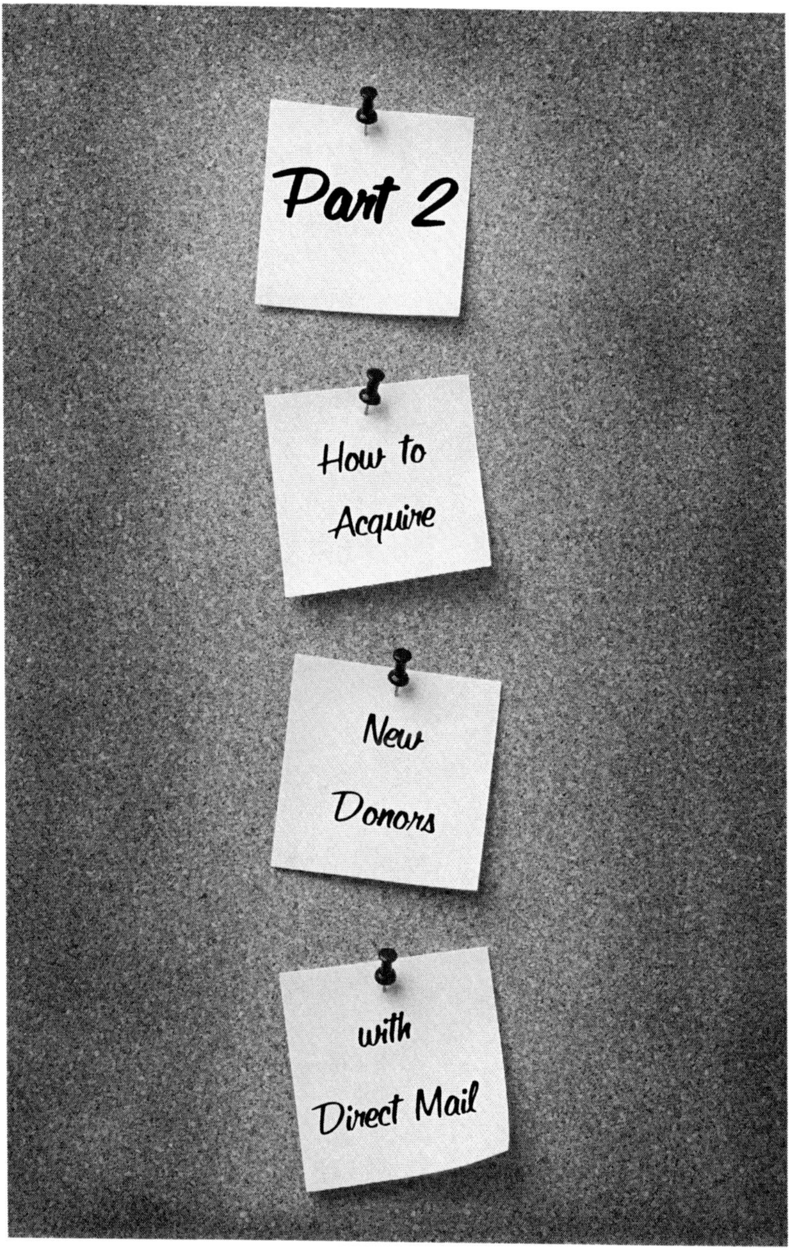
Part 2
How to
Acquire
New
Donors
with
Direct Mail

6

How Direct Mail Donor Acquisition Works

Let's look at a couple of basic truths about how direct mail donor acquisition works. Some of these were mentioned in chapter 1. It's important to go over them again just so you truly understand how direct mail fundraising works, and particularly how donor acquisition works.

Direct mail donor acquisition loses money initially

In his book, *Revolution in the Mailbox*, Mal Warwick talks about a time 30 years ago when you could mail a letter to tens of thousands of people and you would make money on your acquisition. You would gain new supporters and you would not only break even but you would actually have net profit at the end of your mailing. That does not happen today. It's very, very rare. The first thing you should know about direct mail donor acquisition is that it loses money initially.

You should expect your direct mail donor acquisition mailings to lose money. They almost always do. They gain new supporters, yes, but they usually cost at best somewhere between $1.25 and $1 to raise a new donor.

This means that donor acquisition letters are designed to raise donors and not donations. Obviously you want your mailing to make as much money as possible. But your goal is not simply to get money. You're after donors. Not donations.

Now, here's something that I try to do and I encourage my clients to do whenever they hire me to do some consulting for them. It's useful to ignore one set of numbers and fix your eyes on another. The number that you should try to ignore in direct mail donor acquisition is the cost of getting your first donation.

According to James Greenfield in his book, *Fundraising: Evaluating and Managing the Fund Development Process*, you can expect to pay anywhere from $1.25 to $1.50 to raise $1 with an acquisition mailing. That doesn't sound like a very wise use of your resources. You'll have to go to your board and tell them,

"We'd like to spend $1.50 to raise $1," and you might be afraid that they will fire you with that kind of thinking.

But with acquisition letters you need to remember that you should have your eyes fixed on the lifetime value of your donor, not the short-term value of their first gift.

You need to remind yourself, your board members, key volunteers and any colleagues you have that are inexperienced in direct mail donor acquisition, that your goal with acquisition mailings is to acquire friends, not funds. Obviously you want to make money if you can. But that's not your goal. Your goal is to make friends—to acquire friends, not funds.

Let me give you an illustration. Let's say for the sake of argument that you have a donor acquisition letter and you're going to mail it to 10,000 people. They've never given you a gift before. They're all strangers. They know of your organization but they're strangers as far as having any kind of a relationship with you.

And so you write the package. You design it. You print it. You put a stamp on it. You put it in the mail. And let's say it costs you around 60 cents a piece, which is about average. So you're mailing 10,000 pieces, 60 cents each. Then your cost will be $6,000.

Let's say you receive a one percent response rate, which is the industry standard that people expect to receive. So you mail 10,000 pieces. You get a one percent response rate. That's 100 gifts. Let's further assume that the average gift that you get from those 100 people is $30.

So you've got $30 times 100 donors. You have a gross income of $3,000. But your mailing costs, total cost for putting this package in the mail, were $6,000. So if you take away $3,000 from your expenses of $6,000 then you're left with a loss of $3,000.

You actually lost $3,000. You spent $6,000. You earned $3,000. So you still spent $3,000. So your cost for the campaign was $3,000. Are you in trouble? Well, no. Because here's what you tell your executive director or your director of development: "We spent $3,000 but we gained 100 new donors."

And if the numbers are in any way predictable, around 80 percent of them will give again if you do the right thing. Provided you follow up properly and thank them for their gifts and solicit them in the right way the next time, you've gained 100 donors and about 80 percent of them will give again.

So each of these new donors cost you $30. The question that you have to ask yourself and that you have to pitch to your board is this" Are you willing to spend $30 today to raise one donor or a friend who will likely give your organization hundreds of gifts in the years to come, provided they give $50, $60, $70, $80 a year and they stay with you for three, four, five years?

You should be willing to spend that kind of money to make that kind of money. But you must remember that your goal with the acquisition letters is to raise a donor and not a donation.

Incidentally, if you want to read a good discussion of the economics of donor acquisition you should read Stanley Weinstein's book, The *Complete Guide to Fundraising Management.*

I'll just say it again. Donor acquisition mailings lose money. Your goal with an acquisition mailing is to acquire friends, not funds. So that's one key to how a direct mail donor acquisition program works. It loses money initially.

Direct mail donor acquisition needs a popular cause to succeed

Direct mail is an effective way to acquire donors when you have a cause that has broad appeal, either locally or nationally. Let me give a couple of examples of broad appeal. One would be the treatment of heart disease. All across the United States, all across Canada, all across New Zealand and Australia, heart disease is prevalent and so its treatment and cure is a popular cause.

Helping sick children is a popular cause. Caring for abandoned pets, or abused pets in general, is a popular cause. These are popular causes because many, many people have a soft spot for abandoned pets or children that are sickly.

So if your organization is either small or has an obscure kind of case for support then acquiring donors using direct mail is probably not the wisest way for you to go, because you don't have a broad enough base of support. And you'll remember that example I gave you earlier, that organization on the West Coast. They provide temporary shelter to lost exotic pets like lizards, reptiles, snakes.

Most people that I know would not gladly support an organization that provides temporary shelter to snakes—boa constrictors, anacondas. They would be repelled by that type of organization. They would not gladly give money to support a cause that helps snakes when they're terrified of snakes.

So that organization would not be wise to use direct mail fundraising letters to ask people in their community to support a local shelter that will help those kinds of pets. Even though those pets should be helped, the organization that helps them does not have a broad enough base for support.

So if your cause is too obscure or if the area that you're going to be fundraising in is too small, direct mail is not the way to acquire donors. You need a popular cause to succeed.

Direct mail donor acquisition needs volume to succeed

You're not likely to operate a successful direct mail fundraising program if you only have a few hundred supporters. There are some non-profits that only have 800 supporters, and they manage to make money from mailings, but the one thing that they're not able to do is qualify for discounts on postage.

Discounts on postage usually start at 1,000 pieces, depending on what country you live in. So you need to mail at least 1,000 pieces to get a break on postage. Instead of spending 50 cents you'd spend 32 cents for example.

Also, your cost for hiring professional writers and professional designers will be prohibitive if you only mail a couple of hundred pieces. A professional team of writers and designers might charge you $3,000 or $5,000 for producing your package. And if you only mail 1,000 pieces then you're basically adding $3 to $5 to the cost of each piece. That's a lot of groceries.

Direct mail fundraising works best when you mail to tens of thousands of donors repeatedly over time asking for small donations. So it's a volume way of raising money. Because you ask for small gifts, you have to ask many people for those gifts.

Direct mail donor acquisition needs other mailings to succeed

Donor acquisition works only if you mail to those people again and again and again.

Direct mail fundraising usually works when you mail at least eight times a year. That would be four appeal letters and four newsletters at a minimum. So you mail eight times. You'd mail a letter asking the donor for a gift and then you'd send them a newsletter which was simply informative and inspiring. And then you'd send another letter that asks for a gift. Then you'd send another newsletter that was informing and inspiring, and so on.

You'd mail at least eight times a year. Some non-profits mail 12, 14, even 21 times a year. But you need to mail. I recommend to my clients they mail at least eight times a year. People will forget you if you only mail one or two letters a year. You won't be on their radar.

If you only mail two letters a year and your donor misses one of them because she's in Florida then you'll only reach that person once a year and they won't be current and they won't be inspired about what you're doing. They will not have heard from you for many, many months.

So if you don't have enough money in your bank or in your budget to mail at least eight mailings a year it could be that direct mail is not the way to go for your non-profit at the moment. Now you do need to remember that, with renewal mailings, donors pay for themselves, generally speaking. Acquisition mailings lose money, but once you have a donor and you mail to that donor again, that mailing will generally make money.

So you don't literally have to have money in the bank. You can just adjust your cash flow. You can spend the money on acquisition and then recover some of your costs within a few weeks as your donations come in. But you need to be willing to spend that kind of money to mail eight times a year minimum.

Four tests to see if direct mail donor acquisition is right for you

Test #1: Are you well known to many donors?

Some non-profit organizations should not use direct mail as a way to attract new donors. You can ask yourself if your organization one of them. You can take a simple test by asking yourself, "Is my organization well known to many people?"

In chapter 1, we discussed the average response rate to a direct mail donor acquisition mailing. It's about a one percent response rate. This means that you need to mail 100 letters to acquire one donor. And you need to mail 10,000 letters if you want to acquire 100 donors. And you need to mail 100,000 letters to acquire 1,000 donors. This is the unavoidable math of direct mail fundraising.

If you're intent on acquiring a large number of donors, you'll have to mail a large number of pieces. So are you well known to many people? Direct mail is not the best donor acquisition tool for you if you're located in a small town that has a really small pool of potential donors, or if your organization is brand new, unknown.

To succeed at direct mail donor acquisition you need to have broad name recognition for your organization itself, or the support of an individual with broad name recognition.

Test #2: Do you meet a pressing need?

The second test is to ask, "Do we meet a pressing need? Do we have a compelling case for support?"

For example, it could be that in Podunk, Alabama, there is a model train club and they're a fine organization and they raise money and they issue charitable tax receipts. But they don't meet a pressing need. They're a hobby club.

The treatment of heart disease is a pressing need. Global warming and climate change are pressing needs. Diabetes prevention and cure is a pressing need. You need to have a case for support and you need to meet a basic, urgent, human need. If you have a case for support like that, then direct mail fundraising might be the way for you to go.

Test #3: Would you pass a search on Google?

Do you have a track record, an annual report, audited financial statements, a way of proving that you're financially responsible? Can you prove that you're ethical and trustworthy? If people visit your website and there is no history, no description of your board and no description of your management, now is probably not the right time to be acquiring donors using direct mail.

To succeed at direct mail donor acquisition your organization needs a few things. One of them is public proof that you are credible, preferably going back a couple of years. This isn't to say that you can't start from scratch when you're brand new, because you can. It's been done before. But you need to prove to the public somehow that you're a credible organization and that you're worthy of their trust.

Test #4: Can you find donors easily and cost-effectively?
Are potential donors for your organization easy and cost-effective to find? Some donors are easy to find but you have to spend a lot of money to find them. Others are harder to find and still cost a lot of money to find.

I'll just give you this example. My wife and I adopted two boys from an adoption agency in the Town of Mississauga. It's not only an adoption agency but it's an evangelical adoption agency, so they have a pretty narrow focus. They do great work. They place babies in evangelical homes. These are babies that would otherwise be aborted.

So my wife and I adopted two babies through this agency, and, as you can probably imagine, most of their donors have been touched by adoption somehow. They either adopted a baby or they placed their child for adoption or they're the parents or grandparents of adopted children. In some way or another, the donors to this organization have been touched by adoption.

Most Canadians have not been touched by adoption. So this organization does not use direct mail as a way to acquire donors. They do use direct mail as a way to keep in touch with donors and raise funds, but not to acquire them. They don't do mailings of tens of thousands or hundreds of thousands right across Canada hoping to raise money because they don't have a pool of potential supporters that's easy to find cost-effectively.

There are evangelicals all across Canada that would probably give them a donation but those people are not easy to find and they're not easy to find cost-effectively. So direct mail is not the way to go for this organization.

So you need to take these four tests. If you just take these four tests you'll see if you're ready for direct mail donor acquisition. Are you well known to many people? Do you meet a pressing basic human need? Will you pass a search on Google? If someone gets your letter and Googles your organization, what will they find? Will you pass the test? And are you able to find potential donors cost-effectively?

7

Eight Steps for Acquiring Donors with Direct Mail

Step #1: Develop your case for support

You need to start right at the beginning with who you are, who you help, what you do, why you exist. That's what a case for support is. Your case for support covers three basic things:

Your cause

You need to have a cause that has broad appeal and is compelling. There have to be sufficiently large numbers of people in the area that you're mailing to that will find your cause appealing and compelling. When you sit down at night and you turn on the television you will only watch what's compelling. There'll be plenty of shows that you won't watch. They're appealing to some people but not to you. So your cause that you champion has to be compelling and have broad appeal.

Your message

Your case for support should deal with the message that you're going to communicate to your audience. It needs to be clear and it needs to be credible. Somebody receiving your letter doesn't have the advantage of being able to ask you a question on the phone or at their door. They're simply reading your letter and the message you communicate has to be clear, not complicated and difficult to understand. And it has to be credible and not incredible. People have to be able to read your letter, see what you're raising the money for and say to themselves, "This makes sense. I believe in this cause. It is credible."

Your reputation

Are you successful? Do you have a history of using donors' donations to achieve the kinds of goals that you want? Just think of the organizations that you support yourself, the charities to which you send your gifts. You likely send your money to them because they are successful.

Are you trustworthy? That's another question that donors will ask themselves: "Can I trust this organization with my donation?" If you have a good reputation in the marketplace then you will be trustworthy.

So that's Step #1 in direct mail donor acquisition—developing your case for support. It's absolutely vital. There's no point in writing a letter and putting postage on it and mailing it to people until you're clear about your cause, your message and your reputation.

Step #2: Clone your best donors

The second step is finding donors who are like your best donors. If you've been around for a couple of years and you go through your database and simply talk to some of your staff, you'll be able to draw a picture of what your best donors look like. A good donor could be somebody that gives you many gifts. A good donor could be somebody who gives you lots of money. A good donor could be somebody who gave to you recently. Somehow you have to decide what your best donors look like, and then you have to clone them, so to speak. You have to multiply them. There are three things that you should look for in a potential donor:

Capacity to give

Donors have to have the capacity to give. A good direct mail fundraising prospect is somebody who has the resources to support your organization with gifts over time. That's the key—not just one gift, but gifts over time. They don't have to be millionaires, since you're asking them for a small donation. They don't even have to be employed. They can be retired. They can be on a pension because you're asking them to support your organization with a small gift. Plenty of retired people on a fixed income still support their favorite charities. The criteria that you're looking for is simply their capacity or their ability (not their likelihood) to give.

For example, imagine you're a university and someone has just graduated from your school. Let's say they studied medicine and they now have $80,000 in student debt. They are not a likely candidate for a gift. Because they're in debt. But you could write to that same student 10 years from now and they'll be in a position to give. You should keep in touch with them between now and then, but you need to remember that your best candidates for gifts are people who have capacity to give.

Connection with your cause

Donors need to have some kind of affinity with, a natural liking for, or a natural disposition towards your cause. They need to be people who identify with the people that you help, or the cause that you champion. You're most likely to attract financial support and gain new donors when you mail your acquisition letters to people who already believe in what you stand for. They have an affinity with your cause.

Chance of developing a long-term profitable relationship with your organization

Raising funds through the mail is a long-term proposition. What you're looking for in direct mail donor acquisition are donors who will support you over time. One-time donations are fine, and one-time donations are welcome, but if those one-time donations are too small they don't even cover the cost of the mailing. You want donors. Not just donations.

So that means you need to look at every source of potential donors and ask yourself, "What is the likelihood that these prospective donors will not only respond to my mailing with a gift right now, but will follow through in the years to come with other gifts?" Your emphasis has to be on the long term. Not the short term.

So the thing to bear in mind whenever you're looking for new donors is that they should meet all three of these criteria. They should have the capacity to give. They should have a connection with your cause. And they should have a real chance of developing a long-term profitable relationship with you.

Donors should not be just wealthy, with no affinity. I help plenty of non-profit organizations. They all know who Bill Gates is, but Bill Gates does not know who they are. Bill Gates is wealthy, but he has no affinity with their organization. So the people that you want to reach should not simply be wealthy but have no affinity.

And they should not just have an affinity but be bankrupt. There could be plenty of people who really believe in what you do but have no capacity to give you a gift. For example, you may run a homeless shelter. The people in your homeless shelter really respect you. They love you. They know that you care for them and they have a great deal of affection for you and your staff. But they have no money to give you. So although they have affinity, they have no capacity.

When you find a donor that has the capacity to give and has an affinity with your cause and is able to enter into a long-term profitable relationship, profitable for them and for you, then you'll avoid the disappointment that a lot of direct mail fundraisers bring upon themselves in direct mail donor acquisition. And you'll save a lot of money too, because you won't be trying to renew donors who are not likely to renew.

So you need to clone your best donors. That's step number two in direct mail donor acquisition.

Step #3: Find the names of potential donors

The third step in direct mail donor acquisition is finding the names of potential donors. You need to get the names and addresses of people that are likely to support your organization. And there are many, many places you can look to find these people.

Top of the list is **similar non-profit organizations**. I suggest that the first place you should look in your search for potential donors is organizations that have a similar cause to yours. Not a direct competitor but an organization that serves a similar constituency or works in a similar type of work.

People who support those other organizations are the best prospects for supporting yours. Let me give you an example. Let's just say that your non-profit organization advocates for the protection of endangered animals.

You could do a search of lists of similar organizations that are involved in animal welfare and you'd find a list of the following:

- The National Wildlife Federation
- Defenders of Wildlife
- The Nature Conservancy
- Ducks Unlimited
- American Society for the Prevention of Cruelty to Animals
- Sierra Club
- International Fund for Animal Welfare
- People for the Ethical Treatment of Animals

The National Wildlife Federation has 710,000 donors. People for the Ethical Treatment of Animals has 204,000 donors. The other organizations have somewhere in between. If you added all those donors up you'd have a potential mailing list of 3,596,000.

Not all of these organizations will rent you their lists. Some of them will exchange their list with you on a *net name basis*. If you have 10,000 names, you give them 10,000 of your names and they give you 10,000 of theirs. It's simply an exchange. No money changes hands.

The donors and members on these lists are better potential donors than your average citizen for a couple of compelling reasons. First of all, they already know and care about protecting animals. If they support one of these organizations you know that they care about protecting animals. And we're just pretending for the sake of this illustration that your non-profit is involved in helping endangered animals.

They are also known to donate to animal welfare charities. So they not only care about animals, they also donate to those charities. And you know—and this is the important point—you know that they respond to direct mail fundraising appeals, if you're getting their names from a list that uses direct mail to raise funds. So that's one place that you can look—similar non-profit organizations.

Another place where you can find potential donors is **magazine readers**. Again, let's just keep with our illustration here. Pretend that we're an organization that's involved in animal welfare. You can go through a list of magazines and discover that there are magazines aimed at people who care about animals.

For example there's a magazine called *Texas Parks and Wildlife* magazine. They have 133,000 subscribers. There's another magazine called *Wild Bird*. Another magazine called *Wildlife Conservation* magazine. Now, you don't know if these people donate to animal welfare causes but you do know that they're interested in wildlife and animal conservation because they read those magazines. Some of those magazines will rent those lists of people, and you can mail them.

There are some donors who have a **specific interest**. Again, you can go through the mailing lists that are on the market and you'll discover that there's a mailing list called "Tiger Donors." These are people that are known to be passionate about the fight to protect abused tigers and lions. There's another mailing list called "The Elephant Sanctuary." It's the list of the first national habitat in North America developed for endangered Asian elephants. So if your animal organization is concerned with a particular animal or bird or fish, then lists like these will be invaluable to you.

Another place you can look is **kindred spirits**. Let's say, for example, you're a pet owner. Let's say you own a dog. If you live in any city of any decent size there will be an animal shelter for abandoned dogs and cats. And that shelter needs funds. And if that shelter sent you a letter asking for funds to help them find homes for stray pets or pets that would otherwise be put down, you might very likely respond because you have a pet and this shelter has a pet. They know that you're a kindred spirit in the city. They take care of pets. You take care of pets. And so you're a kindred spirit.

There are also things called **compiled lists**. These are lists that the list owners put together. List brokers and list owners will go through census data. They'll go through surveys. They'll read through telephone directories and other public records and they'll compile lists of people and put them into various groups. You may be able to find a compiled list of donors that would help your organization.

For example, there is a compiled list called "Warm Hearted Donors to Animal Causes." These people are what we call "self-reported." Somebody somewhere did a survey of North Americans and asked them, "Do you support animal causes?" And the person on the list replied, "Yes, I do." And so their name was added to this list of "Warm Hearted Donors to Animal Causes." It's a list with 250,000 names.

Another good source of lists is **people that are known to buy through direct mail**. These people are called "Mail Order Buyers." If you can find the list of people who buy products and services by direct mail that are closely related with your animal cause, then you have a source of potential donors.

Let me give you an example. There's a mailing list called "Pet Owners Who Love to Shop by Mail," and there are 13,000,000 people on that list. This is a list of people who shop by catalog. They shop online. And they've responded to surveys and identified themselves as people who shop for their pets using the mail. So if your charity helps animals, you could mail an acquisition letter to these people because you know that they're used to sending money through the mail for a cause that includes animals.

You could also find people who match your **donor profile**. It could be that most of your donors share a common trait. For example, they might all be women. They might all be veterans. They might all be African American. And there's likely a mailing list out there in the vast group of lists of people who fit your ideal profile.

For example, this is hard to believe, but there's a mailing list of "United States Nurses with Pets." These are nurses that own a dog or a cat. There's even a mailing list called "Jewish Vegetarians." These are individuals interested in a Jewish approach to vegetarianism and animal rights. So there is likely a list that will help your organization. A list of people who match your donor profile.

There are also **businesses** that have mailing lists. There may be a business in your town, your city, your region, and if the people that do business with that business fit your criteria, you may be able to rent that list. Or the business may be able to do a mailing for you. They would mail to their list and they would send something of yours along. That's called a piggyback mailing.

There are also **special event participants or guests**. Do you host a banquet every year? Most of your guests will be supporters in one way or another, but they may bring a spouse. They may bring a friend. They may bring a potential donor. If you can get the name and address of people who have attended your banquets or your golf tournaments or other special events, that's one way to acquire a donor.

There are also **newsletter subscribers**. This is popular online. There are plenty of non-profits now and they offer a free newsletter on their website. A potential donor will visit the website and sign up for the newsletter. And they'll read the newsletter week after week, month after month and eventually the non-profit—once they believe they've established some kind of credibility and relationship with that person—will ask them for a gift. So it's a two-step donor acquisition process.

You can also do the same with a print newsletter. You can offer a print newsletter to your potential donors. It might be color. It might be black and white. It doesn't matter. And you mail that to these potential donors month after month, and you decide that after a certain number of months you'll ask them for a gift. You mail them a newsletter, you develop the relationship first, and then you ask for the gift. That's a two-step donor acquisition process.

Another source of donors is **advocates who are not donors.** I'm talking about advocates that you have who champion your cause but do not yet give. For example, Amnesty International is an advocacy-based organization. They petition government. They petition businesses. They petition heads of state to bring about changes when it comes to prisoners of conscience. They have many, many members who are strong advocates for the cause. Not all of them are donors. Some of them simply sign petitions and lobby the government. These people could become donors.

Another source of donors is **lapsed donors**. This seems kind of strange that a source of donations would be people that have stopped giving, but if you take a list of people that used to give to your organization and have lapsed, and you compare that with a list of people that have never given to your organization, and you mail each list the same appeal letter, you will probably discover that the lapsed donors generate a higher response rate and a higher average gift than the people that have never given you a gift. Lapsed donors are a source of funds.

Another source of new donors is your **clients**, the people that your organization serves. Naturally, if your clients are homeless or unemployed, they are not prospects for donor appeal letters. But if your clients are former hospital patients or others who have benefited from your services, then you have a valuable source of potential supporters. These people already know your mission, who you serve and how you help them. They may be your best advocates.

Another group of individuals that knows all about your organization is your **volunteers**. They not only know you, they believe in you. They often know the most moving stories about the people that you help. That's why they give you their time and talents. Now you can ask them to give their treasure as well. Some of your volunteers will feel that their volunteering is as much as they can give, which is OK. You need to make sure your volunteers feel comfortable whether they make a donation or not.

Then there's your **staff**. One advantage of asking your staff for donations is that you know two things about them. You know that they know all about your programs and services. And you know that they have money (you gave it to them). So send them an appeal letter. Or better yet, ask them to join your monthly giving program, with their gift coming right out of their pay each payday.

Suppliers, the businesses that supply you with products and services will often make a donation when asked. So ask! Just remember that businesses don't give—people give—so you must mail your fundraising letter to a person by name, not to a business.

Step #4: Create a package

Now you move on to creating a direct mail acquisition package (which is an outer envelope, a letter, and a few other things). And it should meet some basic criteria:

Simple

Mail a package that is simple. It should have a two-page letter. It could be a four-page letter but it should be at least two pages. The package does not have to have a brochure. I recommend you don't include a brochure unless you have a very compelling reason for doing so. The package should not have any distracting inserts that increase the cost but tend to depress the response. If you mail an envelope with a brochure and a booklet and a flyer and a leaflet and a catalog and a survey, you'll depress your response. So your packet should be simple. No brochure unless needed. No distracting inserts.

Affordable

Your package should be affordable. You can reduce your costs right away by using a standard business mailing envelope, such as a #10. And you can use a standard #9 reply envelope. That's a slightly smaller envelope that fits inside the #10. It's a standard business reply envelope.

Keep your stationery standard, 8½ by 11 if you're in North America, A-4 size if you're in Britain and New Zealand. Reduce your costs further by not using a front-end premium. A front-end premium is something like return address labels, postcards, greeting cards. You can keep your mailing affordable by not relying on front-end premiums, at least not to start with.

You can boost your response rate by offering an attractive back-end premium. In other words, a premium that people have to ask for. They usually do it by giving you a gift. Then they get the premium. But you save money by not mailing that premium up front. And you can even offer an attractive back-end premium for gifts over a certain size.

Magnetic

Your package overall has to be magnetic. Absolutely compelling, gripping, exciting to read and designed to generate a response.

For example, look at the envelope on the next page. The front says, "Your dollar buys twice as much food when we do the shopping." And there's a photo of one girl eating one apple. And then on the back you see there are two children. "Your dollar buys twice as much food when we do the shopping." And you turn it over and, sure enough, there are two children. Each sister is eating an apple.

Step #5: Test the package against your lists

You need to test the package against your lists. In direct mail donor acquisition, you don't mail to all of your potential donors at the same time at first. That's expensive if you've made a mistake. Instead, you do a small test.

Let's say you're going to mail to a total of 100,000 people. You should do a test mailing first of 5,000 or 10,000 pieces, to test the package against a representative sample of those names. If the test does well, you mail to the entire list.

Or, let's say you have five lists you want to test. You would mail 5,000 pieces to each list. What you're trying to do is discover which lists pull the best. Most donor acquisition mailings are mailed to more than one list. Large, large mailers that do acquisition mailings might mail 500,000, 700,00 or 1,000,000 pieces and they might mail those pieces to 5, 10 or 15 lists.

But first of all they do a test of 20 or 30 lists. And they see what the results are. And there are a couple of things that they measure.

The first thing you test is your response rate. That's the percentage of people that respond to your mailing. You aim for one percent. You might be happier with less and you'd obviously be happier with more.

You also measure your average gift. Is it high? Is it low? Is it about average?

You also look at your cost to raise a dollar. You'll be expecting to pay somewhere between $0.98 and $1.50, depending on your case for support and the lists that you're mailing to.

CANADA POST
POSTES CANADA
Postage paid
Addressed Admail
Port payé
Médiaposte avec adresse
3868540
6003958
114/5 xxP1(A)
Alan Sharpe, President
Raiser Sharpe
22 - 30 Adelaide St N
London ON N6B 3N5
Your dollar buys
TWICE
AS MUCH
Food
when we do
the shopping.

191 New Toronto Street, Toronto, ON M8V 2E7

You'll also measure your cost to raise a donor, or your cost to acquire a donor. In direct mail fundraising, the number that we tend to look at is the cost to raise a dollar, but in direct mail donor acquisition, the more important number is the cost to acquire a donor. Because if you know what the lifetime value of your donor is, you know how much money you should be willing to spend to get that donor.

Let's say your average donor stays with you for three years and gives you a total of $100 in donations. If it costs you $10 to get that donor you should be willing to spend that money because you'll spend $10 but gain $100. Or you'll get $90 net revenue from that donor over three years.

So you measure your cost to acquire a donor because you're looking at your lifetime value of each donor and deciding if it is worth spending that amount of money to acquire that donor.

Now I'm just assuming that for this acquisition mailing you're just mailing one package to a number of lists. All that you're testing is your lists. You can also test packages, of course. You can mail two, three, four packages, but you wouldn't want to mail those to all different lists because you'd start getting confused.

All you're doing at this stage is testing your lists to find out which ones deliver the best results—response rate, average gift, cost to raise a dollar and cost to acquire a donor. Then you rollout.

Step #6: Rollout

You now roll out to the entire list. Let's say you've tested five lists and you've discovered that the first two lists are the best. Then you would mail all of your packages to those two super-high performing lists and you would ignore the other three.

So let's say you had 100,000 people that you were going to mail on one particular list. You would test first of all. You might mail 5,000 or 10,000 packages to that list. You'd see how they did. If they did really well, then you'd mail to the other 90,000 people on the list (you'd "roll out" to them). And you'd omit the first 10,000 that you you'd already mailed to in your test, plus those who had responded to the test.

Step #7: Follow up with new donors

The next step in direct mail donor acquisition is following up with your new donors. This is one of the steps that some organizations don't take into account when they launch into direct mail donor acquisition. You'll remember that I said the most important letter in direct mail fundraising is the second letter, not the first.

The first letter acquires the donor but the second letter renews the donor. If all you do is acquire donors who give one gift and then fall away you'll always be losing money and you'll always be in donor acquisition mode.

The important letter in direct mail fundraising is the second and third and fourth letter that gets the donor on board and giving regularly. You need to follow up with your donors. The first thing you need to do is thank them.

You've sent your acquisition mailing. The potential donor has responded with a gift. Now it's your turn. You need to mail them a thank-you letter or a card or a note. There are four things that you need to get right when it comes to thanking your donors:

Prompt—Your thank-you letter needs to be prompt. I recommend that you mail the letter within 24 hours of getting the gift. Some organizations think they can save money by mailing all their thank-you letters at the same time. They process them all on the same day and mail them all on the same day (to get discounts on postage) and so they wait a week or two or three and they get all of their thank-you notes together and they print them all at the same time and mail them. That's not a good idea because it might take a week or two for you to get the gift. And if the donor has to wait four weeks for a thank-you letter it might be six weeks before your thank-you letter arrives. That's too long to wait.

Personal—Your thank you should also be personal. It should be heartfelt. It should be from your heart to the donor's heart. It should not sound like it's being written by a committee at the IRS or by a bunch of lawyers who are dotting the i's and crossing the t's. It should be personal.

Particular—Your note should be particular. Ideally, your thank-you letter should say, "Thank you, Alan, for your gift of $100 that we received today in support of the ABC Fund." It shouldn't simply say, "Thank you for your gift." It should name the amount and the date and what the money was designated for, if anything. It should be a particular thank you.

Positive—Your thank you should be positive. The

overwhelming tone of the letter or the note or the card should be positive. It should be enthusiastic. This is one of the reasons that you shouldn't send a postcard as a way to say thank you. Postcards are impersonal and they tend to look like everybody gets the same one.

You could also follow up by sending new donors and supporters and members a welcome kit. This is not mandatory. But if you have the budget and if it's cost-effective to do so, you should mail your donors some kind of a kit that welcomes them on board, welcomes them to the organization.

If you've ever joined a member-based organization like Amnesty International, you'll know that you get a welcome kit. You get something through the mail that says welcome to the organization. And sometimes it even includes a membership card. And you really know that you're a member because you got a welcome kit.

Inside that welcome kit there are many, many things that I could name. I'll mention them in later chapters. Usually there'll be a simple letter that welcomes you to the organization, welcomes you on board as a donor, a partner, a collaborator with the organization. There might be a little brochure that describes the organization and who they help.

There might be some literature on how they raise their money, how they spend their money. And there might be a newsletter or maybe a copy of their latest annual report. And there might be a list of ways that you can get involved as a volunteer. And if the organization sells products, if they have a catalog of some kind, they might include that, too.

If you can, you should send a welcome kit. It's a great way to encourage people to send you another gift and become more involved.

Step #8: Measure your results

The final step that you should take in direct mail donor acquisition is measuring your results. You should measure what the response rate was of the total campaign. What's the percentage of people that mailed you a gift?

You should also calculate your average gift. You can compare that with previous acquisition mailings to see whether it was higher or lower or about the same. You should also measure your cost to raise a dollar. And see if it's higher or lower.

The nice thing about the cost-to-raise-a-dollar metric is that you can compare it with other fundraising methods and arrive at a valid comparison. You can compare the cost to raise a dollar with a banquet, or the cost to raise a dollar with telephone fundraising, or the cost to raise a dollar online, and so on. And you can see whether your direct mail cost to raise a dollar is competitive with other methods.

You should also look at your cost to acquire a donor. Compare that with other campaigns and other methods. And then you should adjust your package where needed. You may learn after that first mailing that you can reduce the cost of the package without reducing the impact.

You might be able to save money on printing. You might be able to save money on letter shop costs. You might be able to make the letter just a little bit longer, a little bit shorter, and so on. You can do that based on the results of your first mailing.

8

How to Get the Most from Direct Mail Donor Acquisition

Let's just look at a couple of results that you can expect with direct mail donor acquisition. First of all let's look at response rates. Acquisition mailings typically generate low response rates. That's because you're mailing to strangers who don't know you. An acceptable response rate with an acquisition mailing is somewhere between half of 1 percent and 2.5 percent. And the number that everybody throws around in the industry is 1 percent. That's kind of the expected.

Now you may be thinking that a response rate of only half of 1 percent might not sound adequate to you but it's acceptable if your costs are low or your average gift is high. So your response rate is not the only number that you should be looking at, because if your mailings are cheap and if your average gift is high, then a low response rate is fine.

You should also remember that generating a high response rate in an acquisition mailing is more important than receiving a high average gift. Let me just repeat that. Generating a high response rate in an acquisition mailing is more important than receiving a high average gift since the whole point of acquisition mailing is to acquire donors. The higher your response rate the more donors you acquire and the more donors you acquire the more donors you can appeal to in coming months, leading to higher revenue over time.

What would be an average gift? You should expect somewhere between $15 and $45. This depends on your region. It depends on your charity. But anywhere between $15 and $45 is an average gift. Now you should be aiming to break even on your mailing or even lose a little bit of money but you should be thinking lifetime value.

Mistakes to avoid

Mistake #1: Mailing to wealthy businesses or people

There are a couple of mistakes that you need to avoid in direct mail donor acquisition and one of them is mailing to businesses or people that you think are wealthy. Lots of inexperienced non-profits make this mistake. They think that their best prospects for direct mail appeals are businesses or wealthy people.

When they think of who they should send their appeals to they immediately think of Bill Gates of Microsoft. Not Brad Gates who lives right next door. They think of the extraordinary businesses—large businesses, well-to-do, wealthy businesses. And not the ordinary business owners that operate all around them.

Now you'll remember that I mentioned Bill Gates earlier on. If your organization is at all typical, Bill Gates has zero affinity with your cause and he does not even know about you. So he's not a long-term prospect even though he is a business owner and even though he is wealthy.

Mistake #2: Trying to raise start-up funds

Another mistake that some people make is using direct mail donor acquisition as a way to raise start-up capital. So I just want to warn you about this if you're brand new and you need money to get started as an organization. If you're starting and you don't have around $100,000 in the bank, then you should not use direct mail.

You literally cannot afford to use direct mail to raise funds because launching a new non-profit is like launching a new business. You need to spend money to make money. You can't start a non-profit with no money any more than you can start a business with no money.

You need to raise your startup capital somehow. You can borrow it. You can save it. You can get it from angel investors, or a major donor who underwrites that part of the project. But somehow you need to raise the startup capital to start your non-profit and that method should not be direct mail fundraising letters.

As we've seen, most direct mail acquisition letters lose money (but raise donors).

You mail acquisition letters to raise donors. If you need

money to start your non-profit, you should not use direct mail because you'll probably lose money. You won't raise the money that you need to start your non-profit.

Why donors stop responding to direct mail appeals

Why do donors stop responding to direct mail fundraising appeals? This is worth knowing so that you can avoid the mistake of neglecting your donors and having lots of them fall away. The reason that you're doing direct mail donor acquisition is that people stop giving and you have to replace them.

Here are some of the common reasons donors stop responding to direct fundraising appeals:

Some people forget. They simply forget they haven't given you a gift in over a year.

They also **get distracted**. They have grandchildren or a hurricane hits their home or their mom gets diagnosed with cancer. They get distracted and they don't give.

They **lose interest** in your cause.

They **suffer financially**. Maybe they get fired. Maybe the breadwinner in the home suffers an injury.

They **die**.

You mail to them too often. It could be that you pester your donors and they get far too many appeals and so they stop giving for that reason.

You don't mail to them often enough. They don't hear from you often enough and you're never on their radar and so they stop giving for that reason.

You don't listen. They've given a suggestion. They've told you that they want to give in a certain way and you haven't listened to them and so they stop giving.

You treat them like a stranger. Maybe all your letters address them as "Dear Friend," even though they've been giving to you for 10 years. You treat them like a stranger and so they stop giving.

They **feel unappreciated**. Maybe they think that you're just after them for their money. You don't appreciate them as a person.

So they stop sending you gifts.

They **lose trust in you**. Maybe you've experienced some bad publicity recently or for some reason that trust is broken. They lose that trust and so they stop giving.

They **stop receiving your appeal letters**. They've moved to another address. They haven't given you their new address and so the only reason they stop is that they stop hearing from you. And so you stop hearing from them.

You made them angry. Maybe you changed your corporate identity or your executive director has changed her hairstyle and there's something that makes them angry. When some of these donors become angry there's not a lot you can do about it.

They **retire** and they don't have the kind of money they had before to give to your organization.

How donor acquisition integrates with your annual campaign

Donor acquisition is part of a direct mail plan that includes donor renewal, lapsed donor reactivation, and donor upgrading. Donors acquired through direct mail, you should add them to your house list. And they should receive regular mailings from then on. That's how you integrate them into your annual plan. You add them to your house list. Your database. And you send them regular mailings from then on.

The secret to successful direct mail fundraising is not acquisition, but retention—keeping the donors you have. You should aim to acquire donors who remain loyal and generous for a long time and treat them so well that they do so happily. The key is retention. Not acquisition.

Easy ways to reduce donor attrition rates

Your attrition rate is your percentage of your donors that stop giving in any given year.

The first thing that you can do is **thank them** for their donations promptly every time. You can show your donors how you're using their gifts to change the world. Donors want to be thanked and they want to be told that their money is making a difference.

And you should also strike a **happy balance between**

informing your donors and asking your donors for money. Avoid mailing too many newsletters or too many appeals. You should have a balance between asking and informing.

Acquire donors who are likely to remain loyal. In other words, mail to lists that have the best potential donors on them. You're looking for people that will remain loyal over time.

Avoid tactics, such as front-end premiums and sweepstakes, that are likely to acquire one-time or short-term, unprofitable donors. Front-end premiums are those premiums like return address labels and postcards and notepads, the greeting cards that you mail to your donors to acquire them. They're expensive. Sweepstakes and lotteries are expensive too. And they tend to acquire donors who are short term. And give a smaller gift than average. Avoid those kinds of donors. That's one way to avoid your attrition rates.

How to save money on direct mail acquisition mailings through testing

You might be thinking of ways that you want to save money on your direct mail donor acquisition. It could be that you're a little scared of the idea of having to get $100,000 and put it in the mail. So let me just tell you there are ways that you can save money on direct mail donor acquisition and the simplest way is through testing.

Test all your creative package parts—in other words, the envelope, the letter, the reply device, the theme, the case for support. You should test all of that on a small group of people before you mail to an entire list. Never mail to a whole list if you can test a small part of it first.

Test all your lists by mailing to a fraction of the list before rolling out to the whole list. Test your creative package to make sure it resonates with the potential donors. Test your lists to make sure you're mailing the right package to the right people.

And as quickly as possible, establish a control package. A control package is a direct mail donor acquisition package that you use over and over and over again until it stops pulling the way you want it to. You don't have to re-invent the wheel each time you do direct mail donor acquisition. What you're aiming for is a letter, an envelope, and a reply device—a complete package—that you mail over and over again until it stops pulling the way you want.

What you're looking for is the largest number of repeat donors. You want a control package that brings in the largest number of donors who give again, those who give you more than one gift. And you're looking for that package that brings in the largest number of repeat donors at the lowest cost. Those are the two keys. Not just the highest response rate but the highest response rate of donors who give again at the lowest possible cost.

9

How Donor Acquisition Mailings Differ from Donor Renewal Mailings

Your job as a direct mail fundraiser is to make new friends every and keep them for as long as possible. And to do that you need two kinds of letter, acquisition and renewal. Understand the differences between these two letters and you'll improve your results.

Purpose

Acquisition mailings are designed to persuade non- donors to mail you their first gift. They aim to acquire donors. Renewal mailings are designed to encourage past donors to give again. Their aim is to re-new, or re- solicit, existing donors.

Audience

Acquisition mailings are mailed to strangers. Renewal mailings are mailed to friends.

Cost

Acquisition mailings tend to be inexpensive, costing anywhere from $0.50 to $1.00 a piece. Renewal mailings tend to be more expensive, costing anywhere from $0.75 to $7.00 a piece.

Personalization

Acquisition mailings, to keep costs down, tend to be one-size fits-all. They rarely involve any personalization beyond the salutation. Renewal mailings tend to be more involved, and may include personalized salutations, personalized ask strings based on the donor's previous giving levels and personalization in the body of the letter.

Segmentation

Acquisition mailings are usually mailed to everyone on a prospect list. Renewal mailings are usually segmented so that each donor segment in a house list (monthly donors, major donors, lapsed donors, first-time donors) gets a different package.

Premiums
Acquisition mailings often include premiums (personalized note pads, return address labels, greeting cards). Renewal mailings rely less on premiums.

Frequency
Acquisition mailings are mailed only a few times a year (somewhere between one and four times a year). Renewal mailings are mailed around six times a year and as often as 12 times a year.

Response Rates
Acquisition mailings tend to generate acceptable response rates of between 0.5% and 2.5%. Renewal mailings tend to generate acceptable response rates of between 6% and 12%, sometimes as high as 20%.

Net-Effectiveness
Acquisition mailings usually lose money (but gain donors). Renewal mailings almost always generate a net return.

Conclusion

I heard about two executives that were talking. One said to the other one, "I would never read a four-page fundraising letter. Never, ever, ever."

And the other executive said, "Yes you would."

And he said, "No, I wouldn't. I would never read a four-page letter. I don't read those."

And the other executive said, "Yes you would, if you received a fundraising letter that said this letter is all about you. If the letter was all about you from cover to cover, from the beginning to the end, you would read it."

And the other executive had to agree. "Yes, I would read a letter that was all about me."

So don't be discouraged in thinking that you need to have deep pockets, and mail letters that people will not respond to. I encourage you to think of a compelling case for support and think of a way to clone your best donors and write letters that appeal to your potential donors. There is a way that you can raise donors, track donors, acquire donors using direct mail fundraising.

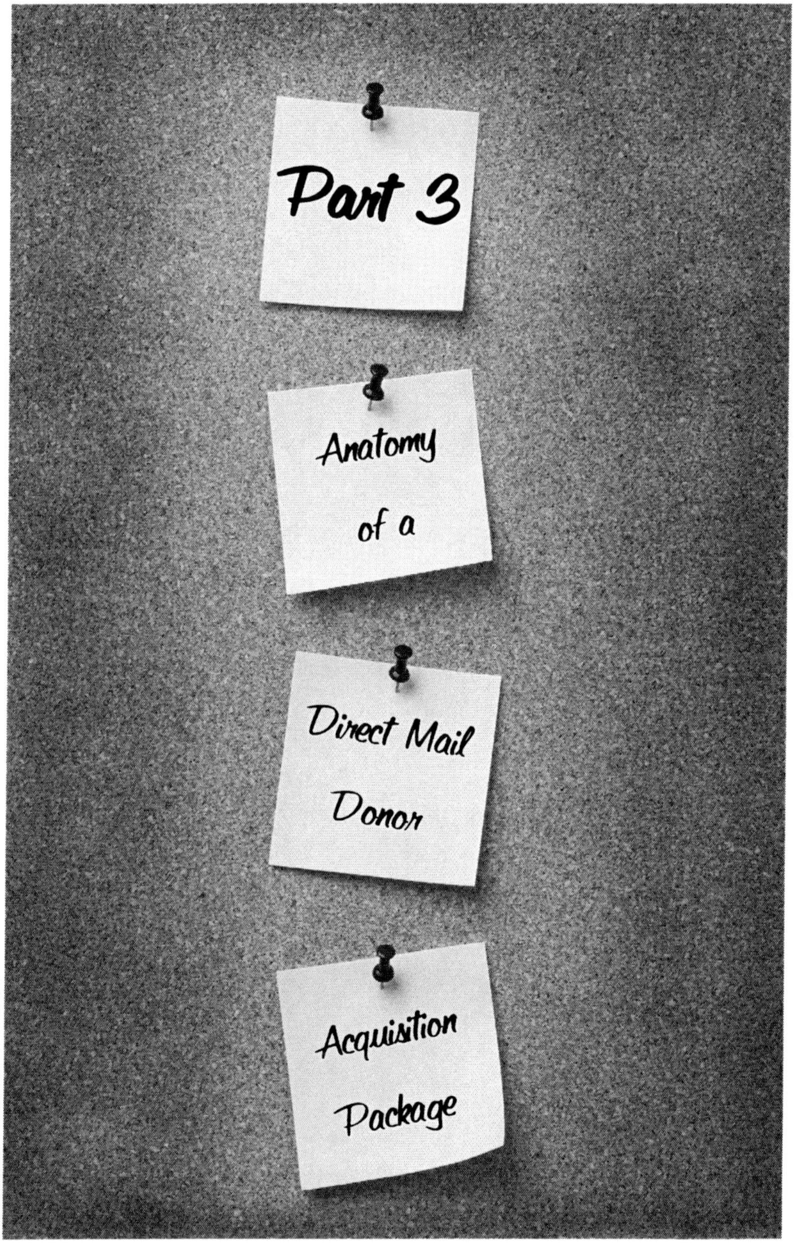
Part 3
Anatomy of a
Direct Mail Donor
Acquisition Package

CANADA POST
POSTES CANADA
Postage paid
Addressed Admail
Port payé
Médiaposte avec adresse
3868540
6003958
114/5 xxP1(A)
Alan Sharpe, President
Raiser Sharpe
22 - 30 Adelaide St N
London ON N6B 3N5
Your dollar buys
TWICE
AS MUCH
Food
when we do
the shopping.

10

Anatomy of a Donor Acquisition Package

The outer envelope

In this section, we're going to look at a direct mail fundraising package that was put into the mail by a non-profit to acquire brand new donors. We're going to look at it piece by piece and line by line and see what we can learn about how a professional organization raises funds and acquires donors using direct mail.

Let's look at the outer envelope first of all (opposite page).

This is the outer envelope, or the carrier envelope, sometimes called the mailing envelope. The first thing that I notice about a package like this is that this is not an envelope that you're used to getting in business mail. Most business mail is sent in what is called a number 10 envelope. This is larger. This is the kind of envelope that you'd get if it was your birthday, or if it was Christmas and you were getting a greeting card from somebody. This envelope is greeting card dimensions. This envelope is six inches tall by nine inches wide.

Right away, this envelope has the advantage of being a non-standard-looking envelope. It doesn't look like a traditional piece of business correspondence, which is an advantage. Coming in an envelope that normally carries a greeting card, it carries that kind of tone and sentiment.

If you look at the top right-hand corner, you'll see that this envelope was mailed in Canada. In the top right-hand corner is the postal indicia. There are three ways that you can put postage on your envelope. One of them is a stamp. That's the most personal. The next way is metered postage, where a little machine puts ink on the paper, and that's done envelope-by-envelope.

The third way is to use a postal indicia, like this, which is usually done at the printer, not at the letter shop. The envelopes are printed in bulk, and there's a little permit number there, 3868540, that the non-profit uses with Canada Post. Because they're mailing tens of thousands, they get a break on the postage. They don't have to pay first-class postage for this mailing.

This non-profit has used a different size envelope, they've used a postal indicia so they can save on their postage, so they're not paying first class, and they've used what a "teaser" on the face of the envelope.

You've got this picture of this girl, close up, eating an apple, with a big smile on her face, and then you've got this little headline, which we call "teaser copy," because it's designed to tease the recipient into opening the envelope. It says, "Your dollar buys twice as much food when we do the shopping." That's a tease.

For example, who is the "we" in, "Your dollar buys twice as much food when we do the shopping?" You don't know. If you turn this envelope over and look at the back, you'll see there's a return address in Toronto, but you don't know who this is from. The organization that mailed it does not identify itself. Now this is a bold step. Some mailers would say that you should always say who you are on your envelope, so that people will know who they're receiving this from. Otherwise, they'll be inclined to throw it away because you'll be anonymous.

I suppose that is valid to a point, but if I got this envelope with these two beautiful girls on it and I could see that it had something to do with charity, I wouldn't throw it away thinking that it was coming from a fraud artist or someone who didn't want to identify himself. So it's a gamble—you have to have the courage to not put your logo or your organization name on your envelope.

You'll also notice from the front of the envelope that they're using a window. Behind it is the reply device that asks for the gift. This organization is also saving money by having the reply device and the address on it showing through the window. That way, they don't have to match the letter address with the envelope address if they use a label or if they laser the address onto the envelope. That saves money at the letter shop stage.

Now you'll notice that this envelope has this "two-for-one" idea, and it's worth paying attention to it now because this whole theme here is carried through the whole package. They've got this girl on the cover, and the headline says, "Your dollar . . ." It's always a good idea to start your teaser copy with the donor—"Your dollar buys twice as much food when we do the shopping."

191 New Toronto Street, Toronto, ON M8V 2E7

You look on the front of the envelope and there's one girl, and she's eating one apple. Then you turn the envelope over (see previous page), which is what most people have to do to put their letter opener or thumb underneath the flap to open the envelope. Sure enough, there's twice as much food—two apples, two girls, two people being fed.

On the front it's one person eating, and on the back of the envelope it's two people. You'll also notice that the back of the envelope has the return address, so the organization is not mentioned but the address is, and so if any of this mail is undeliverable, it'll be returned to the sender.

You'll also notice that the back of the envelope, and even the front, does not have the Web site of the non-profit organization. Some non-profits are inclined to put their Web site address on their envelopes. I think that's a bad idea. It's worth testing, obviously, but I think it's a bad idea because someone might just lay your envelope aside and visit your Web site, and they would likely visit your home page, and they wouldn't be visiting this campaign.

They might just click around and surf around your Web site for a little bit, and then click away to YouTube to watch a man juggling hamsters. You don't want to give your donor anything on your envelope that will distract them and encourage them to lay your envelope aside unopened. That includes putting a phone number on the envelope.

The letter

Let's imagine this has arrived in your mailbox. You're intrigued by this beautiful girl and her sister eating this apple, and so you open the envelope. You're wondering, "What does it mean that we can buy twice as much food with your dollar when we do the shopping?" You open it up, you open up the envelope, and now you're looking at the letter (see next two pages).

It's an 8½ x 11 letter, standard size, and it's in two-color. It's in red plus black. Now you notice that when you print something in red plus black—that's just two colors—the picture of this girl in the top right-hand corner, it almost looks like it's full-color, but it's really just black ink and a little bit of red, so the broccoli looks pink when it would normally look green.

Daily Bread Food Bank

FIGHTING HUNGER

6003958
Alan Sharpe, President
Raiser Sharpe
22 - 30 Adelaide St N
London ON N6B 3N5

Dear Friend,

A mother of twins went to a food bank the other day and we were able to do the seemingly impossible. She left with $60 worth of groceries, but those groceries only cost Daily Bread Food Bank $30. How did we do it?

We didn't do it alone. We did it because of people like you, who care enough to support our important work.

The mother I'm telling you about has to visit a food bank every month to feed herself and her family. Like many others who live in the GTA, she runs out of money before she runs out of month. Hunger, unfortunately, is commonplace across the GTA.

Almost 30,000 children in the Toronto area live in families that rely on food banks every month to make ends meet. Many of these children have moms and dads with jobs, but their jobs don't allow them to cover the costs of rent, utilities, clothes and food for their families.

You see, people who use food banks pay around 73% of their income on rent. After paying for rent and utilities, they have just $4.79 per day left over to cover all other expenses – including food. That doesn't even buy a round-trip ticket on public transit.

And that's why I'm writing to you today.

If you have 99¢ in your pocket, you can buy one can of soup. If we have 99¢ in our pocket, we can buy two cans of soup. At Daily Bread Food Bank, because of our important and essential work in the community, we can negotiate exclusive discounts with food suppliers and buy twice as much food as you can at your local grocer. All I need is your help today to purchase and deliver it to families experiencing hunger.

Daily Bread Food Bank is Toronto's leader in the fight against hunger. Each month we serve almost 75,000 people from food banks across the GTA through our network of 160 member agencies and over 190 food relief programs. Besides running neighbourhood food banks, where people come to access nutritious food hampers, our member agencies also run meal programs, where people receive prepared meals, such as soups and casseroles and staples programs, geared toward newcomers adjusting to life in Canada, which provide items like rice and dried beans.

Over please...

191 New Toronto Street, Toronto, ON M8V 2E7 • Telephone: 416-203-0050 • Fax: 416-203-0049
www.dailybread.ca • e-mail: info@dailybread.ca • Charitable Registration # 11888 1549 RR0001

Because hunger can affect anybody, Daily Bread helps everybody. We are non-partisan and all-inclusive. Our donors and volunteers come from every income bracket, cultural background, faith group and walk of life. Some are motivated by their faith, others by a sense of social justice, and others simply by a sense of fairness. **But the one thing our donors have in common is the belief that no one in Canada ought to go hungry.** I know that you share that belief.

By supporting Daily Bread with a cash donation today, you are supporting the goal of a society in which everyone has enough food to eat. And I'm not just being hypothetical here. Your cash donation right now will help single mothers, seniors, immigrants, people with disabilities and working families in a number of powerful ways.

For one thing, when you give us a donation of cash instead of a can of food, we can buy the food we need the most. Because hunger stems from poverty and other issues our clients face, Daily Bread is also committed to enriching client access to counseling and resources. This type of support allows clients to take control of their lives and improve their circumstances. We must continue meeting the increasing needs of food bank clients, whether it is access to counseling or food.

Not only that, but your cash gift helps us get the food to those who need it faster, since we don't have to sort it. Which brings me to another point. As you can imagine, Daily Bread needs money to put its trucks on the street to get food to those who need it the most, and run its warehouse and distribution facility. **Your financial gift makes sure Daily Bread can carry out its mission of feeding hungry people and working to eliminate the need for food banks.**

You play a vital role in ending hunger in the GTA. You see, we don't receive any money from the United Way. We don't receive a penny from the province or the federal government. We struggle month-to-month to provide the necessary and nutritious food families need. That's why your gift is so necessary - right now, so we can continue this important work.

Please give right now. Buy $100 worth of groceries with a gift of just $50. Or $50 worth of groceries for just $25.

Thank you for caring,

Gail Nyberg

Gail Nyberg
Executive Director

P.S. Your dollar buys twice as much food for those who struggle with hunger when we do the shopping, but only if we have your dollar. So please give generously to Daily Bread Food Bank right now, using the enclosed reply form and postage-paid envelope.

Daily Bread Food Bank

FIGHTING HUNGER

191 New Toronto Street, Toronto, ON M8V 2E7 • Telephone: 416-203-0050 • Fax: 416-203-0049

www.dailybread.ca • e-mail: info@dailybread.ca • Charitable Registration # 11888 1549 RR0001

The letterhead immediately identifies who the mailing is from. It's from the Daily Bread Food Bank. They have a little slogan there saying, "Fighting Hunger." If you look at the bottom of the letter, you can see that address again, 191 New Toronto Street. It's in Toronto. All the contact information that you need is at the bottom of the letter, not at the top. That's a good place to put it. If you put your email address, your Web site address, your charitable number, your fax number, your telephone number and your address at the top of the letter, you make it cluttered. You use up a lot of valuable real estate that is better used with headlines, pictures and your logo.

The letter immediately tells you that it's from the Daily Bread Food Bank. The theme that they established on the cover, of buying twice as much food with your dollar as you can when you go shopping, this whole theme is echoed right here, and repeated with this girl, where she's holding up these two pieces of broccoli—not one but two—with a big smile, and she's asking, "Want to be twice as generous for the same money?"

You see this idea about two-for-one and generosity being repeated. This is very important in a direct mail piece. If you establish a theme on the cover of your envelope, the front of your envelope, you should carry that theme throughout the package. It should be on your letter, on your brochure, on your reply device, and it can even go on your business reply card, or your business reply envelope. When I say a theme, I'm talking about some creative way of describing your case for support. We'll look at that in a second.

You should also use visual continuity. Not only does this envelope and letter repeat the idea of two-for-one, but also the girls on the envelope are holding two pieces of fruit, and this girl on the letter is holding two pieces of vegetable, two pieces of broccoli, so visually it says two and in words it says two. So there's visual and textual continuity.

This letter that you're looking at is a sample and it doesn't have a date, but the letter that went through the mail and was received by potential donors had a date on it at the top left-hand corner. That's important. If you mail a letter that looks like this with no date, it makes the letter look generic and boilerplate, and it looks like everybody got the same letter. Of course everybody did, but if you don't have a date on it, it looks like it is mass-produced and not really a letter that was mailed on a given day—it's just a general letter that all the neighbors get. So you should include a date in your letter.

Salutation

You'll also notice that the letter is what we call pre-populated, with the person's name, address, and donor number. Just above my name there, at the top left-hand corner, you'll see a number, 6003958. That's a number that the mailer can use to track this package. They know that this package went to this person on this date, and that same number appears on the reply device so that they can track this mailing and this list to this campaign, to this donor.

Beneath that address block is what's called the salutation, where it says, "Dear So-and-So." In this case, the organization has chosen to use the most generic, commonplace, bland, impersonal salutation that there is: "Dear Friend." If you've read my book, *Breakthrough Fundraising Letters*, you'll know that this is my hobbyhorse. The only difference between a hobbyhorse and a real horse is that you can get off a real horse. This is, I think, a deadly salutation. I don't think you should call anybody your friend, especially if you don't know them.

If you do know them as a donor, you should call them Alan, call them Bill, call them Jane, call them Samantha, call them by their name. Don't call them friend. It's impersonal. Even, "Dear Mr. Sharpe" would be better than "Dear Friend."

The reason that they use "Dear Friend" is that it's cheaper. It's much cheaper to print 100,000 letters just like this than it is to print them individually personalized with a salutation like, "Dear Alan," "Dear Bill," "Dear Jane." It's much cheaper just to print thousands and thousands of letters than it is to personalize. That's what organizations tend to do with direct mail donor acquisition. They try to save as much money as possible on donor acquisitions, so that's why you have this generic, "Dear Friend." I would recommend you test the generic versus the personal salutation.

Opening line

The opening line—what does it say? It's the most important sentence in your letter, and what does it say? "A mother of twins went to a food bank the other day, and we were able to do the seemingly impossible. She left with $60 worth of groceries, but those groceries only cost Daily Bread Food Bank $30. How did we do it?"

You'll notice that the opening line also carries forward this idea of two-for-one—$60 for $30 or $30 for $60—and the envelope had twin girls on it. Some donors might not have noticed that, but anybody who's paying attention would notice there's this two-for-one, two-girls-who-are-twins idea being carried from the envelope to the top of the letter to the opening sentence of the letter.

This is a good opening line because it involves a person. Whenever possible, you should have an opening line that has a person in it, not a cold statistic, and not just a statement of facts, but a real, live person.

It also begins by telling a story, which is also a great way to start a letter. Rather than saying, "I work for the Daily Bread Food Bank and we need your donation," this letter starts off by telling a story about a mother of twins who went to the food bank and did the seemingly impossible. If you have a story to tell that is dramatic and has lots of human interest and color in it, use that as your opening, rather than opening by talking about yourselves or your need or your organization.

You also see right away who the letter is from. If the donor hasn't paid attention to the logo, right away the letter says this mother left the Daily Bread Food Bank with $60 worth of groceries, but it only cost the Daily Bread Food Bank $30, so the writer has identified who the letter is coming from—the Daily Bread Food Bank.

The case for support

Notice the second paragraph, "We didn't do it alone. We did it because of people like you, who care enough to support our important work." Someone once asked me what the most important word in direct mail fundraising is, and I replied, "It's either "thank you" or "you."

The word "you" should appear in your letter more than the word "we" or "us" or "I" or "our charity." Take out a red pen and circle all the times the word "you" appears in this letter, and see if you think it appears often enough. Take out a blue pen and circle all the times you see "we" or "us" or "our organization." See which one carries the most weight.

The first "you" appears in the second paragraph, "We did it because of people like you." Now in the third paragraph, the writer begins to explain the problem. Every direct mail fundraising appeal should be based on a problem, a challenge, a difficulty that the donor can help the charity overcome. It should be some kind of a conflict. Not just, "We need your money," but a problem, a problem that involves people. Right away, this writer says, "the mother that I'm telling you about has to visit a food bank every month to feed herself and her family." Like many others who live in the GTA—that's the Greater Toronto Area—she runs out of money before she runs out of month. Hunger, unfortunately, is commonplace across the GTA, so right away the writer is telling you, "We're the Daily Bread Food Bank, and there is a mother that went to the food bank and she got twice as much food as she could have if she'd had to buy it herself.

She is like many others who live in our city, and she runs out of money before she runs out of month and she has to visit the Daily Bread Food Bank every month to feed herself and her family. That is the problem that the donor can help the organization solve. You'll notice that the fifth sentence in that paragraph is, "The mother I'm telling you about . . ." There's the word "you" again. The word "you" appears in the second paragraph, and it appears in the third paragraph.

Now you're a non-profit and you're mailing a donor acquisition mailing to strangers. You hope that these strangers fit your profile of an ideal donor, and so you hope that they will be sympathetic to your cause, but you can't just assume that they know who you are, or what you do, or who you help. Somewhere in your letter, you have to explain who you are, what you do, and who you help.

This writer does this in the fourth paragraph: "Almost 30,000 children in the Toronto area live in families that rely on food banks every month to make ends meet. Many of these children have moms and dads with jobs, but their jobs don't allow them to cover the cost of rent, utilities, clothes and food for their families."

You can't assume that the reader knows that there are people in your city who work and yet still can't afford to eat. This writer makes sure that early on the reader is told about the problem that this non-profit is trying to face.

Another "you" appears at the beginning of the next paragraph, the fifth paragraph down. Some people have a prejudice about the poor. They think that the poor are lazy, and if they just got a job they could feed themselves. Some people have a prejudice about food banks, and it's a prejudice that the Daily Bread Food Bank has to face.

One of the obstacles that this letter had to overcome was this prejudice that might be present in some of the readers. In the fifth paragraph, the writer confronts it head—on but in a gentle way, and says, "You see, people who use food banks pay around 73 percent of their income on rent. After paying for rent and utilities, they have just $4.79 per day left over to cover all other expenses, including food. That doesn't even buy a roundtrip ticket on public transit."

Here is the problem that this non-profit faces and that people in the city face, and it's spelled out in specific terms. You see the number "73 percent." "People who use food banks pay around 73 percent of their income on rent." That's a fact, and most people can picture that.

The letter goes on to explain that after these people have paid for all their necessities, like rent and utilities, they have not $5, but $4.79, left over. This is an accurate number. Wherever possible when you're discussing numbers, unless you think you're going to bore your reader to death with being too specific, use a specific number rather than a general one. Use a concrete detail rather than an abstract one.

Rather than saying "people don't have much money left over per day," you say "they have $4.79 left over per day." This is an actual number that's obviously been arrived at through study. It helps your cause. It helps you present your case for support if you can be specific and almost scientific in the way that you present your information, without being pedantic and presenting too much detail.

You'll also notice that the writer at the end of this paragraph tries to describe this plight that people have in a picturesque way. What is $4.79? How could you live on that per day? Well, the writer says, "That doesn't even amount to a roundtrip ticket on public transit." What this writer did is visited the public transit in Toronto, or visited their Web site, found out what it costs to get a roundtrip ticket, and discovered that it costs more to travel roundtrip across the city of Toronto than $4.79.

This is a picturesque way of describing the problem. It would be the same as if you were trying to tell somebody what an acre is.

Most people that live in a city don't know what an acre looks like. If you explain that an acre is an American football field without the end zones, most people can suddenly picture what an acre looks like. Wherever possible, take your need, your case for support or the plight that you're trying to describe, and make it memorable with a picture. Present the need in accurate numbers and draw a picture.

Now you've got this little subhead right in the middle of the page, "And that's why I'm writing to you today." There's the donor again, "you."

Next paragraph, "If you have 99 cents in your pocket, you can buy one can of soup. If we have 99 cents in our pocket, we can buy two cans of soup." This is the case for support. It's basic, boiled down. What the food bank has done is boiled down—excuse the pun—they've boiled down their whole case for support into this: "If you have 99 cents, you can buy one can of soup. But if we have the 99 cents, we can buy two cans of soup."

Now that sounds impossible. How could you buy twice as much food as I can, the donor asks? They explain how. "At Daily Bread Food Bank, because of our important and essential work in the community, we can negotiate exclusive discounts with food suppliers, and buy twice as much food as you can at your local grocer. All I need is your help today to purchase and deliver it to families experiencing hunger." This last sentence of this paragraph, where the writer says, "All I need is your help today to purchase and deliver it to families experiencing hunger," this is what's called an implied ask.

The ask

There are two basic ways that you can ask for a donation. One of them is to say, "I need your help today," and another one, the more explicit way, is to say, "Give a donation." If you want to scare the reader away quickly, then ask for a donation right in your first sentence, or your second sentence or your third sentence.

You're much better off warming up the reader to the whole idea that the reader can help you solve a problem that helps people in the city. You don't have to ask for a gift up front and be explicit about it. You can use what's called an *implied ask:* "All I need is your help today to purchase and deliver it to families experiencing hunger."

Another challenge that this non-profit faces, not only having to explain their case for support and overcome the prejudice that some people have about the poor being lazy and not working, this organization also has the challenge of presenting its credentials. When you send a direct mail fundraising acquisition letter, you're assuming that the people that get the letter don't know your organization very well. They don't know your history, they don't know your founder, they don't know why you exist, where you work. They don't know all the details of who you are, what you do, and who you help.

Particularly, they don't know if they can trust you. Donors today are as skeptical as ever. They might have been burned, they might have seen a story on CNN about non-profits that are shady, and that are run by a bunch of crooks, because it is possible to get a tax-free exemption status and fleece people before the government catches up. So people don't know if they can trust you, so you have to tell them enough about your organization that they trust you. There are a couple of ways that you can do that.

You can explain how long you've been in business. You can name the people that sit on your board or the people that endorse you. If they're famous or well known, that helps your credibility. You can explain that you're a registered non-profit. That helps, too. The Daily Bread Food Bank explains in the last paragraph on this page who they are. They say, "We are Toronto's leader in the fight against hunger. Each month, we serve almost 75,000 people from food banks across the GTA—that's the Greater Toronto Area—through our network of 160 member agencies, and over 190 food relief programs."

Not everybody understands what the food bank does. Some people think the food bank is just a place where you can go and get a can of soup or a packet of pasta, but they do far more than that. They have 160 member agencies and food relief programs. Besides running neighborhood food banks, which is what people think the food bank does, besides running food banks where people come to access nutritious food hampers, their member agencies also run meal programs, where people receive prepared meals, such as soups and casseroles, and staples programs geared toward newcomers adjusting to life in Canada, which provide items like rice and dried beans.

I didn't know that, and so this writer tells me something valuable about the Daily Bread Food Bank. They go beyond simply supplying cans of beans, pasta and nonperishable food items. You must do likewise, presenting your credentials and explaining who you are, so that new donors will feel comfortable parting with their donations.

At the bottom right-hand corner of this letter, you'll notice that it says Over Please. I think this is really silly. That's another one of my hobbyhorses, I suppose. Donors know that they should turn the letter over, and they know that they should continue reading on the other side. One thing that this designer has done, which I believe is a mistake, this designer has finished the page with a period. The last sentence in that paragraph says, "Which provide items like rice and dried beans," period. That's a mistake.

When you design your letter, end your page with a run-on sentence that carries on over the other page. You should never end your first page with a period. This paragraph should have ended, "casseroles, and staples programs geared towards newcomers adjusting to," and then just ended it right there, and the sentence should have continued on page two so the reader, the potential donor, had to turn the page over to continue reading to finish the thought.

Most people don't like finishing a novel halfway through. They like to get to the end and find out whodunit. Most people don't like to read half a sentence and not find out how it ends, especially if it's a provocative, interesting, well-written dramatic story that they're reading. I recommend you end your sentence at the bottom of the page halfway through your sentence, and don't put "Over Please." That's my prejudice, so now you know it.

You've turned the page over and you're now on page two of the letter. The writer continues, "Because hunger can affect anybody, Daily Bread Food Bank helps everybody. We are nonpartisan and all-inclusive." Again, this helps donors overcome any kind of prejudice they might have if they thought that this food bank was run by the Roman Catholic Church, or it's just for Christians, or it's only for the urban people at a certain intersection in town.

They might have a prejudice thinking that it's run by the government, or that they get their funding from who knows where. This letter helps to overcome any of those objections that people might have in their minds by encouraging the reader to know that they are nonpartisan. They are not run by the church. They're not run by Rotary International, or by the Salvation Army. They are nonpartisan and all-inclusive, which is a helpful thing to tell people. That's important.

"Our donors and volunteers come from every income bracket," is another surprising thing to find out. "They come from every cultural background, faith group and walk of life. Some are motivated by their faith, others by a sense of social justice . . ." Here, they're talking about their volunteers—". . . others simply by a sense of fairness." Now you'll notice the sentence is in bold. "But the one thing our donors have in common is the belief that no one in Canada ought to go hungry. I know that you share that belief." There's that word "you" again, putting the donor into the letter. It makes it sound like a conversation that's being had.

In the next paragraph, there's another implied ask. The writer doesn't come out explicitly and ask for a donation in some kind of shrill way, tugging on the donor, but says, "By supporting the Daily Bread Food Bank with a cash donation today . . ." That's an implied ask.

"By supporting the Daily Bread Food Bank with a cash donation today, you are supporting the goal of a society in which everyone has enough food to eat. I'm not just being hypothetical here. Your cash donation right now, [there's another implied ask] will help single mothers, seniors, immigrants, people with disabilities, and working families in a number of powerful ways."

The writer continues, "For one thing, when you give us a donation of cash instead of a can of food, we can buy the food we need the most." You'll see that this writer is now appealing to the mind, presenting a common-sense, rational reason for giving a donation. The writer started the letter with the heart, appealing to the heart—this mother and her twins, she can't make ends meet, she has to go to the food bank. That's appealing to the heart, the emotions. Now this writer is appealing to the mind,

"Because hunger stems from poverty and other issues our clients face, Daily Bread is also committed to enriching client access to counseling and resources. This type of support allows clients to take control of their lives and improve their circumstances. We must continue meeting the increasing needs of food bank clients, whether it is access to counseling or food." The Daily Bread Food Bank calls its clients *clients*, which I think is an unfortunate term, but there you have it.

In the next paragraph, they make another implied ask. "Not only that, but your cash gift helps us get the food to those who need it faster since we don't have to sort it." You see the advantages of giving money rather than giving a can of food? In the previous paragraph, the writer explained, "We can buy the food we need." We don't just have to wait for you to deliver the food and realize, "Oh, we didn't need that can. We needed something else." We can buy the food we need. That's one advantage.

Another one is that we don't have to sort it. Our writer says, "That brings me to another point. As you can imagine, Daily Bread needs money to put its trucks on the street to get food to those who need it the most, and run its warehouse and distribution facility. Your financial gift [here's another implied ask] makes sure Daily Bread can carry out its mission of feeding hungry people and working to eliminate the need for food banks."

Did you notice that colloquial way of writing? In the previous paragraph, the writer begins by saying, "For one thing," and in the second paragraph says, "Not only that," and in the next sentence says, "Which brings me to another point." That's not a grammatical sentence, but this letter is written in a conversational tone, the way you'd talk to somebody over coffee at a local donut place.

In closing

The second-but-last paragraph is a strong close. You'll notice the paragraph begins with the word "you," the most important word in direct mail fundraising. "You play a vital role in ending hunger in the GTA. You see, we don't receive any money from the United Way. We don't receive a penny from the province or the federal government. We struggle month to month to provide the necessary and nutritious food families need. That's why your gift is so necessary right now, so we can continue this important work. Please give right now." That's the last paragraph.

Then comes an emphatic ask, an explicit ask, "Please give right now. Buy $100 worth of groceries with a gift of $50." There's that two-for-one theme, which was established on the envelope, established with a photograph of the girl on the letter, established in the opening sentence, and now repeated again. The case for support is repeated in the final ask, "Buy $100 worth of groceries with a gift of just $50, or $50 worth of groceries for just $25."

If you want to end your letter safely, you can write, "Yours sincerely." You could write, "Yours truly, Gail Nyberg." This letter writer has been a little more creative, and has written, "Thank you for caring."

The signature is in black. I recommend, if your budget allows it, you print the signature in blue. That would mean that this letter would have had to be in black, and red, and blue. It would add an extra color, which would drive up your cost, but it would be worth testing. A blue signature will contrast with the rest of the letter.

This signature is not legible. If you didn't know that this was Gail Nyberg, it might be a little hard for you to read who that is, and so beneath the signature, the person has written her name, "Gail Nyberg." You can read who the person is because the signature doesn't tell you. Beneath her name, she's told you who she is. She is the executive director of Daily Bread Food Bank. Her leadership role in this organization adds credibility to this ask, to this letter. Because she is the executive director, she has executive power, she sets the vision of the organization, and so she knows what she is talking about.

You can also mail a letter that's written by a volunteer or a board member, or even one of the clients. The difficulty of having one of your volunteers or one of your clients write the letter is that they can't really speak with any moral authority about who the organization is, what they do, where they do it, why they do it.

If you're watching the American election campaign at the moment, it would be the difference between having Barack Obama say something about where he's headed, and having one of his volunteer staff say it. Barack Obama has far more credibility because, if he's elected, he will become president, whereas one of his volunteers who might say, "Barack says this, Barack believes that," doesn't have the same credibility. This writer signs her name and gives her job title, so any stranger reading this letter would know who it's from.

Beneath the signature is a postscript, "Your dollar buys twice as much food for those who struggle with hunger when we do the shopping, but only if we have your dollar. So please give generously to Daily Bread Food Bank right now using the enclosed reply form and postage paid envelope." That is the case for support and the ask rolled into one.

Studies conducted years ago show that people read postscripts. So if you put a postscript at the bottom of your letter, people will likely read it, and so you should put there either your strongest case or repeat the case for support in your letter. Just in case someone gets your letter, looks at the back, sees who it's from and reads only the postscript, the postscript tells them, "Your dollar buys twice as much food. It helps the hungry when we do the shopping, but we have to have your dollar. Please give generously."

You'll notice that this letter, if you look at page one, has their address at the bottom. It has their Web site address, their email address and their charitable registration number. On page two of the letter, it has all of this stuff again. I say this is redundant. It's not necessary.

On page two of the letter, they could have left the bottom blank—perhaps included just the logo. There's no need to have the address, phone and fax, and everything else presented twice in one letter. The only reason to do that would be if the two pieces of paper were going to get separated, which they're not likely to do. They're a letter.

The informational brochure

Let's look at the enclosure that came with this package (on the following pages) Inside the package was this little brochure. This brochure measures 5½ x 17 inches, and it folds to 5½ x 8½, so it fits nicely inside the mailing envelope without having to be folded again.

What you're looking at, the mother and her two daughters, is exactly what you would pull out of your envelope. You would then put your hand on the right-hand side and you would open it up, and you'd have a facing-page spread, showing these two girls that you saw on the cover, the girl eating the apple, and on the back, her sister, here they are. They appear again in the brochure.

This brochure addresses the common concerns and maybe even some potential objections that donors have before making a donation. There are plenty of things that donors want to know about your organization before they give you a gift. The place to tell them those things is not necessarily in your letter. They might want to know that you're a registered charity. They might want to know what percentage of your income you get from foundations.

Brochure front

How you can help feed your neighbours.

Give now. Your dollar buys twice as much food when we do the shopping.
At Daily Bread Food Bank, because of our important and essential work in the community, we can negotiate exclusive discounts with food suppliers. Daily Bread Food Bank can buy twice as much food for one dollar as you can at your local grocer.

Please give now...

1. Phone 416-203-0050 to make a credit card donation
2. Donate online at www.dailybread.ca
3. Mail a cheque to: Daily Bread Food Bank 191 New Toronto Street Toronto, ON M8V 2E7

Daily Bread Food Bank
FIGHTING HUNGER

191 New Toronto Street, Toronto, ON M8V 2E7 • Telephone: 416-203-0050 • Fax: 416-203-0049
www.dailybread.ca • e-mail: info@dailybread.ca • Charitable Registration # 11888 1549 RR0001

Brochure back

People within our community are struggling with hunger.

Almost 900,000 people in the Greater Toronto Area go hungry annually because they cannot afford to eat. These people are your neighbours.

Children

Thirty-eight percent of people relying on food banks are children. That's almost 28,500 children monthly who don't have access to regular nutritious meals, which leads to poor health and well-being and can even affect their performance in school. Almost a quarter of these children are hungry at least once a week because their families don't have enough money to buy food. Breaking the cycle of poverty in the future demands investment in these children today – with your help.

Working poor

More than half of the people who are working and using food banks earn a wage of $10/hour or more. The problem is, they are only given part time or casual hours with no benefits. Most of them want more hours, but can't get them.

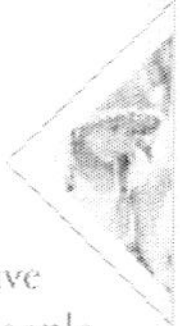

People with disabilities

Nearly half of the people who use food banks report that a disability or serious illness prevents them from working. After rent and bills are paid, many do not have enough for groceries. Thanks to the generosity of people like you, who donate the money that we use to buy food, they find assistance and nutritious food at their local food bank.

Newcomers to Canada

Over 40% of the people who visit food banks in the GTA are recent immigrants. Many are prevented from working in their fields because their professional credentials are not recognized. They are unable to find jobs, even though close to two-thirds have post secondary education. They too go hungry in the land of plenty.

Brochure inside left

Brochure inside right

Help us feed them. FIGHT HUNGER.

Each month we serve over 75,000 people in the GTA through our network of 160 member agencies and over 190 food relief programs. Here's how we'll spend your donation.

Neighbourhood food banks

Our agencies run neighbourhood food banks where people come to access nutritious food. With the help of your donations, we give out two or three day's worth of food per person in each household.

Meal programs

Your support help us provide meals and snacks at hostels, drop-in centres, churches and schools.

Staples programs

We supply rice, dried beans and other staples to newcomers who are adjusting to life in Canada – thanks to financial help from concerned neighbours like you.

Supplementary programs

These community development programs are run by the same people who visit the food banks and receive the food. They are a proactive effort to help people living in low-income areas.

National food sharing system

Daily Bread is a leading partner in the National Food Sharing System. Through food solicitation, warehousing and distribution efforts, we help ensure that donations from the food industry are distributed fairly across Canada.

Finding solutions to hunger

Daily Bread is active in research – seeking out the root causes of hunger, educating the public and advocating for realistic government policies that reduce the need for food banks on behalf of those experiencing hunger.

Advocacy

Daily Bread is committed to enriching client access to counseling and resources. This type of support allows clients to take control of their lives and improve their circumstances.

Daily Bread Food Bank

FIGHTING HUNGER

They might want to know what percentage of your income you spend on fundraising and administration. They might want to know how many cents on the dollar actually goes to help hungry people. They'll have lots of questions like that.

New donors, people that haven't given you a gift before, will have questions. The place to answer those questions is a brochure or a note, or something inside your letter. Usually, that place is not in the body of the letter. What this organization has done is taken their case for support for this particular acquisition, and they've echoed it in their brochure. They didn't mail a generic brochure for this specific campaign. This campaign is all about buying twice as much food for the dollar as a donor can. It features two girls, it features twins, it talks about their mother, and then the brochure does the exact same thing.

It has the skyline of Toronto, and a headline that points at the older girl, "Donate a 99 cent can of tuna, you feed Gabriella." Then a little arrow points at her sister, "Donate the 99 cents instead, you feed Linda, as well." In other words, "We can buy twice as much food with a dollar as you can." The brochure features the mother, too. You see a happy sister, another happy sister, and a happy mother. She looks like she's a single mother, too, just the way that they've shot the photograph.

The brochure, you'll notice, has the logo, Daily Bread Food Bank, and their slogan, Fighting Hunger, on the cover, so you know who the brochure is from. If you separate this brochure from the letter, you still have the logo and you know who it's from. Daily Bread Food Bank knows that brochures and other inserts sometimes get separated from the other contents of the package, like the letter and the reply device, so they've included their Web site address, their phone, their fax and email address in the brochure, and also a reason that you should give a donation.

In this brochure, they take the most compelling statistics and facts that were mentioned in the letter, and repeat them in the brochure just to emphasize their case for support. They tell you a little bit more about the organization—who they are, what they do, where they work.

If you were looking at this as a full-page spread, you would see that written right across the top of these two inside panels, these two facing pages, is a headline, "People within our community are struggling with hunger. Help us feed them. Fight hunger." They present a fact and they present a call to action. They have an action-oriented headline. This is not a brochure that just tells you a bunch of stuff that you need to know about the Daily Bread Food Bank. It's a brochure that's designed to move you to give a gift. It's not only informational;—it's also motivational. You're supposed to do something with this brochure.

You'll notice there's a subhead on the left-hand panel. The headline says, "People within our community are struggling with hunger." Beneath that headline, there's a subhead, and it's a cold statistic: "Almost 900,000 people in the Greater Toronto Area go hungry annually because they cannot afford to eat."

That's just a fact about 900,000 people. So the writer makes it more relevant: "These people are your neighbors." Well that kind of brings it home, doesn't it? It's far more personal this way. What the writer has done is present the four people groups that the Daily Bread Food Bank helps. Children, there's the headline, and there's a picture of children. Working poor, there's the headline, picture of a person working. People with disabilities, there's the headline, and then spread across the gutter between the two pages is a picture of a person with a disability. Newcomers to Canada, and there's a photo there, too.

They help four groups of people, and each of them is represented on this left-hand panel. They mention the working poor, and this helps the organization explain to potential donors that the Daily Bread Food Bank does not help the lazy particularly—they help the working poor. They explain in the brochure here, in the bottom left-hand corner, "More than half of the people who are working and using food banks earn a wage of $10 an hour or more. The problem is, they are only given part-time or casual hours, with no benefits. Most of them want more hours but can't get them. In other words, they're not lazy. They're industrious, but they can't get more hours."

If you look at the next paragraph, it's on the right-hand side, the headline is, "People with disabilities." Just beneath that subhead there's a paragraph, and in the middle of that paragraph is the sentence, "After rent and bills are paid, many do not have enough for groceries. Thanks to the generosity of people like you, who donate the money that we use to buy food, they find assistance and nutritious food at their local food bank." This is an implied ask.

Over on the right-hand side, you'll see at the very top of the page there's that subhead, another fact, "Each month, we serve over 75,000 people in the Greater Toronto Area through our network of 160 member agencies, and over 190 food relief programs." This is a fact that was mentioned in the letter, but it's reiterated in the brochure in case the two of them get separated, but also to emphasize the most important things that people need to know about the food bank. Then the writer explains in red ink, "Here's how we'll spend your donation."

This is one of the most vital questions that donors have when they're asked to give a donation. They get a mailing. It's from an organization they've never supported before. It asks them for a gift. One of the first questions they want to have answered is, "What will you do with my donation?" It's a key point.

In a way, this is an implied ask: "Here's how we'll spend your donation." It doesn't say, "Here's how we'll spend it if you give it." It simply assumes that you will give it and here's how we'll spend it, so it's an implied ask. It includes you in the transaction, even though you haven't given a donation yet. There are, I think, seven ways that they will spend your gift. They'll spend it on neighborhood food banks, meal programs, staples programs, supplementary programs, and so on.

You'll see that plenty of these details don't belong in the letter. They would make the letter too formal and too factual, and they would weaken the human interest and drama that the letter contains. That's why you find them in the brochure.

The back panel of this brochure has an empowering headline, "How you can help feed your neighbors." It's worth remembering that any kind of insert that you put into your direct mail package should be a complete sales proposition in and of itself. You don't want the ask to be in your letter, and then the brochure just have a bunch of facts in it. The brochure itself should also motivate and inspire, and tell the donor how to make a donation. Even an educational insert, like this brochure, should be inspirational. It should present your case for support, and if possible, it should keep the emotion and the enthusiasm and excitement that you had in your letter—they should carry over into your brochure. So the headline says, "How you can help feed your neighbors."

You'll see there are three ways to help, and they're spelled out really, really clearly on the page. There's a great big numeral one, great big numeral two, great big numeral three. The opening sentence, though, of this final panel says, "Give now." There's the ask. "Your dollar buys twice as much food when we do the shopping." There's the case for support, again. It was repeated throughout the letter, it's on the envelope, it's in the brochure, and it's on the final panel of the brochure, the theme and the case for support.

Then you're encouraged, "Please give now," and they tell you three ways you can give. You can give by phone, you can give online, or you can give by mail. You'll notice you can also give by credit card by phone, you can give by credit card online, or you can give by cheque through the mail.

Number three says you can give by cheque, and they give their address. Right beneath that, they give their address again, which is redundant. Nevertheless, if all somebody was looking at was how they could give, and if they saw the word "cheque," they could mail their cheque right away.

It's important that you include your address, because the business reply envelope that came with this package might go missing. Maybe the person will mail it, and someone else will find this brochure and they'll want to give a gift. You have to show them not only that you need their money, but you need to show them how to give—pick up the phone, go online, mail a cheque.

If you ask for a cheque, then you have to give your address. Incidentally, these are the three most popular methods of giving: phone, online, and mail. So this organization has offered all three.

The reply device

Now let's look at the reply device (opposite). This is an unusual reply device because it's an 8½ x 11 sheet of paper. Most reply devices are much smaller. They're the same dimensions as the reply envelope, usually, just a little smaller. This is an 8½ x 11 piece of paper. It's folded once across the middle, just as the letter is.

You'll notice at the top left-hand corner, it says, "Yes, I would like to support the fight against hunger," and then there is a number above my name, 6003958. That's called a key code. A key code is what the organization put onto the reply device so they could track this mailing, and track the list that was used. Let me just give you an example.

☑ YES! I would like to support the fight against hunger

6003958 114/5 xxF1(A)
Alan Sharpe, President
Raiser Sharpe
22 - 30 Adelaide St N
London ON N6B 3N5

Single Gift Option:

Here's my single donation of:

❑ $75 ❑ $50 ❑ $25 ❑ Other $ ____

❑ My cheque payable to Daily Bread Food Bank is enclosed.

❑ I prefer to use my: ❑ Visa ❑ MasterCard ❑ AMEX

Card No: ____

Expiry Date: ____ Signature: ____

Telephone: ( ) ____ Email: ____

Monthly Gift Option:

I prefer to make a monthly gift of:

❑ $20 ❑ $15 ❑ $5 ❑ Other $ ____

❑ I have enclosed a cheque marked VOID.
❑ I prefer to use my: ❑ Visa ❑ MasterCard ❑ AMEX

Card No: ____

Expiry Date: ____ Signature: ____

Telephone: ( ) ____ Email: ____

Monthly giving is the best way to to help end hunger in Toronto. Your on-going monthly commitment is the easiest, most cost-effective way of giving.

Your monthly gift will be deducted on the 15th or 21st of each month.

You are in complete control. You can contact us at any time regarding changes to your monthly donation at: (416) 203-0050 ext. 241

Who you're helping

"Sometimes I have to skip meals to make sure my kids have enough to eat. Fresh fruits and vegetables are a luxury for us, as often I can't afford them."

Joyce, single mother of 3.

"From the food bank I get rice, noodles, milk, bread and baby food."

Solange, single mother of 4.

"Just to feed my son, I have come to a food bank."

Peter, parent of 2.

"There were times we didn't eat because of pride. It was difficult to make that first trip to the food bank."

D.W., husband and parent of 1.

Giving Online gets your donation working immediately for hungry people in our community. Visit www.dailybread.ca today and click on the DONATE tab.

Daily Bread Food Bank

FIGHTING HUNGER

191 New Toronto Street, Toronto, ON M8V 2E7 • Telephone: 416-203-0050 • Fax: 416-203-0049

www.dailybread.ca • e-mail: info@dailybread.ca • Charitable Registration # 11888 1549 RR0001

Let's just say that this mailing was the first acquisition letter of the year, and it was mailed to List A. Let's just say that this organization does four acquisition mailings in the year, and this is the first. Let's just say that they had a choice of 10 mailing lists to send this letter to, and they chose to mail it to five of those lists.

They also wanted to make sure they tracked this particular package because it was the, "We buy twice as much food for a dollar as you can" package. What the organization would do is create a key code. They would use a combination of numbers and letters that would tell them that this was the first mailing, and it was mailed to one of those five lists, and it was the package that was the, "We buy twice as much food for a dollar as you do" package. The key code would contain that information.

The simplest key code might have the number 01, which means that it's the first mailing of the year, and then it would have the letter A, meaning that it was List A, out of A,B,C,D, and E, and it would have the numerals 01 again, which mean, this is the "We buy twice as much for food for one" mailing.

Thus, "01A01" means: First mailing of the year, List A, the "two-for-one" mailing.

That key code would be put on the reply device, so that when the donor fills this in and mails it with her check, the organization gets this reply device and they look at that key code and they put that into their database. They say, "This gift from this donor was motivated by the, "We buy twice as much food as you do for $1" mailing. It was the first one that we mailed in the year, and it was from List A."

They would also send this same letter to List B, and List C and D and E, and so on. Then at the end of the year, they could look through all the results and they could say, "Oh, the list that generated the most gifts, and the highest revenue and the best response rate was List C, or List D," because they kept track of it.

The key code is usually put on by the letter shop, or you provide it in the data that you give to the letter shop. You track each campaign by tracking the key codes on the response devices. The only way that you can really keep track of how your mailing does, is by looking at the reply devices and seeing that key code. That tells you what you mailed, it tells you who you mailed to (which list), and it tells you when you mailed. You put that into your database. Once it's in your database, you can use that information for years and years to come to track the results of that mailing.

You'll notice that the reply device starts with "Yes!" This is a tactic that's used in direct mail fundraising, where you take the donor and you put the donor into the reply device, so that they are the one saying, "Yes! I would like to support the fight against hunger."

Rather than you saying, "Give a gift today," when the donor gets to this particular piece of paper in the package, the donor reads what she is thinking (or supposed to be thinking). This statement is written as an affirmative, as a positive personal commitment that the donor is making, and tries to capture in one sentence the benefit of making a donation.

Now you'll notice here as well that the potential donor's name and address are already printed on this reply device. This might have been showing through the window on the mailing envelope. Printing the donor's name and address on the reply device is likely to improve your response because the donor doesn't have to do anything.

If this reply device had a place for my first name, last name, address, city, ZIP, state, and so on, it would be more work for me to do, and so I might not be as likely to fill it in. I'd say, "Oh, I can't be bothered," and I might not give a gift, or I might not be inclined to write all that in.

You'll also notice that this organization gives donors two ways to give a gift. They can give a single gift, or they can join the monthly giving program. Those options are big and bold. The organization could also have named these "Option 1" and "Option 2" to be just a little clearer about that.

Let's look at Option 1, where it says "Single Gift Option, Here's my single donation of . . ." You'll notice that the organization puts the potential donor into the reply device again. The donor is the one saying, "Here's my single donation of," and this row of numbers here is called an ask string or an ask ladder. "Here's my gift of $75, $50, $25, Other."

This ask string starts at the highest number and works its way down to the lowest number. Ask strings normally start at the bottom and work their way up the ladder to the highest number. This is worth testing. You may find that if you structure your ask string (also called an ask ladder) in this way, you get a higher average gift. You may find that the opposite is true. You should always leave an Other option, as well.

This is also a good place to capture an email address. You'll notice here that the organization has done that. If you're paying by credit card, you put in your card number, the expiration date, your telephone number, and your email address. This is a good place to capture it. If you want to solicit subsequent gifts by email, and if you want to keep your donors informed by email, this is the way to do it. You get their email address. It's much less expensive to follow up with donors by email. Younger donors prefer email to mail, so this is a good place to capture them. They give you the choice of giving by cheque or giving by credit card, and they include the top three most popular credit cards. They even tell you who to make your cheque payable to. You make it out to Daily Bread Food Bank.

The other option is monthly giving. Normally, when you're doing a direct mail acquisition piece, you ask the donor for a gift. Usually it's a gift of cash by cheque or credit card. Most organizations do not ask a brand new donor to join a monthly giving program. That requires more commitment. Giving a gift every month requires more commitment on the donor's part than simply mailing you one gift. Again, this is worth testing. I've done mailings for Doctors Without Borders, where the reply device had the monthly giving option first, and then the single gift option second. Again, this is worth testing to see what kind of result you get.

This monthly giving program doesn't have a name. It's just called the monthly gift option, where you can tell them your credit card number or give them a cheque, and they will take out the money every month. I suggest that if you have a monthly giving program, you give it a name. Give it a really, really good, evocative, compelling name.

For example, Doctors Without Borders has a monthly giving program called Partners Without Borders. The donor is part of the solution. Habitat for Humanity has a monthly giving program that's called Hope Builders. They don't just build houses—they build hope. Daily Bread Food Bank should have the same thing. They should give that monthly giving option a name, so rather than saying, "Join our electronic funds transfer program," or "Join our monthly gifts program," they should tell people to, "Join Pantry Partners, our monthly giving program." I just made that name up, and it's not a great name, you'll agree, but you see my point.

You'll notice underneath the monthly gift option that the ask string starts at $20 and works down to a smaller amount. The cash gifts started at the large amount and worked down to the smaller. The monthly gift option starts at the larger and works its way down to the smaller, as well, but you'll notice that the ask string starts at a much smaller denomination.

If they're asking you for cash, they start at $75. If they're asking for a monthly gift, they start at $20. The reason for this is that most people will not give you a monthly gift that is the size of a single gift. For example, I might give an organization a gift of $100, and I might do that once a year, but I wouldn't give them a gift of $100 12 times a year. I might give them a gift of $15 once a month for the year.

You'll also see that under the monthly giving option they explain the benefits of joining the program. "Monthly giving is the best way to help end hunger in Toronto." Monthly giving helps people that are needy. "Your ongoing monthly commitment is the easiest, most cost-effective way of giving for you." They could have put in that phrase at the end. With monthly giving, you don't have to write a cheque, you don't have to find an envelope, you don't have to put a stamp on it, you don't have to go to the mailbox. It's easy, cost-effective and convenient for the donor. These benefits are worth stressing when you're asking for a monthly gift.

The logo and the address are at the bottom of the reply device. This is worth mentioning. The reply device, of course, you fold up and include with your cheque or credit card payment. You put it into the postage-paid, self-addressed envelope and mail it back to the organization. But let's just say somebody loses the return envelope. All they have is the reply device. Who do they mail it to? Well, this organization is really smart, and at the bottom of their reply device they print their full address, telephone number, fax, Web site—everything that anybody needs to know to mail in a gift. It's important that you do that.

2007 Donor Survey

Because we need to find more caring people like you.

Please take a moment to complete this brief survey. Your responses will be kept in the strictest of confidence. They will only be used by Daily Bread Food Bank to help us learn more about our current donors and most importantly, how we can find more caring people like you to support our fight against hunger.

1. Please indicate your age group:
   ❑ 25-34 ❑ 35-40 ❑ 41-50 ❑ over 50

2. Your profession is: ______________________________

3. What type of magazines do you read? (Please check all that apply.)
   ❑ business or finance ❑ world news/politics ❑ medical/health ❑ sports
   ❑ fashion ❑ interior decorating ❑ other (please indicate) ______________

4. Do you contribute to other charities? ❑ Yes ❑ No
   If yes, which ones? ______________________________

5. Tell us why you give to Daily Bread Food Bank: ______________________________

   ____

6. Which of the following goals do you think are part of Daily Bread Food Bank's mission? (Please check all that apply.)
   ❑ Feed hungry people locally
   ❑ Educate people on how to save money when shopping for groceries and preparing meals
   ❑ Teach poor people in local communities how to grow their own food
   ❑ Eliminate the need for food banks
   ❑ Deliver excess fresh food from restaurants, etc. to social service agencies and soup kitchens
   ❑ Lobby government to change/adopt policies

7. What is your impression of the following organizations?
   Even though you may not be aware of some of them, we would still like your general impression of each organization.

	very positive									very negative
Daily Bread Food Bank	10	9	8	7	6	5	4	3	2	1	0
Second Harvest	10	9	8	7	6	5	4	3	2	1	0
Salvation Army	10	9	8	7	6	5	4	3	2	1	0
Covenant House	10	9	8	7	6	5	4	3	2	1	0
United Way	10	9	8	7	6	5	4	3	2	1	0

8. If you said no to monthly giving, please tell us why. ______________________________

   ____

   ____

Please mail this completed survey in the postage-paid envelope provided.

Thank you for supporting Daily Bread Food Bank.

Daily Bread Food Bank

FIGHTING HUNGER

191 New Toronto Street, Toronto, ON M8V 2E7 • Telephone: 416-203-0050 • Fax: 416-203-0049

www.dailybread.ca • e-mail: info@dailybread.ca • Charitable Registration # 11888 1549 RR0001

The survey

Not only has this organization included a brochure, which might depress response, but they've included a survey (opposite page), which might also depress response. The more you give a donor to do, the more work you give them, the less likely they are to give a gift, generally speaking. But everybody likes to give their opinion. I do. You probably do. If somebody says, "What do you think about this?" you'll probably give them your opinion.

This survey is real simple, about eight questions. They want to know your opinion as a potential donor. What are some of the questions that they ask in the survey? First of all, they ask you, "What type of magazines do you read?" You would tick those off. You read fashion magazines, you read interior decorating magazines. The reason they want to know this is they want to know what kind of list they can rent the next time they do an acquisition mailing.

Let's just say that they mail this acquisition package, they get these surveys back and they discover that a really large percentage of their donors read interior decorating magazines. For their next acquisition mailing, they could rent a list from an interior decorating magazine, or magazines, and they could mail a test package to those subscribers to those magazines, and see if they generate a high response and high average gift at a cost-effective figure. That's the reason that they're asking question three. They want a source list of people that are like you, if you respond to this package.

They also want to know why you gave. That's question five, "Tell us why you give to Daily Bread Food Bank?" That's important to know. People will give you many answers. You'll notice that this isn't an either/or question or a multiple choice question. You have to write your answer in your own words. This type of question is used in qualitative market research. It's not quantitative. Everyone will give you different answers. You add them all up and you may decide that there's a picture emerging, a trend emerging as to why people give. You can use that to your advantage and to the advantage of your donors.

Question six is also about motivation. "Which of the following goals do you think are part of Daily Bread Food Bank's mission?" Feed hungry people locally, eliminate the need for food banks, and so on. They give you these options, and they ask you, "Which of the following goals do you think are part of Daily Bread Food

Bank's mission?" This helps the organization discover the level of awareness that there is in the community for what they do, where they do it, who they help, and what kind of a difference they make.

It could be that when they get these survey results in, they discover that there's a great gap in the perception of potential donors of the work the Daily Break Food Bank does. Perhaps many people are mistaken as to what they do, or maybe everybody knows about one particular thing they do, but many don't know about another part of their work. Answers to this question help the organization shape their case for support in upcoming mailings.

Question seven asks about the person's impression of some of their competitors: Second Harvest, Salvation Army, Covenant House and United Way. These are competitors for not just the work that Daily Bread Food Bank does, such as Second Harvest—they provide food, the Salvation Army provides food—but some of these organizations also compete for the potential donors' dollar. This survey helps Daily Bread Food Bank discover what the potential donor thinks about Daily Bread Food Bank's competition.

Again, just in case the donor hasn't noticed it, at the bottom of the page, there's the address, phone number, Web site, everything that the potential donor needs to know to mail in the survey. At the bottom of the survey it says, "Please mail this completed survey in the postage-paid envelope provided." It should also have said, "With your gift." "Please mail this completed survey in the postage-paid envelope with your gift." That would have been a better way to conclude that call to action.

The reply envelope

The final part of the package is the business reply envelope (opposite page). The reason it's called a business reply envelope is that it's postage-paid. You'll notice at the top right-hand corner, there's the indicia again. This is a business reply indicia. It's different from the one that's on the mailing envelope. It's got the permit number for the mailer.

What the organization has to do is pay a fee to be able to use this service, and they pay for every one of these envelopes that is returned to them. They can mail out 100,000 of these envelopes inside their direct mail appeals, it doesn't cost them a penny in postage. Only the ones that are mailed back are charged to the non-profit. This is worth testing as well.

Business reply envelopes generally generate a higher response rate than plain envelopes that say, "Please put your stamp here," because if you ask for a stamp, you're asking the donor to do something. They have to find a stamp, and then they have to put it on the envelope. But if they put a stamp on, that saves you postage, so you can save money. That's worth testing.

You could test a business reply envelope and a plain-Jane one that has no postage on. A compromise is to print a statement that says, "If you put your postage stamp over the top of this indicia you save us postage." That is exactly what happens. If the donor puts postage on, the postal service does not charge the non-profit.

11

Why Donor Acquisition Letters are Longer

Should you mail a one-page letter or a two-page letter? Neither. Mail a four-page letter. I'm talking about donor acquisition letters. The ones you mail to strangers, asking them to send you a gift. The most successful acquisition letters are longer than your typical renewal letter. Here's why.

Renewal letters, by definition, ask current donors to renew their support. So these letters assume that donors understand who you are, what you do, who you help, and why you are a worthy cause that deserves the donor's support.

But a donor acquisition letter usually lacks all of these advantages. It must assume that the reader knows little about your organization and your mandate. Which means an acquisition letter can't simply ask for another gift, since the reader has never given before. An acquisition letter, instead, has to ask for a first-time gift. And that requires more than a simple request for a gift.

Acquisition letters, even though most of them begin "Dear Friend," are written by strangers to strangers. So introductions are in order. Your organization must introduce who you are. You must describe what you do, and who you help, and where you operate, and so on. This takes time, and so it takes words, and so it takes space, more space than one page of a sheet of 8.5 x 11 inch paper.

Another reason that donor and member acquisition letters are often longer than two pages is that you have more objections to overcome. Current donors trust you. Strangers don't. That's why many acquisition letters describe how the organization spends each donated dollar, something you'll rarely see explained in a donor renewal mailing. Commonplace in acquisition packages is a description of the percentage of each dollar spent on programs, administration and fundraising.

Another reason acquisition letters often run to four pages and longer is inertia. Potential donors can think of all sorts of reasons not to support your cause. They are like cars without gas. Or, the stay with the analogy, engines without sparkplugs. Your letter must act as the gas that propels the car forward, the spark that ignites the fuel. That can rarely be accomplished on one page. Even the most compelling causes need more than one page to tell their story and inspire people to act.

Review

Your direct mail fundraising program has three goals. Your first goal is to acquire new donors. Your second goal is to renew those donors, to turn them into friends that stay with you for some time. Your third goal is to upgrade those donors, or to develop the relationships, so that they don't just give gifts every year, but they also join your monthly giving program, or they give larger amounts of money, or they give more frequently, or they join your donor's circle, or they become a major donor. You try to upgrade them somehow.

Ideally, they would leave a gift for you in their will, or they would take out a planned giving instrument of some kind. Acquisition, renewal and upgrading. Those are the three goals that you face in your program.

In the next sections we're going to look at donor renewal—how you get a first-time donor that you've just acquired, and renew them and inspire them and inform them so that they give you a second, a third, and a fourth gift, and become good friends of your organization.

We're also going to look at how you measure your results, what you should measure, and when and why. We're going to look at how you put together a whole years' worth of mailings, what a calendar looks like, how you block off the various parts of the year, what you mail, when you mail it, and why you mail it.

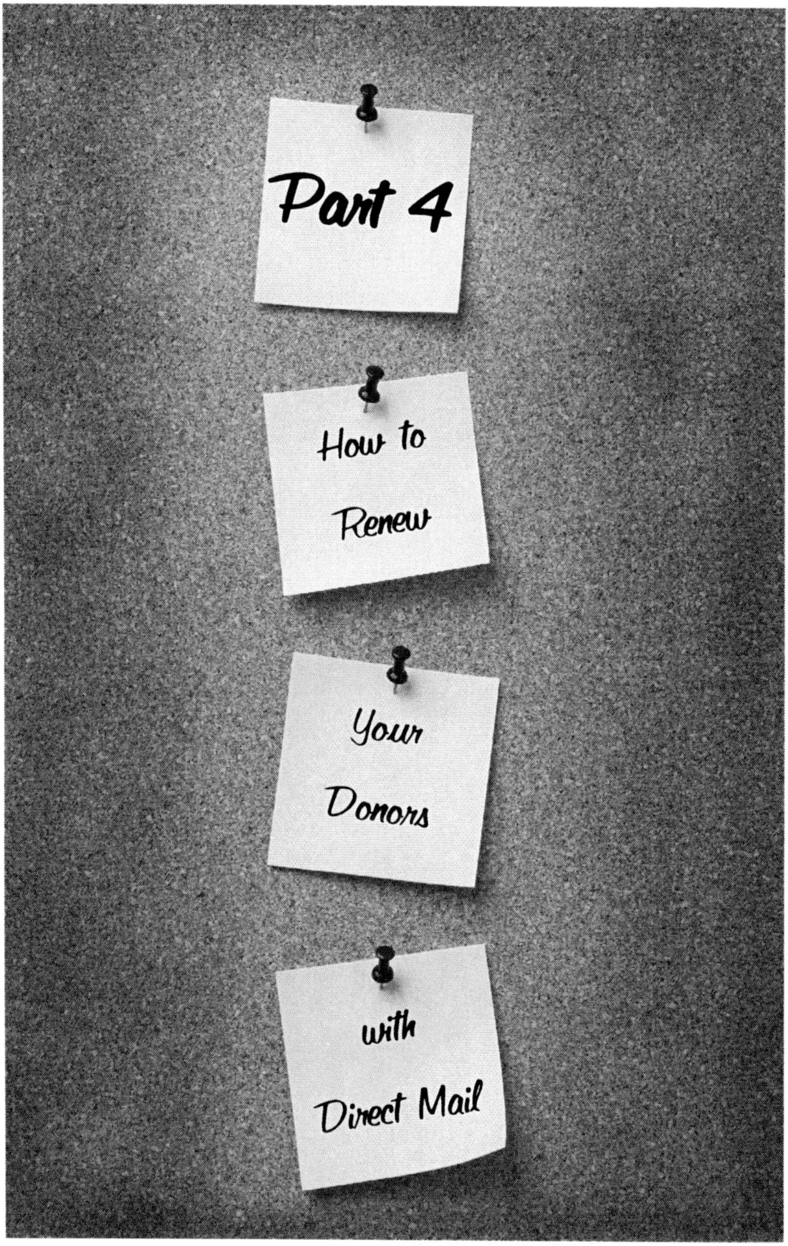
Part 4
How to Renew
Your Donors
with Direct Mail

12

Why You Must Renew Your Donors

I grew up in a home where a couple of the people drank alcohol and got drunk. There were two members of my family that were drunk pretty regularly for most of my childhood. When I got older, I went to Al-Anon meetings and I went to Alcoholics Anonymous meetings, and I discovered that in Alcoholics Anonymous they talk about something called "the elephant in the living room."

It's a funny kind of dynamic when you're living in close proximity with somebody who has a drinking problem, because almost always the person with the problem denies that there's a problem. They are in denial. They don't seek help, they get drunk, they make a nuisance of themselves and a fool of themselves, and they hurt people's feelings.

When confronted with it the next day or a few days later, they deny that anything happened, that they were responsible. They deny that they have a problem. It's an unusual way to grow up, because, as a kid you grow up thinking, "There's something wrong in my home but nobody seems to want to talk about it."

In Alcoholics Anonymous meetings they talk about this elephant in the living room that is apparent to everybody but nobody wants to talk about. In direct mail fundraising, we have an elephant in the living room. It's destructive and lots of people know that it's going on, but nobody really wants to talk about it. The elephant in the living room is abysmal conversion rates.

The conversion rate is the percentage of your first-time donors that convert to being second- and third- and fourth-time donors. In other words, it's the percentage of people who respond to your acquisition mailing with one gift, who subsequently give you a second and third and more gifts. If you're able to get them from giving one gift to giving two or more, you are said to have converted them from being a one-time donor.

The elephant in the living room is that only 35 percent of new donors acquired by direct mail ever give another gift. That's according to Steven Hitchcock, of Mal Warwick and Associates of Berkeley, California, a well respected, excellent direct mail fundraising agency.

Only 35 percent of new donors acquired by direct mail ever give another gift. If you look at that the other way, that means that 65 percent of new donors give only once. I call this the elephant in the living room because there are some charities that are always in donor acquisition crisis mode.

Some of them mail premiums, such as greeting cards and return address labels, and they rely heavily on mailing things to people—knick knacks, trinkets and treasures—to lure people into giving a gift to the charity. But they attract a very poor quality, low-dollar, un-loyal donor, so they have to mail another acquisition mailing, and another acquisition mailing, and another acquisition mailing. They're always in crisis mode because they're attracting the wrong kinds of donors.

They suffer from this elephant-in-the-living-room syndrome. Rather than retaining their donors, they're always in acquisition mode. The challenge for non-profit organizations is to face this uncomfortable fact, this sobering fact, I might call it, and realize that they need to encourage first-time direct mail donors to give again, and again, and again. The secret to success in direct mail fundraising is not acquiring new donors but acquiring donors who give again and again. It's making friends for life rather than acquiring one-time donations repeatedly.

Why you must renew your donors

Why must you renew your donors? Well, the first reason is that donors acquired through direct mail usually generate net income only after making a second donation. That's because acquisition mailings usually lose money. There was a time when you could send a letter to a stranger and they would respond with a gift, and postage rates were low and printing costs were low, and the cost of list rental was low, or lower, and you could make money on your acquisition mailings.

You might spend 80 cents or 75 cents to raise one dollar. That's not true today. Almost all donor acquisition mailings lose money but gain donors. If you lose money and gain a donor, that means you've had a net loss, as far as money goes, and so you need a second or third gift to recover your losses. Donors acquired through direct mail usually generate net income only after they've made a second gift. They pay for themselves, as it were, with their second gift, sometimes their third gift.

The second reason that you must renew your donors is that re-soliciting existing donors, going to your house file of donors and asking them for a gift, is likely to perform five to eight times more profitably than going out and trying to acquire the exact same number of donors who give the same amount of money and are first-time donors.

It's five to eight times more profitable to ask people you know than it is to look for people that have never given a donation before. This is true in business. Just about every retail business will tell you it's much more expensive to go out and find a brand new customer than it is to invite an existing customer to come back to your store and give you their business again.

The third reason that you have to renew your donors is that the donor who gives you a small donation today by direct mail is the donor that will ultimately—you hope, and with a little bit of work on your part—give you a slightly larger gift, perhaps volunteer, perhaps join your monthly giving program. One day, maybe, he or she will give you a major gift, perhaps sit on your board. Then, when they die, they might leave you a bequest in their will or take out a planned giving instrument in the later years of their lives.

Most people that make it to the top of what's called the giving pyramid—the major donors, the legacy donors, those high-value loyal donors—most of them started further down the pyramid, and many of them started by giving a one-time gift in response to a direct mail appeal. You have to renew your donors at the bottom of the pyramid if you want to gradually move them up the pyramid, or if you want them to move themselves up the pyramid to becoming your most loyal, faithful, generous donors.

What all of this means for you and me is that the most important gift in direct mail fundraising isn't the first gift, but the second. What's most important in direct mail fundraising isn't the first mailing that acquires the donor, although that's obviously vital, because without the mailing, you don't get the donor. But what's more important than the first mailing is the second mailing, and the third and the fourth, those mailings that keep the donor. Those mailings that renew the donor.

These organizations that I know of that are always in donor

acquisition crisis mode, they're always mailing premiums, they're always mailing sweepstakes, they're always trying to find new donors because their first-time donors fall away at such terrible rates.

The place they should be concentrating their scarce financial resources, and the place you should be concentrating your time, energy and your scarce financial resources, is not more and more donor acquisition, but better donor conversion. You need to spend your time and your money turning a first-time donor into a repeat donor.

Donor conversion, as I mentioned, is simply the process of turning a first-time donor into a repeat donor. Some people call it donor renewal, which is also the act of persuading donors and members to renew their support year after year.

In this section, we're going to look at how to convert these first-time donors. You've acquired them—now you must convert them into repeat givers.

Avoid donors who never renew

This may sound kind of funny, but the way I look at it is you should write your second letter first. You're going to send a direct mail acquisition package out to your potential donors. I recommend that, before you do that, you sit down and write your second letter first.

In other words, you write the letter that you're going to mail to new donors after they've come on board. You could even write your thank-you letter first, and put together your welcome kit, which we'll talk about in a minute.

If you think really carefully about what you're going to do with your new donor once you get the donor, you'll be very careful about how you acquire that donor. If you are mailing premiums, for example, and you know that some people will respond to your mailing simply because you mailed them a premium and they feel guilty, you'll know how much work you have ahead of you in your second letter, to get them to give again.

The first time, they gave out of guilt and obligation. How are they going to give again when you talk to them about your mission and the people you support? It helps if you write your second letter first. You don't have to physically do it. You can simply do it in your mind. Before you sit down and craft your acquisition package, decide what you're going to mail to any new donors that respond to your appeal. You'll avoid some costly mistakes.

For one thing, you'll avoid the acquisition methods that tend to attract once-only donors. If you mail them address labels and notepads, and greeting cards and calendars, and decals and bumper stickers, knick-knacks, trinkets and treasures, you'll probably get a higher response rate than you will without those premiums. You'll probably attract larger numbers of donors and maybe even more money, but you'll have a disadvantage on your hands. I almost guarantee it.

If you mail premiums at the front end, in other words if you mail the premium rather than offer it in exchange for a donation, you will attract gifts that are smaller. Plus, not only will your gift be smaller in dollar size, but you'll tend to attract donors who are less likely to give again because they gave out of guilt, out of obligation. You mailed them a nice knick knack and they feel obligated to send you something in return. Now your results may vary, but I recommend that you test to find out for yourself.

The same holds true for emergency appeals. They attract a certain type of donor. If you were around when Hurricane Katrina hit in 2005, when it hit New Orleans and that whole southern coast—the Gulf Coast—you'll know that the Red Cross, the Salvation Army and lots of other charities mailed direct mail appeals that were very, very successful in raising money for that hurricane relief.

The percentage of new donors that gave to that hurricane appeal, who then went on to give again and again the same organization but for other emergencies, was low. There are people that will respond to emergencies. They want to help the people in New Orleans. They want to help people who are struck by a hurricane, an earthquake, a flood, a famine or a Tsunami, but they're giving because of the emergency. They're not giving because of the organization or the case for support, in particular.

Emergency appeals that are mailed to strangers work well at generating immediate income and they attract new donors, but they have a lower likelihood of gaining donors who will repeat their giving over time. This has been proven. Now your case may vary. You need to make sure that your direct mail acquisition packages are written and designed to attract long-term donors from the beginning. Attracting a long-term donor from the outset is easier and less expensive, and easier on your nerves than trying to persuade a once-only "emergency donor" to give again.

Donors demand three things before they give again

Fundraising consultant Penelope Burke wrote a book called *Donor-Centered Fundraising*. She wrote a Canadian edition and she wrote an American edition. She's come to some startling findings that are very helpful. She interviewed hundreds of donors and hundreds of executives and volunteers who work for charities across North America. She asked them, particularly the donors, "What does a charity have to do before you will give them another donation?"

Donors told Burke in large numbers, "Before I give another gift to a charity, they have to show me that they received my gift and were glad to get it." Charities normally do this with a thank-you letter, and we'll discuss that in a minute.

The second thing that the charity needs to do is, "Show that my gift was put to work as I intended. If I designated the money to a particular cause or program at the charity, they need to show me that they are using my gift the way I intended and the way I designated."

Finally, "They need to show me that my gift is making a difference. I not only want to know that they got it and that they're using it, but that it is making a difference, changing the world."

Those are the three things that Burke discovered that today's thinking donors want out of a charity. You can see here the role that your donor renewal program has to take if you are to encourage first-time donors to ever give you a second and third and subsequent gifts.

13

Thank-you Letters, Cards and Notes

Let's take a look at thank-you letters. Penelope Burke discovered that donors want to be thanked, and they want to be thanked in a certain way. She also discovered that they want to be informed about how their gift is being used. You can thank them with a thank-you letter and you can inform them with a newsletter, and then you can ask for your subsequent gift with what's called a renewal letter. These are the three keys to successful donor renewal; thank-you letters, newsletters, and donor renewal fundraising letters.

Four reasons you must mail thank-you letters, cards and notes

1. It's the right thing to do

Saying thank you is simply the right thing to do. You may know of some organizations that say, "We will acknowledge all gifts larger than $10." If you're poor and you mail them a gift of $5, or $6 or even $3, they won't even acknowledge you. You'll never know that they got your gift, and they'll show no thanks whatsoever. I say that's wrong. Anytime anybody gives you a gift, you should thank them. It's the right thing to do.

2. Remind donors that they made the right decision

You also need to remind your donors that they made the right decision. If you've ever had buyer's remorse, you know what this is all about. Buyer's remorse is what happens when people buy a high-ticket item, and right after they've bought it they go home and they think, "Oh, I shouldn't have bought it. I shouldn't have bought that jewelry. I shouldn't have bought that car. I shouldn't have bought that exotic vacation. I shouldn't have spent all that money." They regret what they did. They have remorse.

Donors can have the same thing. If a donor gives you a large gift or even a small gift, and you don't thank them, the weeks go by and they think, 'Oh, I shouldn't have given them that money. They obviously don't need it, and they're not thankful for it." I suppose you could call it donor's remorse. You need to remind donors that they made the right decision, and you do that with a good thank-you letter.

You need to remember, too, that your donors have plenty of choices about where they donate. The typical donor in North America is a female, 60 years of age or over, and supports more than 10 charities. If you don't thank her for her gift, she will likely give to someone else. You need to remind her that she made the right decision.

3. Thank-you letters boost revenue over time

A third reason that you should mail thank yous is that thank-you letters boost revenue over the long-term. This is not their primary aim. We'll look at that in a second. Your goal in sending a thank-you letter is not that your donor sends you another gift right away using the reply device and the envelope that you included in your thank-you letter. That's tacky.

The primary aim of a thank-you letter is to say thank you. It's been shown over time, and Penelope Burke proved this, that if you thank people for their gifts, they are more likely to renew their support than those who are not thanked, and so a simple thank you boosts income.

You'll also find that loyal donors give more money than uncommitted donors. Those donors that you thank and that become loyal are going to increase your bottom line more than those who are uncommitted.

4. Thank-you letters increase donor loyalty

Another reason that you should send thank-you letters is that they increase donor loyalty. We tend to gravitate towards people who show an interest in us. I know this is true of me.

If I'm at a party and I don't know anybody, and somebody comes up and is charming and delightful, and shows a real interest in me, I tend to like them and I tend to want to spend time with them at the party.

We tend to shop where we're treated well. We like shopping where we're treated like a special customer. We tend to be loyal to those places and to those people and to those businesses that show an interest in us and that treat us fairly.

How do thank-you letters increase donor loyalty? They show you're thankful. This sounds redundant, obviously. You mail a thank-you letter, you say thank you, and the thank-you letter shows you're thankful. But those organizations that only give you a thank-you letter, or acknowledge that you're living, if you give them a gift of $10 or more, they show by not sending a thank-you letter that they're not thankful. Thank-you letters increase donor loyalty because they show that you're thankful. You've actually written it down and made an effort.

They also show that you're organized. This is not such an obvious point, but if you're on social assistance and you get your check every month on the same day of the month, you know that the Social Security organization is organized. It's a bureaucracy, but it's organized. They're faithful that way. You know that the bank takes the money out of your bank account for your mortgage every month on the same day. You know that they're organized. If they took it out on a different day every month, you would think they were disorganized.

Organizations, charities, will send you an income tax receipt at the end of the year for your gifts. If they do, you know that they're organized. If you thank your donors promptly and consistently for their gifts, they'll know that you're organized, and they'll be more loyal to you.

Thank-you letters also show that you are predictable. That's a third reason that thank-you letters make people more loyal. They show you're thankful, you're organized, and you're predictable. We tend to be more loyal to people that we know are not fickle. Somebody said that a thankful heart enjoys blessings twice: When they're received and when they're remembered. That's a good reason to send thank-you letters as part of your donor renewal program.

Thank your donors using the four P's

Let's look at four ways that you should thank your donors. These are pretty easy to remember: the four P's of thanking your donors. Remember, we're doing this because it's the right thing to do, but also because it boosts revenue, boosts donor loyalty, and increases the chances that a first-time donor will give you a second gift. I would suggest that the easiest way to generate a second gift is to thank your donor profusely for the first one. (That's not one of the P's, by the way). Donors who are not thanked for their first contribution are almost guaranteed not to make a second one. Here are the four ways that you thank your donor:

#1: Thank your donors Promptly

Mail your gift acknowledgement within 24 hours of receiving the gift. You may say, "Alan, that's impossible. We're a huge organization. We couldn't possibly thank our donors within 24 hours." I say if you mail it within two days, three days, you're doing all right. But don't make the mistake that some charities make in sending all their gift acknowledgements and all their thank-you letters at the end of the month.

What they do is they gang them up, they batch them up, they accumulate them over the month. They take all the gifts they got on the first, second, third and fourth, and they save them until the end of the month and then they send all the thank-you notes on the same day. They do this because it saves postage. They mail thousands of thank-you letters in one day, and they get the discount postage rate.

The problem is the donor that gave on the first doesn't get a thank you until four weeks later, maybe five. Each day of delay that you take in thanking your donors adds to the impression in your donors' mind—and in your new donors' mind, if you've just acquired them—that you're either ungrateful, disorganized or unprofessional, or all three. That's not an impression you want to leave. So thank your donors promptly. I recommend you do it within 24 hours of receiving their gift.

#2: Thank your donors Personally

The second "P" is that you thank your donors personally. I know an executive director of a charity up here in Canada, and he was the executive director of another charity for 20 years. Every night he took home with him a pile of thank-you letters, and he signed every single one by hand for 20 years.

He did it when his children were toddlers, he did it when they were teenagers, and he did it after they'd left home. Sometimes he signed 300 thank-you letters in one evening. To my knowledge, this man never tested his method against sending a generic computer-generated gift acknowledgement that was not signed, and didn't have a hand-written little note. But I think you can imagine which method worked best at increasing the new-donor conversion rates that are so vital, and attracted subsequent gifts, the personal thank you as opposed to the generic computer-generated gift acknowledgement.

Thank your donors personally. The best way to thank a donor is face-to-face, and with major donors we do this all the time. We know how important it is if someone gives us a gift of $500,000. We don't mail a note. We pay a visit. We know how important it is to go face-to-face with them and thank them.

Of course, you couldn't possibly thank every one of your direct mail donors face-to-face, not if you have a good, healthy, robust, successful program. You'll have thousands of donors. But face-to-face is still the best way.

The second best way to thank them is by phone. Nothing beats getting a phone call. You hear their voice, they hear how thankful they are. That's the best. If you can't visit face-to-face, then phone. If you can't phone, write. Send a note or a card or a letter. Here are some best practices to follow when sending a thank you:

Address the donor by name. Do not address your thank-you letter, "Dear Friend." If they were a stranger, they are a stranger no longer. They've given you a gift and so you should call them by name. Nobody calls their friends "friend." They call them by their name. They say, "Alan." Your letter should say, "Dear Alan."

Make your opening line a zinger. The opening line of your thank-you letter should absolutely surprise and delight the donor with its originality and power. For example, you could start your thank-you letter by saying, "Thanks for your recent gift. I did the math, and your kind gesture will help us lay 550 bricks in our new school project in Bolivia. So I thank you today—the children in Bolivia will thank you in January when the school is completed."

That is an original opening sentence. Don't start your thank-you letter by saying, "We are in receipt of your gift," or, "The Board acknowledges your above contribution."

Acknowledge the donor's thoughtfulness and concern. Don't just thank them for their gift, but thank them for being thoughtful and for being concerned about your organization.

Use a real signature. Wherever possible, have a living, breathing person sign the acknowledgement with a real pen and real ink. Don't use a stamp if you can have a real person sign it. Don't computer-generate the signature if you can have a real, living person sign the letter.

Use a closed-face envelope. Penelope Burke also discovered that you're more likely to be successful if you mail your thank-you note or card in a closed-face envelope. In other words, an envelope that doesn't have a window. It's closed-face.

Use a first-class stamp and don't have any teaser copy on the outside. Just a plain envelope, closed-face, addressed to the donor. I received one a couple of weeks ago. It was a personal thank-you letter, hand-written, and the envelope was also hand-written and it had a stamp on it. It made quite an impression on me when I saw that in my mailbox.

Don't use a postcard. Postcards are impersonal, and that's the last impression you want to make when you're personally acknowledging a first-time donor that you're hoping will give to you again. Postcards look boilerplate, generic, mass-produced. Plus, because of privacy legislation, you can't personalize a postcard with the gift amount and the date the way you can with a letter. So stick with something that goes into an envelope.

#3: Thank your donors Particularly

You need to thank your new donor for this first gift in particular. You must acknowledge that they are a new donor, and that you're very grateful for their first gift. Avoid generalities. Shun anything that sounds generic and boilerplate and just overused, the kind of thank you that everybody would get.

Be particular so that your donor knows that your gift acknowledgement, your thank you, is coming from a grateful person, not a gift acknowledgement module in some donor software application. They want to know that they're being thanked by a person, not a computer.

There are a couple of ways that you can be particular in your thank-you letter. You can mention the gift amount and you can mention the date received. The amount and the date, those are two simple ways that you can be particular, and they will impress your donor. Your donor will know that they are being thanked for a particular gift that they gave at a particular time.

You could also mention the designation of the gift, or the particular campaign to which the donor responded. They might have given money to a campaign that you ran on adding a new wing to your hospital. It might have been called the Our Hospital Has Heart Campaign. They designated their gift towards that, and so your thank-you letter could thank them for their gift that they gave on a certain date, of a certain amount, towards a certain campaign. You can be particular. You can refer to the project or the issue or the emergency that prompted that gift. This is especially important for a first-time donor if they've designated their gift.

You can also mention the type of gift that they gave. They might have mailed you a cheque, they might have given online, they might have pledged money to your organization. They might have given you a gift in-kind, which is a little unusual in direct mail fundraising, but you can mention the type of gift that they gave, if you want to be particular in your thank-you letter.

You should say what you're doing with the gift. You'll remember that Penelope Burke discovered that this was vital to donors before they give again, so you can say why you're thankful. Say, "We're thankful for your gift because it will help us do the following . . ." or, "We are using your gift to do the following . . ." That's why you're thankful.

Now if it's possible to say in your letter, "We received your gift in this morning's mail. Thanks a million," then you could say that. You should be as original and particular as you possibly can be in your thank-you letter.

#4: Thank your donors Positively

What you're trying to communicate with your donors is that they've done more than simply mail you a cheque, mail you a donation. You should try to communicate to them that they've joined with other like-minded citizens in supporting a worthy cause. You should try to communicate that the donor has joined with a select group of other donors, other supporters. They've done more than give a gift—they've joined a cause. They've joined arm-and-arm with others like them.

Praise them for their involvement—thank them for participating in your cause. Show them warmth and enthusiasm. Be positive in the letter. Don't simply discharge your duty of thanking the donor and including an income tax receipt. Be warm and enthusiastic.

I also recommend that you don't ask for another gift. Don't ever do it. You haven't earned the right to a second gift just yet. If you're thanking them for their first-time donation, you haven't even spent it yet, and so you shouldn't be asking them for a second one.

Penelope Burke discovered that 53 percent of individual donors surveyed said that asking for another gift in the body of a thank-you letter is rude. Eight percent of those people, who have received that kind of a solicitation in a thank-you letter, said that they would stop giving if that happens.

Eight percent is a lot of people. If you want to scare away eight percent of your donors, ask them for a second gift. You might be thinking, "But Alan, we always include a business reply envelope with our thank-you letters, and they always generate net income. They pay for the mailings." I say don't do it. You've got to think long-term when it comes to direct mail fundraising, and you're alienating the 53 percent who think it's rude, and eight percent will leave you for good. So don't do it.

Calcutta Concern, Inc.

Alan Sharpe
38 Wethered Street
London ON N5Y 1G9

Wednesday, September 27, 2008 **10**

2 Dear Alan,

This is just a quick note, but it comes from my heart to yours as I head out the door for my flight to India. Thank you for your gift of $125, which we received this **3** morning. Your generosity will make an immediate difference in the lives of teenage mothers in Calcutta. I am going to make sure of that.

You'll remember from my letter of August 25, 2005 that this year marks the 10-year anniversary of Calcutta Concern. I know that we got here only thanks to the generosity and concern of people like you, people who share our vision of delivering **4** emergency medical help to populations in danger in Calcutta and surrounding regions, and speaking out on behalf of those we help. I hope you are with us when we celebrate our 20th!

5 For your gift, for your moral support and for your steadfast commitment to the work of Calcutta Concern, I thank you.

You'll be glad to learn that our infant intervention program in Calcutta is growing as anticipated, thanks to you. The word is getting out, and more and more mothers **6** are bringing their infants in each morning for a free nourishing breakfast and medical check-up. The work is hot and tiring, but we press on, knowing that we must reach as many people as possible before the monsoon season is upon us.

7 I must dash. I'll conclude with a final heartfelt THANK YOU to you for remembering us—and the people we help half a world away—with your gift.

8 Here's to your health!

9 *Melinda Jacobs*

10 Melinda R. Jacobs, M.D.
Executive Director

11 *P.S. If you'd like to follow this exciting project in more detail and see the marvellous difference that your gifts make among teen mothers in Calcutta, please read my daily journal at www.CalcuttaConcern.org/journal.*

23 Maple Drive, London ON N7R 1G9
Tel 519 1234-4567 Fax 519 123-4567
www.CalcuttaConcern.org

Anatomy of an effective thank-you letter

1. The date helps donors see that this is not a form letter, and reminds them at year end (tax time) of the charitable donations they made during the year, to whom, for how much, and when.

2. Not "Dear Friend." This letter is a personal thank you from the heart of the executive director to this donor. Even though the executive director does not know Alan personally, she writes to him as a friend, which is to say, by name.

3. This novel opening sentence reveals the personality of the writer and clearly shows that this letter was written on a particular day, by a particular person, for a particular reason. Openings like this resonate with donors, who want to be acknowledged by a human being and not a computer. This opening sentence obviously only works for the day on which it was mailed. A less-specific opening (one that does not mention boarding a flight to India) would be necessary for gifts that are acknowledged after this date. Note that the writer acknowledges the donor's gift by date and amount.

4. The writer nurtures her relationship with the donor, continuing the "dialogue" of previous letters. The writer thanks the donor a second time, and shows how she is grateful not only for the donor's generosity but also for the donor sharing the organization's mission.

   Restating your mission in each letter, however briefly, helps your donors appreciate what you do, who you help, and their role. Notice the humour and warmth of the concluding line, and how it reveals something of the personality of the writer.

5. Another thank you. You should aim to thank your donors at the start, in the middle, and at the end. This thank-you shows the writer's gratitude for the giver as well as the gift.

6. Now the writer shows in concrete, easy-to-understand ways how the donor's previous gifts are hard at work today, changing lives and making a difference in the world. Donors need to know that their contribution, however small, accomplishes the goals of the donor in supporting your organization.

7. The conclusion echoes the beginning—a nice touch. Another heart-felt thank you, this time showing that the donor's gift was actually felt around the world and not just at head office where it was received and receipted.

8. The writer closes with a personal and idiosyncratic salutation. Try to end your letters in a fresh, original way every time.

9. Use a real signature whenever possible, in an ink that contrasts with the body of the letter. Otherwise, us a high-quality scanned signature that looks authentic when printed.

10. In case the signature is illegible, the donor will still know who this letter is from, since the writer puts both her name and her job title beneath her signature.

11. The writer encourages the donor to learn more about the mission of her organization, and the project that the donor supported with his gift, thus strengthening the relationship between the donor and the non-profit.

14

Before You Ask Again, W-I-N Them

Your first-time donors need a reason to give again. You're not going to get their second gift automatically. Your donors are busy. They receive appeals from other causes that are just as worthy as yours. Because they're new, because you've just acquired them and they've only given you one gift, they likely do not know your organization all that well.

They're not as familiar with you as others are about how you started, who your founder is, how long you've been in business, who you help, where you work, how you spend your donors' money. They're not as familiar with you as they are with other organizations. This means that you have some work to do between receiving a donor's first gift and asking them for a second one. You can't just ask them for a gift right away. You need to do something to develop that relationship with the donor. I suggest that after you've received a first gift from your donor, you win them to becoming new donors. W-I-N. You win them.

Welcome your donors

You give them a welcome. You've already thanked them for their gift. You've mailed them a thank-you letter or a card or a note, and now you mail them a welcome. This is usually called a welcome kit, or a new-member package. If you join any kind of membership organization, like Amnesty International, or the World Wildlife Fund, or Greenpeace, they will mail you more than just a letter. It'll be a package, and they'll mail you that within a few weeks of receiving your gift and your membership application.

The goal of a welcome kit is to inform and inspire your new donors. You want to help them see that they've made the right decision in mailing you a gift, and that you are an organization that deserves their continued support.

This welcome kit that you put together and mail to new donors is the tool that you use to continue building on this relationship that you've just started. They sent you a gift, and you mailed them a heartfelt, personal, prompt, particular thank-you letter, and so you've started this relationship. You wrote to them, they wrote back, you've written to them, and now you mail them a welcome kit.

You can put into the welcome kit just about whatever you want. It's whatever you think is important to develop this relationship, inform your donors and inspire them to give again. Don't put anything into this welcome kit that will simply distract and bore your donors. The emphasis is on informing them and inspiring them, so that when your appeal letter arrives they're ready for it.

You could include a welcome letter, signed by somebody in your organization, that's nice and warm and friendly, and thanks them not just for their gift but for becoming a member or joining your organization—becoming a partner in the work that you do.

You could have some literature in there that describes your work, where you work, who you help, the people that you help.

If you've got any kind of history as an organization and you'd like your donors to know where you've come from, and any kind of major accomplishments that you've had over the years, you can include that, too.

It could be that your organization receives honor gifts, or gifts in memory of loved ones who have departed. You could mention those, including a card and a reply device in that welcome kit so that people could use those honor cards and memory cards.

Maybe you sell products. You might sell books, CDs, you might sell resources for your members, for donors. You might have a catalog of those resources, or a couple of fact sheets. You could include these in your welcome kit.

You may have a newsletter. You could include a copy of your newsletter, a copy of your annual report.

It could be that you always like to know why people joined your organization and what they care about. You may wish to know more about your particular donor. What does she like about your organization? What are you doing well? You could enclose a little survey in the welcome kit, asking new donors a series of questions, and include a business reply envelope so they can mail it back to you.

You can tell new donors about volunteering opportunities at your organization. Maybe you've got field offices, regional offices. Maybe you have a drop-in program some evening or day of the week, where your volunteers can come and help out. You can have a list of those. You can either have it on your Web site and direct your donors there, or you can print it off and include it in your welcome kit.

If you are a member-based organization, you would obviously include a membership card with the member's name on it.

You may want your donors to know that they can contact your major giving officer, your planned giving officer, your special events officer.

You may want to tell them that if they change their address or want to get in touch with you, they should phone a certain person, at a certain office and at a certain phone number. You could include a directory of staff, and invite the new member, the new donor, to get in touch with you. You'd also want to include in your welcome kit all the full contact information for your organization, your Web site, particularly if you have more than one, your email address, and any locations you have that are important to the donor—local addresses, for example.

One thing that new donors are concerned about is how an organization spends their dollar. You'll notice that quite a few donor acquisition letters and packages include a buckslip or a note of some kind that says, "Here's how we spend your money." It usually features a pie chart, and shows the percentage of money that goes towards fundraising, overhead, capital expenditures, program costs and so on. Ideally, your program costs are around 80 cents of every dollar, and your overhead and fundraising and all the others are around 80 cents on the dollar. You could include that same little buckslip or lift note in with your welcome kit to reinforce that you are good stewards of the donors' money and that you spend it well.

Another thing that's happening these days is that donors are getting a little bit more particular about how the charity corresponds with them. Some donors will tell you, "I don't want you to phone me, ever." Some will say, "If you do get in touch with me, I want it to be by email. Don't mail me anything. I want to save trees." If you really want your appeal letters and your correspondence with your donors to be donor-centered, you should include something in your welcome kit that lets them choose how you correspond with them. They may say, "Correspond with me in Spanish," or in French or in English. They may say, "Don't exchange my name with any other organization" or "I never want you to telephone me." They may tell you, "I only want to hear from you once a year, and that's at Christmastime. Don't send me any special appeal mailings." If you want your correspondence to be donor-centered, give your donor a way to opt in or opt out of the ways that you correspond with them, and the kind of asks that you make during the year.

Involve your donors

The second thing you need to do is get your donors involved. The "I" in WIN is for involved. Before you ask them for a second gift, ideally it would be great if you could get them involved in your work in some way. Involved donors are statistically more likely to give you another gift, and they're likely to give you more money than donors who are not involved.

If you read Kent Dove's book, *Conducting a Successful Fundraising Program*, you'll find that he discovered that in 1993—which is quite a while ago—the average gift among households with volunteers was 55 percent higher than among households with no volunteers. Fifty-five percent higher. Households with volunteers give more money than those without volunteers. Volunteers are involved in the organization. If you can get your first-time donors involved, they are more likely to renew and give you another gift. So get them involved.

Perhaps they can't volunteer. Well, you could get them to sign a petition, if you're involved in any kind of advocacy. You could get them to answer a survey. You could get them to volunteer on the phone or volunteer where they are. You could invite them to phone you. You could invite them to visit your Web site, or drop in for a tour of your facility. You could invite them to sign up for your weekly email newsletter.

If you've got a store, like the Goodwill does, or like Habitat for Humanity does, where they sell used building supplies, you could invite them to visit your store. Involvement leads to commitment, and commitment leads to greater levels of giving. Not only welcome them, but involve them somehow.

Give your donors News

You also want to give them news. That's the "N" in the WIN. The thing to remember about donors is that they're really what somebody called pre-donors. They've given you only one gift. They've attended one ballgame, but they're not fans yet.

They're somewhat aware of your cause. They probably know a little about the work you do and the people you serve, but they don't have the breadth and depth of knowledge that loyal, long-term donors have. To transform your brand new donor into a long-term loyal supporter, you need to educate them, and you need to inspire them. The more that a first-time donor knows about your organization and the needs you meet, and the people you help and the work you do, the more likely they are to support you again. You need to inform them.

Now, as Penelope Burke discovered, if you want to attract that vital second gift, the most important thing to tell your donor is what you did with his first gift. Donors want to see proof that you are using, or have used, their last gift the way that the donor intended. If you don't prove this to your donor, they're not likely to give again.

If all that you do with your donor, from the time they give you their first gift, is ask them for more funds and ask them for more funds, and never inform them about how you're using their last one, then they'll feel like that little drawer that you have in your office for petty cash.

They'll feel like an automatic banking machine. They won't feel like a valued supporter and a partner in your mission. They'll fall away. They won't renew.

You need to keep your donors informed. You need to inform them initially about who you are and what you do and who you help, and then you need to keep them informed over time. This is a vital, vital part of donor renewal. Here are some ways you can inform your donors so that they're more likely to renew.

You can mail them an update, showing them how their donation is at work. Let me just give you an example of how an organization did this with a major donor. I know of a major donor in the United States, and he's an engineer. The chancellor of the university knew that the university needed a new boiler system for the university. It would cost $1 million. They needed all the pumps and pipes and equipment to pump the hot water around the campus. Their old system was dilapidated and worn out and rusty.

The chancellor found a donor that was willing to underwrite the whole project, and it was this engineer. The chancellor got a Polaroid camera—this is in the olden days—and he went to the plant, and he went through the doors and he took Polaroid pictures of the plant as it was. The floor was watery and there was rusty water everywhere. The pipes were all rusty and they needed to be replaced.

After the project was completed, he took photographs that showed the brand new plant, brand new gleaming pipes, the new pumps, the new system. The floor was finished and dry and painted. The place looked gorgeous. Then he went to this individual donor. The chancellor paid him a call, and sat down with him over a coffee and showed him these Polaroid pictures. It brought tears to the eyes of this engineer. He was so excited that this organization had used the money the way he wanted. He saw with his own eyes that his donation had made a difference. He saw the before, he saw the after, and he knew that he was the cause for it. He was a partner with the university. That would be the ideal way to give your donors news. You'd give them updates on how you're using their donations at work.

A simple way to update your donors is to mail them a newsletter, and we'll look at that in a second. If you don't have a newsletter, then you can mail what Tom Ahern calls a Newsyletter. You might not have the budget, the time or the staff to actually put together a multi-page newsletter. Well, you can mail them a letter that's got lots of news in it.

You could involve your volunteers, get them to pick up the phone and phone your donors with an update on your work, and how the donor is making a difference.

Another way to spread the news is to announce an upcoming event. Send invitations to your donors and invite them to something. It can be an online event, a live event, it can be a banquet, a golf tournament, a run, something that you're doing. That's another way to spread news.

If you've got an email program and you've got email addresses, you can email a progress report rather than mailing it.

It's also important that you give them the kind of news that they're looking for. If your donor designated her gift to a particular cause or a particular program, then send that donor information about the cause or the issue that she responded to with her first gift. Show the difference that the donation is making today.

If you run a child sponsorship program, giving your donors news is easy because you have updated photos of the child and letters written by the child. That's the best news that the sponsor could possibly get.

You might have been written up in the newspaper. Some journalist might have visited your site and written nice article about you. You might be on You Tube. You might be on CNN. This is the kind of news that you can send to your donors to show that there have been recent successes that were made possible by the donor's generosity.

MEDECINS SANS FRONTIERES
DOCTORS WITHOUT BORDERS

VOL. 2, NUMBER 2, SUMMER 2000

THE WORLD'S LEADING INDEPENDENT MEDICAL RELIEF ORGANIZATION

AT THE HEART OF
WORLD CRISES

Mozambique
After the floods

David Morley, our Executive Director, spent some time working at an MSF project in Mozambique where Canadians' donations were used.

Six weeks ago, almost nobody lived here in the village of Chequelane. But when the Limpopo River flooded its banks, people fled the valley, looking for higher ground. The inhabitants of Chokwe came this far, 40 kilometres from home. Now 80,000 people live here in Chequelane.

Photo by MSF

On the common land around the village, a mixture of pasture, scrub and trees, a tent city has been struck. There is a bustling market. A big green tent is city hall, and there are numerous church tents.

The camp has been here for about a month, and now people are afraid the cholera outbreak in Maputo will make its way here. The camp administration has asked us to prepare a Cholera Treatment Centre. If cholera starts

CONT'D ON PAGE 3

EDITORIAL *by David Morley*

People
before **profits**

When we demanded that all people worldwide receive access to essential medicines, some of the people who congratulated us on the Nobel Prize called us idealists who don't understand the realities of the marketplace. That's good—it proves we are on the right track.

Seventeen million people die each year because they lack access to essential medicines. Ninety percent of them are among the world's poorest. In most cases, they are suffering and dying not because the medications to help them do not exist, but because they cannot afford the cure.

Must we now say to our patients, "I'm sorry, I cannot treat your disease; you must die of market failure"?

For market failure is the prime factor in these and so many other preventable deaths. The world's poor are not a lucrative market, so drug companies ignore them.

We are lobbying governments and drug companies to loosen patent laws and allow the production of more generic drugs. We want more drugs to be declared as *essential medicines*, which will make them more affordable to the world's poor. We also want more research into developing more effective treatments for diseases like tuberculosis and sleeping sickness.

We have the knowledge we need to help many of the world's poorest, people who are suffering from disease. Taking action, developing the medicines and making them available, is just a matter of political will. We must put an end to a system which says, if you can't pay, you die, and replace it with one where the needs of the sick come first. ■

15

Use Newsletters to Boost Donor Loyalty

Let's take a look at newsletters and why they're important at donor renewal. Newsletters do three things, and they all begin with the letter "I."

Newsletters inform your donors. Donors act like investors. They want to know that their investment is delivering a return on that investment, so you need to inform them.

Newsletters inspire your donors. Donors give from both sides of their brain. They give from the emotional side of their brain and they give from the rational, logical side of their brain. When you inform them, you appeal to the rational side of their brain. When you inspire them, you appeal to the emotional side of their brain. Donors give from both sides.

Donors give from the head and they give from the heart, and so you not only have to inform, but inspire. Remember, you face competition as far as your donor is concerned. Your donor has a finite amount of discretionary money every month to give to charity. She likely supports more than 10 charities, and so you face competition for her donation. You need to inspire her to give to you, and to give again.

Newsletters involve your donors. You need to involve your donors. You can help your donors advocate, for example. You can give them a way in your newsletter for them to get involved by advocating for your cause—signing petitions, phoning their MP, phoning their member of Congress. You can give them something meaningful to do that helps you advance your cause.

You can do all three of these things with a donor newsletter. You can inform, you can inspire, and you can involve. That's the beauty of newsletters.

Nine common donor newsletter mistakes to avoid

I want to look at nine common mistakes that people make with newsletters, and how to avoid them. We will be discovering the positive by looking at the negative. If you pay attention to these mistakes and avoid them, you'll produce a knockout newsletter. Remember, your newsletter is designed to inform and involve and inspire your donors.

Mistake #1: Focusing on the institution and not the donor

The first mistake you want to avoid is focusing on the institution and not the donor. This is a classic mistake that new non-profits make and that very, very old non-profits make. They talk about themselves.

When you pick up their newsletter, you read stories about the board: "The board did this and the board did that." All the members of the board went off to some retreat in the woods and they discussed the strategic plan, and you see photographs of them at this retreat, sitting around a table looking interested.

Maybe there'll be a history lesson in the newsletter, describing the history of the organization in minute detail.

Sometimes you'll see organizational charts showing the executive director, the chairman of the board, all the regional offices. The focus is on the institution and not on the donor, which is a mistake. Avoid this one.

Mistake #2: Cliché photographs

Another mistake that people make in their newsletters is that they have lots of cliché photographs, and there are at least three that are well known in the non-profit world. You see these all the time. I hope they're not in your newsletter. You see them in the newspaper, too. Journalists that are invited to public events run by charities hate to take these kinds of photographs. They dread them.

One of them is ribbon-cuttings. You've seen these. There'll be a group of people all dressed up in their best dresses and suits. They'll be standing in front of a doorway, and there'll be a great big ribbon stretched across the opening. Someone or a group of people will be carrying oversized scissors and they'll be cutting the ribbon. It's a cliché photograph. You should avoid it.

Another one is a line of men in suits. Sometimes the mayor will be there. There might be a token lady or two present. They'll all be carrying shovels. They'll maybe have the shovels in the ground with their foot on them, and they'll be looking at the camera with these awkward grins on their faces, because they're in suits and their shoes are getting all muddy, and they're having this photo taken for the ground-breaking ceremony. Journalists hate these photo opportunities, falsely called. They offer only old, tired, hackneyed, cliché photographs.

Another one is the jumbo cheque. You've seen that before. Journalists call this the grip-and-grin photograph, where two people, the person giving the check and the person receiving the check, are standing there in front of the camera. They're gripping each other's hands in a handshake, they're grinning at the camera. They're holding this huge cheque. It's a cliché photograph that's been done to death, and so you should bury it. Don't include it in your newsletter. Use original photographs.

Mistake #3: No captions

Another mistake that some non-profits make is that they don't put captions under their photos. They have photographs all over the newsletter, and it's not obvious to every single donor what each photo is depicting, what it's saying, what it's communicating. Most photographs are not self-explanatory. Most photographs are not worth a thousand words. You need to have a sentence under each photograph that explains what it is that the donor is looking at. You need to help them understand, so put captions under your photographs.

Mistake #4: Not giving opportunities for donors to get involved
Another mistake that non-profits make is that they don't provide any opportunities for the donor to get involved in the newsletter. All the donor can do is read and look at the pictures. No petitions. No quizzes. No crossword puzzles. No answers to frequently asked questions. No product order forms. Nothing in the newsletter that involves the donor in any meaningful way. That's a mistake.

Mistake #5: Infrequent mailings
Some organizations mail their newsletters infrequently. They don't mail them often enough. You need to remember that your donors are bombarded with appeals from other charities. Many donors, especially those on a fixed income, give out of discretionary funds. They only have so much money per month that they give to charity, and they give to whoever comes first.

I read some research that was done by a focus group in the west. They asked the group, "Who do you give to every month?" Quite a few of them said, "Well, we give to whoever asks first." If your newsletter arrives late in the month, or doesn't arrive frequently enough, other charities that arrive in the mailbox more often than you do will get the donors' money. You need to mail frequently enough.

I suggest at least four times a year—once a quarter. If you don't mail more than four times a year, they'll forget you. You won't be on their kitchen table. If you only mail once or twice, you won't be in the top of their mind.

Mistake #6: Too many pages
Another mistake that charities make is that they mail a newsletter with too many pages. Donors are busy. You're busy, they're busy. When a donor gets a newsletter that is too thick, that has too many pages, or is too large and has too much reading to do, it just looks too intimidating, too daunting.

They may just lay it aside, or maybe just browse through it in a token way. It's a mistake to mail a newsletter that's too big.

Mistake #7: Sending a newsletter that is too fancy

If you mail a newsletter that's full-color, glossy, and that has really, really gorgeous photography and is beautifully designed, your donors may think, "Oh, you're not being a very good steward with my donations. My money is going towards this expense rather than going towards helping the people that I want it to help." Or they may think, "You don't need my money. If you can produce a newsletter like this that is obviously expensive, you don't need my donation," and they'll give somewhere else. That's a mistake you can avoid in your newsletters.

Mistake #8: Not using enough "make-a-difference" language

The kind of language that you should find in a newsletter is, "Your gift is making a difference. Because of you, our donors, we can do the following . . . Donors make a difference. Money makes a difference. Donations make a difference." You need to have that kind of make-a-difference language. One key to donor loyalty and donor renewal is proving that a donor's gifts are furthering your donor's cause, and that you're grateful for those donations the donor, because they're making a difference in the world. They are, and you are, with their gifts.

Mistake #9: Talking about programs and not about people

Donors give to people to help people. They don't give to programs. They don't give to policies. They don't give to institutions. Donors give to people to help people, so your newsletters should talk about people, not about programs, but about the people in those programs that are doing the work and that are being helped by the work that you do.

Those are nine mistakes to avoid. If you can manage to avoid all nine in your newsletters, you'll have a knockout newsletter that renews your donors over time.

16

How to Craft Fundraising Letters that Renew Donors

The three keys to donor renewal are thank-you letters, newsletters, and renewal letters. You need to mail fundraising letters to your donors over time that encourage them and invite them and ask them to renew their support. Your thank-you letter thanks them, your newsletter inspires and informs them, but your renewal letter actually asks them to renew their support. This is the third vital part of a donor renewal program. So how do you do that? How do you actually write a letter that inspires a donor to give a gift?

One thing you should do with every fundraising letter is make it a thank-you letter. Every time you sit down and write to a donor and ask them for a gift, thank them for their last gift. Thank them for being a donor, being a supporter, being a member. Acknowledge that they have a history with you.

I'm doing some consulting at the moment with a charity. Every letter that they mail says, "Dear Friend," and they mail them to non-donors and donors alike. The problem there is that when you mail the same letter to people who have given and to people who haven't given, you end up treating your donors as though they haven't really given, and you treat your people who haven't given as though they have given.

You have to moderate your language so that you try to appeal to everybody, but you water it down. The donor doesn't really feel that you know that they're a donor if you're writing to both audiences.

So write a letter that acknowledges the donor's history with you. Treat them as people and not as paycheques. Write your letters from your heart to their heart, not from your institution to them. Write the letter as coming from a person and going to a person, and showing that you appreciate them as a person and not just as a source of money.

Use make-a-difference language. Describe in your letter how

the donor's gift is actually making a difference in the world, and how a donation today—a repeated donation, repeated support—will make a difference today and tomorrow. Look to the past and look to the future, but in both cases use make-a-difference language.

Ideally, you should think like your donors. Think about what motivates them. Think about what they give to, why they give, and write your letters that way. For example, I'm doing some consulting at the moment with a hospital. They surveyed their donors recently and discovered that 86 percent of their donors are 45 years of age or older, and about 68 percent are 55 or older. That's a certain demographic.

Right away, they have a rough idea of how these people think. They also know that the topic of heart disease resonates very strongly with these donors because they are 55 years or older. It's when you get to that kind of age that you begin to notice that lots of your friends have heart disease. Your parents might have it, your uncle might have it, your grandparents might have it, and your friends are starting to get it.

This hospital would be wise to structure some of its fundraising appeals around the topic of heart disease, because the donors that they appeal to know about heart disease and think about heart disease. Also, this hospital has great expertise, not only in cardiac research, but cardiac patient care. This hospital should think like its donors so that it can write renewal letters that resonate with them.

What logically follows from this is that you should tie your ask into, or make it correspond with, your donors' interests. If your donor gave you a particular gift for a particular campaign, then you would be wise to ask them for another gift for that same campaign if your donor software and your strategic plan allows for that, that is, if your board allows you to make asks for restricted campaigns or designations, not just for your general fund. Make your ask correspond with what you know the donor is interested in.

Personalize everything you mail them. Every letter, every bulletin, every update, every thank-you letter should be personalized in some way. For example, I know a hospital, and every time it sends a renewal letter to its donors, it says in the first paragraph, or the second or third—somewhere on page one—it says, "We are very grateful to you for your last gift, which was for___" and then they name the dollar amount, "and which we received on ____" and they name the date. They always mention the dollar value and the date of the donor's last gift. Doing so proves that the letter is personal for that donor. It's not the same letter that every other donor is getting. They address them by name. They never call them, "Dear Friend." Personalize everything you mail your donors.

Four goals of renewal letters

Let's look at a couple of goals that you could have for any of your renewal letters. It's important when you're running a donor renewal program, and you're encouraging first-time and second-time donors to give again and again, that you know why you're writing and what goals you have in mind.

Donors renew their support with cash, obviously, but they also renew with their commitment. You not only want them to renew with a gift, but you want to win their hearts and minds every time. That's why renewal letters are so vital. They help you maintain your broad base of support year after year, cost effectively.

What you need to remember, too, and we discussed this before, is that renewal letters are part of a year-long program, usually called the annual giving program. But annual doesn't mean you mail just one letter annually, because you shouldn't. You need to be in your donors' mailbox more often than once a year. "Annual giving program" simply means you look at your fundraising efforts as a year-by-year activity that lasts for 12 months.

You need to persuade your donors to renew their commitment every year. They need to give every year. That's what donor renewal is all about.

Goal #1: Renew donor commitment

The first goal of donor renewal letters is obviously to renew donor commitment. Some donors only give once a year. You need to make sure that you get that once-a-year gift. Others give more regularly. They might give three, four or five times a year. Some will give you gifts during the year, but sporadically, and you can't predict when they're going to give.

As James Greenfield says in his book, *Fundraising*, "Donor

renewal is not automatic." Every letter you mail should aim to re-motivate, re-invigorate, and rejuvenate your donors, and encourage them explicitly and implicitly that they are to renew their commitment to your organization. Not just give another donation, but renew their commitment to your organization and the people that you serve.

Now if you send a series of renewal letters, the first renewal letter that you mail during the year will obviously ask them to renew their support, but donor renewal is really a year-long activity. It takes place at every contact you have with every donor. It might be a phone call. It might be a personal visit. It might be their presence at a banquet or other event. In every case, every communication you have with your donor is getting them to recommit, to renew their commitment to your organization in one way or another.

Goal #2: Renew donors' gifts

A second goal of your renewal letter is obviously to renew their gift. You want not only their commitment, but you actually want them to send you another donation. That's obviously a goal of every renewal fundraising letter, to raise funds, so you have to ask for a gift in every renewal letter that you mail.

Whenever possible, you should make mention of the last gift that your donor sent, and how much it was for and when they sent it. You should thank them again for their support. You also need to remember that the most effective renewal letters are those that ask for funds for a specific need, usually a project that you have on at the moment. You need to ask for the donation. That's one of your goals with the renewal letter.

Goal #3: Upgrade donors' gifts

A third goal that you could have—you don't have to have this in your renewal letters—is to ask your donors to upgrade their gift. Not only do you want them to renew their support and send you a donation, but, if at all possible, you want them to increase the amount of their gift. This is optional.

In some of your letters during the year (perhaps towards the end of the year), you have this option of asking your donors to renew their support at a higher level.

You could ask them for more money or ask them for a simple

percentage increase. You could say, "I'm inviting you to increase your commitment by 10 percent this year to help us keep pace with inflation and to help us meet our ambitious goals for the coming 12 months." You can do the math at the front end, and show them what that dollar figure would be of the 10 percent increase of their support, based on either their last gift or the amount that they give you per year.

Goal #4: Convert annual donors to monthly givers

A fourth goal of your renewal letters is converting your annual donors, who respond to your direct mail appeals, to monthly giving. This is not a goal that you have to have, but if you have a monthly giving program, this could be one goal of your donor renewal letters, to convert some of those donors to monthly donors.

You could mail them a letter whose primary goal is to persuade them to become monthly donors. You could spell out all the benefits that the donor enjoys and that you enjoy by them giving monthly.

If you prefer, you could include a postscript at the end of the letter, inviting the donor to give you a monthly gift every month rather than simply a one-time gift. If you didn't want to mention that in the body of the letter, you could simply include a buckslip or liftnote in the package that describes your monthly giving program and invites the donors to sign up.

Mail a series of renewal appeals

What you need to remember, too, about renewing donors, is that you need to mail a series of renewal appeals. If your non-profit is a member-based non-profit, then producing a series of membership renewal mailings is natural. You do it all the time. You know that you first mail a letter that asks them to renew their support, and then you mail them a reminder letter, and then you mail them another reminder letter. You may even send them a last-gasp, "This is your final chance to renew your membership" letter.

You can do that because memberships expire, so it's easy for you to say, "Your membership is about to expire." Memberships usually last a year, and your members expect to renew their membership, or at least be reminded to do so.

But even if your organization does not have members, you can still think of your donor renewal series as a member renewal series, where your goal is still to persuade them to renew their support over time. If you're a membership-based organization, you would naturally write, "Your membership is about to expire. Please renew." If you're not a membership-based organization and you simply want your donor to renew her support, you would simply write, "I'm counting on you to renew your support this year."

You need to expect to ask several times before you can secure that elusive second gift. Not everybody will respond to your first renewal letter. You should expect to ask them once, twice, three, maybe even four times a year before they'll give you a gift.

Mail at least four renewal packages during the year. Mailing more than once makes economic sense, because even a renewal mailing that only breaks even can perform better than an acquisition mailing. Don't just mail one letter a year hoping to renew your supporters. Remember this, too: mail your second ask sooner rather than later. Don't delay too long before you ask them for a donation. Don't be afraid that you're going to annoy your donors somehow with mailing them too many solicitations during the first year. Tests have shown over time that the longer you wait to renew a gift, the lower your renewal rates will be. So mail sooner rather than later.

Think friends, not funds

Direct mail fundraising is about relationships. It's not about revenue. Obviously, you're mailing to make money. You have to have net revenue, otherwise you can't exist as an organization. But the only way to generate sustainable income through the mail is to build relationships with your donors—relationships that are built on trust and that are mutually beneficial. You benefit and the donor benefits.

This means your goal with every letter you mail to your donors is not to raise funds, but to raise friends. To put it another way, the aim of every fundraising letter is to retain donors first, and to raise revenue second.

You can see how vital it is to your organization to keep the donors you have. In the fundraising profession, we call this donor retention, and donor retention is all about loyalty, the donor's loyalty to you and your loyalty to your donor. The most effective way to increase and sustain donor loyalty is to write heartfelt personal thank-you letters that you mail promptly, to inform your donors, inspire your donors, and involve your donors with donor-centered newsletters, and to send donor-centered, compelling renewal letters until the donor renews.

Treat donor groups differently

You should never mail the same letter to everyone in your database. You have people in your database who have given you a gift of $20 and they gave it three years ago. You have others who have given you a gift of $20,000 and they gave it to you last month. Both people should not both get the same letter.

You may have some people in your file that subscribe to your newsletter but they've never given you a gift. They should not get the same letter as people on your list who have given you gifts every month for five years. You should never mail the same letter to everyone. You should segment your file and treat different donor groups differently. That's the secret to effective fundraising.

Treat high, medium and low donors differently

You have some donors that give you large amounts of money or they give very frequently. They are your high donors. They should get more attention than your your low donors, who give either very little amounts of money or who give very infrequently.

In the middle you have your medium donors. You should treat them all differently. Not only should they not all get the same letter, you should not be mailing them the same amount of mail. In other words, you may write to your high-end donors eight times during the year. If you're writing to them eight times a year you should not be mailing to your low donors eight times a year too. You'll be wasting your money. You might be better off just writing to your low donors once or maybe twice a year.

Spend time and money on your most promising donors

Spend your time, your money and your effort—the kind of mental and emotional effort that you put into your direct mail fundraising program—on your most promising donors. You should spend your time, your money and your effort where it promises to deliver the highest return on your investment.

Think recency, frequency and monetary value

The simplest way to start segmenting your database is to look at recency, frequency and monetary value of the gifts. In other words, look at your database and ask yourself, "Who gave a gift most recently?" They should get more attention than someone who gave you one gift years ago and has not given you a gift since.

You can also segment according to frequency. Who are the donors in your file who give you the most gifts or give most frequently? Donors who give you gifts five, six, eight times a year should get more of your attention and more of your time and more of your energy than donors who give you gifts infrequently, such as once every few years.

You can also segment according to monetary value. Donors who give you a large amount of money should get more of your attention than donors who give you small amounts of money, unless the donor who gives you small amounts of money gives you those gifts every single month, year after year. I'm just talking about the overall monetary value of your donors over time.

Part 5
Testing,
Tracking
and
Analyzing
with
Confidence

17

Your Data Never Lies (but it Misleads if You Let it)

I once worked as the Director of Development for a national charity in Canada. They had always hosted a large, lavish fundraising banquet once a year in Mississauga. The staff, right from the executive director all the way down to the receptionist, including all the development staff, thought that this banquet was the organization's most successful fundraiser of the year.

Shortly after I joined, they asked me to conduct a comprehensive development audit to measure the profitability of their various ways of raising money, including this famous annual banquet.

So I started with the sacred cow, the annual banquet. I created an Excel spreadsheet. I went back five years and began entering the costs, including the venue, catering, table and chair rental, lighting, sound, the honorarium that we paid the speaker, the cost of printing the invitations, the postage for the invitations, and every other related cost for this particular event, excluding salaries and fixed overhead.

Then I looked at the gross income that had been generated from this event over the last five years, and entered that in my spreadsheet. I subtracted the expenses from the gross. I looked at the net. What a surprise I got.

What looked like their most successful fundraiser was actually their least effective fundraiser. Just to give you an example of what I mean, in 1999 they spent 89 cents to raise one dollar. They didn't realize that their best fundraiser, as they thought it was, was actually a financial flop year after year. And that's because they always published and celebrated the gross income that they generated from the event, and never looked at their net income, or at least they didn't publicize the net income.

And so they talked about all the money that they brought in year after year, but once they had deducted their expenses, they were effectively spending 89 cents to raise a dollar, which is a very expensive way to raise a dollar. And when I spoke to the executive director about this, he said, "Well, we also use the banquet as a communications tool, to reach our many audiences." And he tried to backpedal and explain that their best fundraiser wasn't only a fundraiser. It was also for publicity, which was true. But if you're looking at an event as a fundraiser, you need to do a little better than spending 89 cents to raise a dollar.

Now, when it comes to direct mail, you can avoid their mistake, and you can avoid lots of other mistakes by learning the most common ways to measure your success. And then use those measurements, those metrics, as a way to arrive at an accurate picture of your accomplishments, how you're doing. I like to say that the knowledge is in your numbers. All you need to do is uncover that knowledge and use it to your advantage in carrying out your mission.

Your data never lies

The nice thing about direct mail fundraising is that your numbers never lie. If you mail 100 pieces and five come back, then you know that you've got a five percent response rate. That's a fact, and nobody can argue with that.

If you spend $1,000 and you raise $2,000, then those numbers speak for themselves. They don't lie. But the way that you analyze your numbers can mislead you if you're not careful.

Let me give you an example. I get e-mails and phone calls just about every week from potential clients, and they ask me, "Alan, if we hire you to write our fundraising letter for us, what kind of a response rate do you think you could generate?" And the assumption, of course, on the end of the phone is the higher the response rate, the better. Everybody knows that generating a high response rate is a good thing, and that generating a low response rate is a bad thing. That's why that's one of the first questions they ask me. "What kind of a response rate can you expect to generate for us?" That's a good question. Sort of.

But the answer I give is rarely what they want to hear. To simply quote an average response rate would mislead them. If I told them that my last package, for example, generated a 36 percent response rate, they might say, "Oh, great. When do we start?" But I would be misleading them, because high response rates do not necessarily mean profitable results, and neither do low response rates necessarily mean poor results. So I don't tell them what response rate they can expect. Here's why.

I could craft a direct mail appeal that featured a photo of a starving child on the envelope, and inside were lots of dramatic stories and horrendous accounts of poverty and distress and despair in, let's say, the African continent. And I could lay so much guilt on you that you would respond, and so would all of your neighbors, and that package might generate a 20 percent response rate.

But because you gave out of guilt and fear and manipulation, and not because of the innate worth of the campaign and the people behind it, you might only give a small gift. So small that the average gift for the whole campaign might end up being something like two dollars. So we'd end up with a 20 percent response rate, which is good, but an average gift that is off the chart in the wrong direction and so low that you'd lose money.

Or I could craft a package for you that generates a response rate that is only one half of one percent, but generates an average gift of $2,000. That's possible, and that's better than the high response rate and the low average gift. So to simply look at your response rate alone is misleading.

The problem with direct mail fundraising arithmetic is this: you need to understand and use more than just one measurement. When you walk into the grocery store, you don't buy a bunch of bananas based on price alone. You pick them up and look at them. You squeeze them, you smell them.

You wouldn't choose a lifelong mate based on looks alone. At least, I hope you wouldn't. You'd consider other things about them: their character, for example, and their age. You wouldn't do it just on looks. And you shouldn't measure your direct mail fundraising success by one ratio or one formula alone, such as response rate.

You need to look at each campaign and you need to look beyond each campaign, and you need to look back to your previous results and you need to look forward to your anticipated results. You could be satisfied today with a direct mail program that generates an average gift of $35. You might be satisfied with that, but never realize that over half of your donors who give $35 give you just one gift and never give again.

If all you do is focus on your average gift, you'll be misleading yourself, not realizing that the very people who give that gift fall away and you have to find people to replace them. So your average gift doesn't tell you the whole story any more than your response rate tells you the whole story. Your data never lies, but it does mislead you if you let it.

18

Testing Your Donor Acquisition Package

Let's go right to the very beginning of your direct mail fundraising program, and start with acquisition. Let's look at the things that you test and the things that you measure when you mail a direct mail donor acquisition package, designed to acquire a brand new donor that doesn't know you yet. You have five goals with your first test.

Goal #1: Test as many lists as possible

You want to test as many lists as possible to discover which ones deliver the most responses. You remember that in direct mail donor acquisition, you generally rent lists, or you exchange lists with other non-profit organizations. And if you're a sophisticated mailer and you're going to mail, let's say, 100,000 pieces of mail, you don't want to mail all of those pieces to one list without testing it first.

So you take 5,000 pieces and mail them to a representative sample of what you think is a good list, and then measure your response rate, your average gift, your cost to raise a dollar and your cost to acquire a donor. You do this with as many lists as you can afford to test.

Then, if the results are suitable, you mail the same package to the lists that performed best. But you test first. And you test as many lists as you can afford to, to discover which ones deliver the best results. Not just the most responses, but also the lowest cost to acquire a donor and the highest average gift.

Goal #2: Acquire as many donors as possible

Your second goal with your first test—and this is with all tests too, of course—is that you want to acquire as many donors or members as possible. With an acquisition mailing, your goal is not to make money as much as it is to acquire donors or members. The more, the better.

Goal #3: Recover your costs

Of course, another goal is to generate enough income to recover a substantial part of the cost of your test mailing. You don't want to lose your shirt, or your blouse. If at all possible, you'd like to make money, but you at least want to recover as much of your mailing costs as you can.

Goal #4: Discover which acquisition package performs best

The fourth goal that you have with your testing is to discover which acquisition package performs the best. Ideally, you'll be testing lists and you'll be testing packages. You might test a 5 x 9 envelope against a #10 envelope. You might test a four-page letter against a two-page letter. You would test these things against each other to discover which one performed the best.

Goal #5: Discover if direct mail is a cost effective way for your organization to acquire donors

And finally, your fifth goal in testing is to discover if direct mail is a cost effective way for your organization to acquire donors. This is your main goal with your first test when you're starting out in direct mail fundraising.

Create your test package

The first step that you have when it comes to testing acquisition mailing packages is to create what we call a test package. This is a package that you will mail to all the lists that you're testing to see how it performs. And at a minimum, it has to contain the carrier envelope or the mailing envelope that everything goes inside. It has to have a letter, a reply device, and a return envelope.

I recommend that if you are starting small, that you create just one package for your initial test mailing. If you're mailing hundreds of thousands of people, then you can afford to mail two packages and test which package works the best and which list works the best. But if you're starting small, and maybe you're only mailing to 10,000 or 20,000 names, create just one package and make it the best package you can.

Don't go cheap. Spend as much as you can afford. You can always cut costs later. Don't go as cheap as you possibly can on writing and design and printing and postage only to discover that, after the results come in, you think, "Oh, if only we'd used color instead of one color, or four colors instead of one color, or if only we had used that little buckslip or that premium or something that we had thought about using."

We don't know if any of these would make your package perform better. You'd have to do another test to find out. So don't go cheap just for the sake of going cheap. Spend as much as you can afford. Cut costs later.

This includes hiring a professional writer, professional designer and using color printing. It doesn't have to be four color. You could use black plus one color. And it includes using a premium, if you think it will boost response and attract long-term donors.

You could include a freemium, which is something that doesn't have any intrinsic value but helps you communicate your case for support. A hospital I recently wrote a package for mailed a letter that was written by one of their patients who had lost her daughter as a baby at the hospital. The hospital included a facsimile of the patient bracelet that the baby girl wore in the hospital.

In and of itself, that patient bracelet didn't have any intrinsic value. The donor couldn't use it for anything the way they could use a return address label or a greeting card (two popular direct mail fundraising premiums).

A freemium helps you communicate your case for support in a compelling way, and it often makes your package lumpy, which makes it more likely to get opened.

Choose lists to test

You have to choose the lists you're going to test. When it comes to testing an acquisition mailing, you need to mail enough letters to have confidence in your results. Direct mail fundraising consultant Mal Warwick of Berkeley, California, says you need to mail at least 30,000 letters.

You need to test lists that are large enough to roll out to. In other words, if you're going to do a test that is statistically significant, you don't want to mail just 10,000 pieces total and test just 2,000 names. The list has to be large enough that you can test a portion of it and then roll out to the whole list.

In other words, if you're mailing to 100,000 names, you'll

want the list to be 100,000 and you'll want to test just 10,000 of those names. If the list is really, really small, then it's not worth your while to test. You wouldn't get statistically valid results.

You need to mail to a number of promising lists, as many as you can afford, so that you discover which tests work the best for you. You want to test lists of people who are already donating to organizations like yours or causes like yours. They will be the best candidates for giving you a gift.

You also want to test lists of non-donors, people that aren't known to donate to any causes, such as magazine subscribers who read magazines that cover a topic that is similar to the kind of work that you do. And you don't necessarily know that those people are donors, just that they are magazine subscribers.

A valid list test is a mailing of 5,000 names. The rule of thumb that we use in direct mail fundraising is that you need to generate at least 50 responses to have an accurate picture of whether that list is good or not. And if you're going to get 50 gifts, then that means you would need to mail at least 5,000 names and get a response rate of one percent.

Since the response rate that everybody works on these days is one percent, a valid list test is a mailing of 5,000 names. This is what I mean by making sure you have a list that's large enough to roll out. If the list you're renting is just 5,000 names, you can't really test it, because your test would be your mailing and you'd have no other names to mail to after you got your test results.

Make sure you do what's called a merge and purge. A merge and purge is usually done by the letter shop. You will rent a list or a couple of lists and the mailing house will take all of those lists from organization A, organization B, magazine C and so on, take all those lists from different companies, different non-profits and merge them all together. And then the letter shop will purge from that master list the names of all the people that are already in your house file. They purge those names so that you don't end up mailing your own donors an acquisition package. You don't treat them like strangers.

And they also do it so that you don't end up mailing one person five or six pieces, because lots of individuals in North America support more than one charity, and their name might be on more than one list. And if you don't do a purge, then you'll mail that same person many times and turn them off. And if they're a donor and you mail them many times, it'll turn them off even more. So make sure you do a merge and purge.

Make sure that the names you test are selected randomly on an "nth name" basis. That's a true random selection. Let's say you have a list and you want to test the names in it. You wouldn't just take the first 5,000 names. You would select every other name, or you would select every 10th name or every 15th name or every 20th name. By selecting your names on an nth name basis, you get a representative sample of the list that's not skewed by the people being arranged alphabetically or by ZIP code or by some other false way of selecting them.

How to budget for a typical mailing

One of the most important numbers to know in direct mail fundraising is how much you have to spend to acquire donors and to raise money. This is the problem that the charity I was hired by kept making with their annual banquet. They were always looking at their gross income and never at their net. And, of course, your net income is the amount of money you have left on the table after you've subtracted your expenses.

So you need to know how much you're spending. One exercise you have to do is figure out what it costs you for a mailing. You need to have a budget for a typical mailing. You need to figure out what your costs are and then record them every time you do a mailing. Let's have a look at what these are.

Take a look at the simple spreadsheet on the next page.

On the left hand side you've got the expense items, and over on the right, in the first column is your budgeted cost for each of those. And then there's a simple formula that's calculated to figure out what that cost is per thousand and what that cost is as a percentage of the total budget. This is called your mailing cost. It's all the direct costs involved in creating, producing and mailing your package.

Copywriting, design and production would be called creative. That's a creative expense. You might hire a writer, hire a designer and hire a photographer. Then you have your production costs, which include printing: printing your envelope, your letter, your reply device, all the printing that's involved in the mailing.

You might have an expense for list rental. If you're mailing to

Sample Budget for Direct Mail Acquisition Test Mailing
Prepared by Raiser Sharpe

Letters to mail	30,000		

Item	Budgeted cost	Cost per 1,000	Percentage of total
Copywriting	$ 4,500.00	$ 150.00	15.0%
Design and production	2,300.00	76.67	7.7%
Printing	3,256.24	108.54	10.9%
Data processing*	3,269.18	108.97	10.9%
Mail preparation*	3,125.67	104.19	10.4%
List rental	3,000.00	100.00	10.0%
Postage	10,500.00	350.00	35.1%
Premium	0	0	0
Total costs	$ 29,951.09		100%

* Data processing includes address correction and merge-purge
* Mail preparation includes folding, inserting and sorting

your house list, this is obviously not an expense. But if you're mailing an acquisition piece, you will likely have to rent some names. So your budget includes the cost of renting the lists, the cost of the letter shop to do the merge and purge.

There are some other services that the letter shop will do for you. One of them is comparing your list against the national change of address database. And they will automatically correct the names for you of people that have registered with the post office.

There are also other letter shop costs. They'll charge you for sorting the pieces, inserting the envelopes and the letter and the reply device into the envelopes. They'll charge you for sealing them, for lasering the address on to them, for metering them or putting indicia on them, for bundling them and for taking them to the post office.

You'll obviously have to pay for postage. Not just the cost to mail the package, but also the cost of processing the business reply mail you receive from your donors. You can include that as a cost of raising a dollar. And any mail that you get back from the post office that was undeliverable you'll likely have to pay for, too.

You may include a premium or a freemium in your package, and you should include that in your budget so that you have an accurate picture of what it costs you to put something into the mail. This is essential, this step in direct mail fundraising. It's essential for calculating your net income. You don't want to be always working on gross, but instead on your net income.

Measure the same costs campaign by campaign so that you accurately compare campaign results. Sometimes you'll use a premium and sometimes you won't. But generally speaking, your creative, your printing, your list, your letter shop and so on, you should measure every single one of those things consistently, measure the same costs campaign by campaign, so that you're always comparing apples with apples, oranges with oranges.

And remember that mailing costs rarely include indirect costs. They rarely include staff salary, overhead, such as your building rent and electricity.

Sample Results for Direct Mail Acquisition Test Mailing

List	Pieces mailed	Response count	Response rate	Gross income	Average gift	Cost to raise a dollar	Cost to raise a donor
1	5,000	52	1.04%	$ 1,024.00	$ 19.69	$ 4.87	$ 76.30
2	5,000	39	0.78%	432	11.08	11.56	116.92
3	5,000	96	1.92%	2,400	25.00	2.08	27.00
4	5,000	48	0.96%	1,200	25.00	4.16	79.00
5	5,000	108	2.16%	702	6.50	7.11	39.72
6	5,000	44	0.88%	960	21.82	5.20	91.63

19

Tracking Your Results

You're going to have to track your results, and this goes for whether you're mailing an acquisition package or mailing a renewal package to existing donors. Either way, you have to track your results. You need to know at the end of the day how many pieces of mail came back to you and in five years, 10 years, 15 years from now, you need to be able to look at this very same campaign that you're doing today and be able to make some sense of it.

And you do that with a thing called a key code, or a source code. Below is a donor reply device, the little coupon that people fill in when they mail in a gift. In the bottom left corner of that card is the key code, circled.

Yes, I want to help Greenpeace to preserve the planet for our children

☐ OPTION 1: Monthly contribution
I have completed the form on the other side.

☐ OPTION 2: Single contribution
❑ $35 ❑ $60 ❑ $100 ❑ $250 Other $____________

As a monthly donor or with a donation of $60 or more, you will receive a subscription to Greenpeace magazine

6003958
Alan Sharpe, President
Raiser Sharpe
22 - 30 Adelaide St N
London ON N6B 3N5

06P2A-105-A

1616710000004

I want to make my contribution by:

☐ Cheque or money order (payable to Greenpeace)

☐ Credit card ☐ VISA ☐

____/____/____/____
Card number

____/____ ____________
Expiry Date Signature

____
E-mail

For Greenpeace to maintain freedom of action on environmental issues, your donation is not eligible for income tax credit.

You need to track your results, and one reason you use this source code is you need to identify the source of all new donors. In 10 years from mow, you need to be able to go back into your database and pick up any name of any donor and be able to look back historically and find out how you got that donor. Did you get them by phone? Did you get them through a special event? Did you get them through direct mail? And if you got them through direct mail, this source code or key code will tell you where they came from.

You also have to identify which lists each new donor came from. If you're doing an acquisition mailing, you need to code your reply device so that you can look back and say, "This donor came from list A" (or list B or list C). We'll look at that in a second.

Later on, once you've done a couple of mailings, you'll want to identify the creative package to which the donor responded. For a mailing that you do in the spring, you may mail two packages, and you're doing that to test package A versus package B. And so in this little code that you put on to your reply device, you also want to track the package.

A source code or key code is simply a group of letters or numbers, often it's a combination of the two. Sometimes it's little marks and colors that are used on the reply device. And it helps you discover the effectiveness of your mailing lists and your asks and your creative and so on.

Let me just show you how you put together a simple key code. For example, the key code 01A/D12 tells you several things. That key code could simply tell you that this is the first mailing of the year—01. It also tells you that it's package A of four packages that you mailed. See, it's A/D. In other words, it's package A of A, B, C, D; four packages. And it was mailed to list number 12. That doesn't mean that you mailed to 12 lists. It simply means that you took lists of names and you tested them all, and you numbered all of those lists. And then you mailed to three or four or five of those lists, and one of those lists that you tested was list number 12.

So that's a simple key code that helps you track when this package was mailed and the year, which package it was, and which list it was. You could use that key code to go back and discover a lot about your packages, your donors and the success of your mailings. Here are a couple of tips.

Give each list the same code in all your tests. In other words, if you're mailing to the Amnesty International list, call that list number 12, and always call it list number 12. Give each list the same code in all tests. So if you do 10 tests between now and who knows when, and if you always mail to the Amnesty International list as a test, always call it list number 12. You want to track your results accurately year after year.

Keep a master list of all your list codes so you can refer to it and always know what number 12 means or what number 8 means or whatever letters and numbers you use to code your lists.

Make sure that all your list codes are unique and mutually exclusive. If you've got a list called number 12, make sure that there's not another one called number 12. And also make sure that you don't have a package called number 12 or a time of year called number 12. It should be mutually exclusive.

The other advice I have, and this is going to save you a lot of time and effort and energy and grief, is that you should **only code what you need to track**. Only code what doesn't appear elsewhere in your database. For example, you don't have to keep track in your key code of the date of the mailing, because that will be taken care of in the description that you have of the whole mailing and will also be reflected in the date that you get the gift. Only code what you need to track. Be rigorous about that.

Follow these eight rules of testing

Rule #1: Test things that are significant

Don't test a blue signature versus a red signature. It's too expensive of a test. Don't test Times Roman versus Arial. Test things that are significant. In other words, test a six-page letter versus a two-page letter. Test a full-color package versus a black and white package. These would be significant tests.

Rule #2: Test things you can control

You can control your printing, you can control the length of the letter, you can control the photography, and so on. Don't test things that you have no control over—for example, mailing during a recession. You could have no control over that in the future.

Rule #3: Make your test large enough to be significant

Mal Warwick recommends 30,000 pieces to have a significant test. I say you need to mail at least 5,000 pieces to get 50 responses at a one percent response rate. Fifty responses is considered the minimum number you must generate to achieve a trustworthy test.

Rule #4: Test one thing at a time

If you mail a package and it does really, really well and you think, "Oh, we can improve this package," don't do a test where you mail a similar package but you change the headline and you change the teaser copy on the envelope and you change the reply device and you change the postscript, because if the second package outperforms the first package, you won't know what was responsible for the improvement. Was it the teaser copy on the envelope? Was it the headline? Was it the reply device? Was it the postscript? You won't know. Test one thing at a time to be sure.

Rule #5: Don't let large gifts skew your results

When you examine your campaign results, you see gifts of $25, $35 and $45, which is typical. But then you see a gift of $15,000 in response to the same campaign. That number will skew your results if you let it. Your spreadsheet for this campaign may tell you that the average gift was $92, but that's because of this unusually large gift. If you take this one gift of $15,000 out of your calculation, your average gift will likely be closer to $36.

So be careful about large gifts. Remove them when you're doing calculations to measure what your net income will be. Expect your average gift and your cost to raise a dollar to be skewed by large gifts.

Rule #6: Acquire loyal donors in the greatest numbers at the lowest cost

Concentrate on acquiring loyal donors in the greatest numbers at the lowest cost. Enough said.

Rule #7: If you are starting out in direct mail, aim to acquire as many donors as possible

If you're just starting in direct mail and you're obviously starting with donor acquisition, aim to acquire as many donors as possible, not to make as much money as possible. Success in the mail comes after the first gift.

Rule #8: Test every time you mail

If you're mailing to a large number of people, always test something. Test two asks, test the ask string on your reply device, test the teaser copy, test the length of the letter, test the signatory, test something of significance every time you mail. You'll learn a lot, and you'll improve your packages and your approach over time.

What to test

Test **prospect lists**. When I talk about significant tests, this would be a significant test. You find as many lists as you possibly can and you test as many as you can afford to test to see which lists perform better than the others.

Test the **size of the initial gift in your ask string**. The ask string is that series of numbers that you put on a reply device where the donor says, "Yes, I would like to give a gift of" and then there's a range of dollar figures.

The first number might be $50, and the next one is $75, the next one is $100 and then there's "other." Well, that initial number is a vital number. Tests have shown that if you increase the size of the initial suggested gift, you can increase your revenue.

To give an example, a non-profit mailed some test packages, and in some of the packages the gift string started at $20, then it went to $50, then it went to $70. And they did a test against that where the initial gift was not $20, but $30, and the next one was $80 and the next one was $100 and so on.

Then they measured the difference between those two initial asks in that ask string. You should test those. Sometimes you can get a better response rate if instead of asking for $30, you ask for $29, or you ask for $31.

Test **premiums, front and back end**. If you're doing acquisition mailings and you're mailing return address labels or greeting cards or notepads and things like that, test a package that has a premium and a package that does not have a premium, and see what difference it makes in your response rate, your average gift and your cost to acquire a donor.

You can also test your back-end premiums. Those are the premiums that you keep at your office and mail to anybody who asks for one. Usually in the reply device, they tick a box saying, "Yes, I would like to receive my free book" or whatever the premium is.

Test **involvement devices**. An involvement device might be a petition or a donor survey. You can do a mailing and split the mailing in half and mail half of the people the survey and the other half no survey, and see whether the package with the survey increases the response rate and the average gift, and your cost to raise a dollar, obviously, because the survey will cost you printing and it might even bump up your postage rate a little bit.

One thing you can test, and it's an inexpensive test, is to take the exact same acquisition package that you're mailing year after year and just test it by **changing the outer envelope**. Keep the letter the same, the reply device the same. Keep everything in your control package the same, but just change the outer envelope and see what difference it makes. It's an inexpensive test.

Test **personalization**. I recommend that you always personalize your letters. They should always say Dear Alan or Dear Wendy. They should not say Dear Friend. But if your letters do say Dear Friend or Dear Colleague or Dear Alumni or Dear Friend of the Hospital, you should test Dear Friend of the Hospital with Dear Alan and see which of those performs better.

You should test personalizing the letter too. In the body of the letter, you might say, "Alan, thank you for your gift of $45, which we received on the 8th of August, 2007. We really appreciate your gift." That would be a personalized letter, where my gift amount or the date of my gift or even my name or something else about me is mentioned in the body of the letter. It's personalized. You should test that against no personalization.

Test **the length of your letters.** You likely have people on your board that say you should never write a four-page letter. No one will read it. Well, test that and find out. Never mind what the board member says, you should test a four-page letter against a two-page letter, and a six-page letter (I've seen them) against a four-page letter. You may be surprised to find that people read long letters, particularly acquisition letters. Test and find out.

And you should always be testing **new packages**. Every year or every other year, you should be putting a brand new package into the mail and testing it against your existing packages to see which one performs better. So you're not just making incremental changes and incremental tests where you test just a different headline or a different teaser or a different something like that, but you actually test a brand new package: different size, different length, different color, different dimensions: something brand new, different.

Avoid these mistakes

All right, here are some mistakes that you should avoid in your testing, and particularly in your acquisition mailings:

Avoid the mistake of **designing a package that acquires lots of donors who give you one gift and never renew**. Don't be like the organization I worked for and brag about the high response rates you get with your acquisition mailings (three, four, five percent response rate), which sound terrific but come from donors who give once and never again. You need to acquire donors who are likely to renew. That means avoiding any tactic that is likely to acquire a one time, not-very-loyal donor.

Avoid the mistake of **watching your response rate only**. Don't get into the habit of just asking your annual giving officer, or if that's you, don't make the mistake of just looking at your campaigns month after month, year after year and just asking which one generated the highest response rate. It's not the only thing to measure.

Don't make the mistake of **watching your cost to raise a dollar instead of your cost to raise a donor.** This is for acquisition I'm talking about here. Your whole goal with an acquisition mailing is to acquire donors, and when you acquire a donor it may cost you $2 to raise a dollar. And you could never run a sustainable fundraising program where you spent $3 to raise a dollar. But in donor acquisition, you're looking at your cost to raise a donor, rather than your cost to raise a dollar. So don't make the mistake of watching your dollars instead of your donors.

Don't make the mistake of **designing a control package that is tied to current events**, such as an election or a natural disaster, such as Hurricane Katrina, or something that's in the news, such as a coup in Pakistan. A control package is a letter, an envelope and a whole package that you're going to mail repeatedly, a couple of times a year. You're going to use it for as long as you possibly can, until it starts to flag and the results start to fall.

The whole idea is that you don't keep reinventing your control package. That's expensive. You keep mailing the same one until it starts to flag. You don't want to have a control package that is successful today precisely because it's tied to current events, but will fail six months from now, once current events have moved on. So don't tie it to today's news or trends or fads. You want your control package to work for years.

20
Analyzing with Confidence

There are over 10 things that you need to look at when you're measuring your results. Each one tells you something slightly different about your success at direct mail fundraising.

#1: Cost per thousand

One thing we looked at earlier was your mailing cost. It's the total amount of money you have to spend to put a campaign into the mail.

But there's a popular number that's used in direct mail, and particularly in direct mail fundraising, and it's called cost per thousand. It's one of the most common measurements. It's an important measurement because it's an objective way to compare your mailing costs campaign by campaign.

When the total number of packages that you mail is different, the cost per thousand will always give you an accurate picture, assuming that you're not way off in your numbers. I mean, you might mail 100,000 packages one year, and a couple of months later, you might mail 105,000, and then a couple of months later you might mail 90,000, but your cost per thousand is an accurate number that helps you measure the cost from one campaign to the other. You can look at one campaign and think, "Oh, wow, the cost per thousand was pretty high compared to this other mailing that we did."

The cost per thousand is usually expressed as a dollar figure and then a slash with the letter M. M is simply the Roman numeral for thousand. Sometimes the cost per thousand is called CPM, cost per thousand.

When you get a quote from a printer, letter shop or list broker, it will often refer to CPM, cost per thousand. Now you know.

#2: Cost per piece

Another effective measurement is cost per piece. Not just the cost per thousand, but the cost per individual piece. And namely, how much money you have to spend to reach each individual person in your list with your message.

Again, it's an objective number, and it's an easy way to compare your mailing costs from one campaign to the other. You have an Excel spreadsheet and you're looking at six mailings that you did this year, you can compare your cost per piece from one to the other to the other, and you can see which one of those campaigns cost you the most and which one cost you the least, and then you can look at other metrics, such as your response rate and your average gift and your cost to raise a dollar, and compare those with your cost per piece. Sometimes by increasing your cost per piece, you can increase your average gift.

You should compare your cost per piece with your average gift to get an approximation of how much you must spend per piece to raise your average gift amounts. So let's say your cost per piece is 80 cents and your average gift is $35. Then you know, roughly speaking, you need to spend at least 80 cents per piece to raise a gift of $35.

Now, naturally, you're going to want to keep your cost per piece as low as possible. You don't have to spend lots of money that you don't need to. In other words, you don't have to mail first class if you can get a discount postage rate. You don't have to use expensive stationery if you don't want to. You'll want to keep your cost per piece as low as possible, but you also should remember that you don't have to reduce your cost per piece if that's going to affect your response rate or your average gift.

You may find, for example, that if you have a cost per piece of 80 cents and you increase it to 85 cents by hiring a professional writer or a professional designer or by getting the letter shop to do some data work for you in personalizing your letter, you may find that the extra five cents that you spend per piece boosts your response rate and boosts your average gift. So it sometimes pays to increase your cost per piece, and you know that once you start testing and tabulating your results.

#3: Response count

The next thing that you want to measure is your response count. This is simply the number of pieces that return to you in the mail. You need to know what that total number is so that you can calculate your response rate.

You should calculate this number at the same interval

following each campaign. Some organizations will keep track of what their response rate was after the eighth week, or after the third month, and they'll write that down. Now, years and years after a mailing, you're obviously accurate in looking back, but if you did 12 mailings a year, one in January, one in February, one in March and so on, it would help you to look at what your response rate is after one month or after two months and do that for each of those mailings so that you are always comparing apples with apples. You're always measuring your campaigns at the same interval. That way you can compare your results from one mailing to the other and have a valid comparison.

Remember that your response count for each mailing will rise as the size of your donor base rises. So if you only have a mailing list of 10,000 names, the number of people that respond will be a certain number. But if you mail to 100,000 names, the number will rise. And so your response count isn't an accurate way to compare your results with others as much as your response rate is.

#4: Response rate

Your response rate, by definition, is the percentage of people that responded to your mailing. This is an important number because it measures the breadth of interest in your cause. If you have a high response rate, that shows you had broad appeal. If you have a low response rate, that shows your appeal generated less interest. So your response rate tells you how broad or how wide the interest is in your cause.

You should note which appeals pull the highest response rate and try to figure out why. If you look at your mailings year after year after year, you'll generally find that the last mailing of the year, usually mailed around November, tends to pull in the highest response rate. That's for a couple of reasons.

People are more charitable at that time of year, and if you're a Christian charity and you're mailing a Christian Christmasy type appeal, you'll generate your highest response. Christmas is an important holiday for Christians. And it's also the time of year when people have to maximize their income tax returns, and they do that by giving before the year ends. You may find that your highest response rate is at another time of the year, but you should note which appeals pull in the highest response, figure out why, then try to copy those results.

Don't look at your response rate to tell you how successful your campaign was. Your board and your executive director might say, "What was our response rate?" It's not enough. You need to factor in other measures, such as your net income and your average gift, which we'll look at in a minute.

Now, obviously, the trend for a healthy organization is to have response rates that at least remain steady. Sometimes they go up, sometimes they go down a little bit, but you want to look at your response rate over time and see that it is remaining steady or climbing just a little bit. You can't expect your response rate to go up and up and up every year, even though your mailing list might grow in numbers.

Your mailing list might go from 10,000 one year to 100,000 the next year, and your response rate might remain at 12 percent. You can't expect it to keep going up. Your net income will go up and your response count will go up, but your percentage response rate will generally stay about the same. It might even climb just a little bit.

And obviously, a sign of trouble is when your response rate starts to plummet. That shows a lack of interest in your appeals, or in your organization. That's something to watch out for.

#5: Gross income

We discussed gross income at the beginning. It's simply the total amount of money that your direct mail package raises.

If you send out your appeal and it generates $100,000, then that's your gross income, $100,000. You need to calculate this number so you can make sense of all of your other numbers: your net income, your cost to raise a dollar and so on. You can't figure those out until you know how much money you brought in overall, total.

Now I'm belaboring this point, but you need to remember that this figure can mislead you and your board if all you do is look at your gross. Until you've subtracted your expenses, you don't know whether your mailing made money, lost money or broke even. So don't let your gross income mislead you any more than you let your response rate mislead you.

Measure your gross income at the same interval following your mailing. You could do it after the eighth week after your mailing drops, or you could do it three months later. It's a helpful way to see how much money a typical mailing generates within a certain amount of time, so that you're always looking at the same number.

And it also helps you tell your executive director, "If we drop a letter in the mail now, within eight weeks we will probably generate such and such an amount of money, based on historical precedent." Your gross income figure helps you make valid comparisons between campaigns.

#6: Net Income

Net income is the amount of money you have left over after you've subtracted your expenses. And the reason that this is an important number is that it's the only number that matters to your chief financial officer. Your net income is the only income you can use to fund your cause.

You have to spend money to make money, but at the end of the day, it's only the money that's left over after expenses that you can use to help the poor, help the needy, help the people that you help in your organization. And you calculate your net income by subtracting your expenses from your gross income. That's easy to do.

Net income is the bottom line in fundraising. It's the reason you get up in the morning, to generate net income. It's the number that you can't survive without. You can't survive without bringing in net income. Measuring your response rate is important, calculating your average gift is important, but at the end of the day, net income is the only number that really matters in all your fundraising. So just remember when you're boasting to colleagues, when you're telling the press or the media how much you raised with a particular mailing, remember that the bottom line is your net and not your gross.

#7: Average gift

Your response rate measures the breadth of interest in your cause, and the higher your response rate, the more people are interested in your cause. But your average gift measures the depth of interest in your cause. It measures the degree to which people are interested. If you have a really high average gift, that shows that your donors are very, very excited about what you're doing. The high response rate tells you that many people are interested, but your average gift tells you how much they are interested.

And, obviously, the larger your average gift is, the better. But you need to remember, this average gift figure can be skewed upwards by just a few large gifts. You want to avoid that. Don't just do a simple calculation in Excel that takes your gross income and divides it by your response count and calculates your average gift. That will mislead if you have a few particularly generous donors.

You want your average gift to remain steady over time. You want it to go up a little bit if you can. Obviously, you want to bump it up, but you should watch your average gift, because if your average gift starts to decline, it shows that the level of interest in your cause is starting to wane.

#8: Average cost per gift

Your average cost per gift is the amount of money you have to spend to generate one gift. This helps you manage your fundraising costs. It doesn't tell you about revenue or how successful you are. It simply tells you how much money you have to spend to raise one gift, and it helps you manage your fundraising costs.

Average cost per gift is a meaningful number when you compare it with your average gift. After all, you might spend a small amount to generate a gift, but if that gift is also small, then knowing what your average cost per gift is ain't that helpful. But if you compare your average gift with your average cost per gift, you know how much you have to spend to generate a gift.

This is a great number for looking at to trim your mailing costs. When you know that you have to spend so much per piece and so much to acquire one gift, then you can look at those two numbers and decide if it's possible to reduce your mailing costs without sacrificing your response rate or your income.

#9: Return on your investment

Your return on investment is a score. It's usually expressed as a percentage that tells you how effective your investment in mailing cost is at generating net income. This is the number that your chief financial officer will want to know, and it's helpful if you have an Excel spreadsheet, to put this number right in the far right column. You can look down the column, that ROI column, at all of your mailings and see which one generated the highest ROIs. That's a really quick way to see which of your campaigns was successful. Not necessarily which generated the highest income, but which ones generated the highest return on investment.

In other words, which campaign raised the most by spending the least amount of money. Now, in the for-profit world, they simply call this the profit. And obviously, you want to keep this number as high as you possibly can.

#10: Cost to raise a dollar

Here's one of the most common metrics in direct mail fundraising. Cost to raise a dollar is simply what it says. It's the amount of money you have to spend to raise one dollar of income. It's useful in comparing the cost of direct mail fundraising with other methods.

If you wanted to compare the effectiveness of direct mail fundraising against special events, banquets, special runs, telethons, telemarketing, grant proposals, even personal one-on-one solicitation, this is an accurate way to measure cost from one to the other.

For example, your cost to raise a dollar in direct mail fundraising might be 35 cents. But your cost to raise a dollar in major gift fundraising might be 5 cents, because a face to face solicitation might raise a $50,000 gift. Your cost to raise a dollar might just be a few pennies.

In direct mail fundraising, your costs are higher per donor and per mailing, and so this number helps you measure the success and effectiveness of one method against another. You are comparing apples with apples when you're looking at cost to raise a dollar. You simply divide your mailing costs by your gross income, and that tells you what your cost to raise a dollar is.

Now, again, you don't want to use this number in isolation. This is simply measuring your costs. It's not telling you your whole success story. It only tells one part of your success.

Obviously, you want your cost to raise a dollar to be as low as possible, but there are times when your cost to raise a dollar is high and is still acceptable. One example would be direct mail donor acquisition, where your emphasis is on acquiring donors rather than raising money. Your cost to raise a dollar might be a dollar and five cents, but you've raised a donor. And, like I said, it's one of the most effective and most common ways of measuring fundraising success.

#11: Cost to acquire a donor

Closely related to cost to raise a dollar is your cost to acquire a donor. You can use this same number for special events, for telemarketing, for face-to-face fundraising, for direct mail, for the Web. You should always know how much it costs you to acquire a donor.

Some methods are a little bit hard to figure out, because some donors will just come out of nowhere and decide to give you a donation. But if you track your responses with response devices and key codes, you can figure out how much you had to spend to acquire each donor that you have in your database.

You simply divide your net cost by the number of donors that you acquire. For example, if you mail 1,000 packages and each one costs you a dollar, then your total cost of mailing is $1,000. If you get a one percent response rate, that means 10 people responded. Assume these donors give you a total of $750, that's your gross income.

That means you didn't cover your costs. You spent $1,000, but you only raised $750. So you had a net loss of $250. If you divide that $250 by your 10 donors, your cost to raise a donor is $25.

The best way to measure your success in direct mail donor acquisition is to examine your cost to raise a donor, not your cost to raise a dollar. I've said it before. It's worth repeating. This is especially important when you have to argue with your board of directors or your executive director or your director of development. Your director of development might have a planned giving background or a major gifts background and not be used to spending money to acquire donors.

The whole concept might be foreign to him, so you need to know what your lifetime value is of a donor and be able to argue that it makes sense to spend money to acquire donors.

When you compare the results of your donor acquisition mailings over time, you'll discover that some lists perform better than other lists, some packages perform better than other packages. Your goal is to find the lists and the packages that acquire the greatest number of loyal donors at the lowest cost. Your goal is not simply to have the lowest cost to acquire a donor. You should be looking at your lowest cost to acquire a donor who stays around for some time and gives more than one gift.

#12: Net income per thousand pieces

This is a number that some non-profit organizations use and some don't. It's particularly popular with organizations that mail millions of pieces every year because if they mail millions of letters and they can save a penny or a quarter of a penny on each piece, then they can save some serious money.

And so one way they measure their success is not net income per piece, but net income per thousand pieces, because they're always mailing in the tens or hundreds of thousands. So your net income per thousand pieces is obviously the net income you get for every 1,000 pieces that you drop in the mail.

Again, this is a common unit of measurement that helps you measure your results against those of similar organizations. If you're comparing yourself against other charities, you can find out what their net income per thousand pieces is, generally speaking, and make an accurate comparison with your results.

#13: Renewal rate

Now here's a number that you're going to want to look at, and this is not campaign specific. Cost to raise a dollar, net income per thousand, those are numbers that are tied to particular campaigns, and you track those campaign by campaign by campaign. Here's a number that you're going to want to follow in terms of your direct mail fundraising program overall. You need to make sure that the donors that you acquire stay with you for some time and that you don't have a revolving door in your organization where donors come in the front door, they go around the revolving door and they go right back out again and only give you one gift.

Your renewal rate is simply the percentage of donors who renew their support each year with a gift. The renewal rate is usually a percentage and it's usually based on yearly giving. So if you have a donor that gave you a gift last year and if they give you a gift again this year, then they are said to have renewed their support. If you had 100 donors last year and this year you have only 90 donors, then you had a 90 percent renewal rate. Ten of them fell away, or 10 percent fell away, but 90 of them renewed and gave you another gift.

Now, obviously, the higher your renewal rate is, the better you're doing. Your renewal rate tells you the success of your fundraising efforts over time. If you have donors that repeat their gifts year after year, it shows that you're managing to keep your donors. They're staying loyal to you, and you're doing something right. You're probably doing a lot of things right.

You can increase your renewal rate by concentrating your money and your resources on securing that vital second gift. And you can improve your renewal rate by thanking your donors properly for every gift that they give you. You should send a note within 24 hours. You should thank them personally, thank them promptly, thank them particularly, thank them positively.

You should get them involved in your organization as much as possible. You could mail them a welcome kit. You could send them petitions, ask them to take part in various initiatives that you're doing. Involve your donors and they're more likely to renew their support. You need to remember that getting second and third and fourth and subsequent gifts from your first time donors is eight times cheaper than going out, trying to find first time donors that will give you the same amount of money. So you need to be spending your money not on acquiring and acquiring, but acquiring and renewing those donors that give you one gift.

Healthy organizations have healthy renewal rates. They renew large numbers of their donors every year, or a large majority of their donors renew their support every year, depending how you look at it. And poor renewal rates are a sign of trouble, because if you have a large percentage of your donors that are not renewing their support every year, it shows that their interest in your cause is short lived.

Now, it could be that you've done something wrong organizationally, strategically. You've changed your focus or you've shifted the kind of work that you've done or you've had a scandal or terrible press, and that has resulted in people falling away. But if you consistently have poor renewal rates, it shows that people are not interested in your cause over time, and that's a sign of big trouble.

#14: Attrition rate

If direct mail fundraising was a coin, on one side of that coin you would have your renewal rate, which is the percentage of your donors that give again or renew their support. On the other side of the coin would be your attrition rate. That's the percentage of your donors that fall away every year or lapse. We sometimes call them lapsed donors. For whatever reason, they stop giving, and your attrition rate is the rate at which donors do not renew their gifts every year, and it's usually expressed as a percentage.

For example, if you had 100 donors last year and this year only 90 of them gave again, your renewal rate is 90 percent. Your attrition rate is 10 percent. And most non-profit organizations have an attrition rate of somewhere between 8 and 15 percent.

Many of those people stop giving for reasons that are beyond the control of the non-profit. Some of them die, some of them lose their jobs, some of them retire and they're on a fixed income, and for reasons beyond the control of the non-profit they lapse or they fall away. So because many of these reasons are beyond your control, you don't have as much control over your attrition rate as you would like.

Now, monitoring your attrition rate helps you know what percentage of your donor file you need to replace each year through donor acquisition. For example, if you look at your numbers for the last 10 years and you discover that your attrition rate has always been about 10 percent, then you need to figure out what that is in terms of actual people.

Keeping with our example, if you had 100 donors last year and now you only have 90, your attrition rate is 10 percent and that means 10 people fell away. This is a vital number to know, so that you know how many of those people you have to replace every year. This year you'd have to replace 10 donors through donor acquisition just to keep your donor base from shrinking.

Now, a more helpful number to know is the number of donors who fall away each year, rather than the percentage. You may know that your attrition rate is 11 percent, but that won't really mean very much to you. But once you know what the actual number of donors is, that number tells you the exact number of donors that you need to replace each year. So look at your attrition rate as a percentage, but also bear in mind that that percentage represents actual, real, live individuals that have stopped giving.

You should also remember that high rates of donor attrition can sometimes be attributed to the way that you acquire the donors in the first place. If you have lots of donors that come and go and come and go, if your attrition rate is consistently high, it could be that you're acquiring the wrong kinds of donors in the first place. Maybe you used sweepstakes, maybe you used premiums, or you used other devices that lure first time donors who give one gift and never give again.

It could be that your attrition rate is high because you don't follow up with donors. It could be that you're acquiring perfectly good donors but your renewal methods are poor. You don't thank them soon enough, you don't send them welcome kits, you don't write to them again soon enough, you don't send them a newsletter. They give a gift and you just never really correspond with them much after that. That can also be a sign or a reason for a high attrition rate. Sometimes you're acquiring the wrong donors and other times you're simply not working hard enough to renew the ones you have.

#15: Donor loyalty

Another number to look at is donor loyalty, sometimes called average tenure. It's the percentage of your donors that stay with you for one year, two years, three years, four years and so on.

It's always helpful to go through your database, go back historically to maybe 5 or 10 years and figure out how many donors that gave 10 years ago are with you today. And you can figure out what that is as a percentage of the number of donors that you had back then. And then do the same for nine years ago, eight years ago, seven years ago and so on. It's helpful to know how long your average donor stays with you in terms of years, and also what their lifetime value is, the amount of money that they give you over their "lifetime."

If you do this going back 10 years, look for trends in donor loyalty. Ideally, the percentage of active donors that you have this year who have been with you for two years or more is larger than it was five years ago. A healthy non-profit organization wins and keeps the support of its donors and members. So you want to have the highest donor loyalty possible. In other words, you want your donors to stay with you for as long as possible.

Put all your numbers on one spreadsheet

On the next page is an Excel spreadsheet. It's available for sale from my website, and I call it the Direct Mail Fundraising Return On Investment Calculator. In direct mail fundraising, you really only need to know four numbers in order to know how well you're doing and where you need to polish your program.

You need to know:

1. how many pieces you mailed
2. how many pieces came back
3. how much money you spent
4. how much money you earned

If you know those four numbers, you can make a lot of sense of your program. Two of those numbers have to do with what you mail, or the pieces of mail, the mail that goes out and the mail that comes back. And the other two numbers have to do with money, the money you spend and the money you earn.

You'll see here from this Excel spreadsheet that on the left hand side, if you create a spreadsheet like this, you can simply put on the left hand side the first mailing of the year, the second mailing, the third, the fourth and so on. You'll see there that there are seven mailings in the year for renewal, and beneath that there are four acquisition mailings for the year. And beneath that you could also have major donor mailings, and you could also have special appeals. You divide them up as much as you think is important for you.

And if you just look across these columns, you'll notice that once you've put into the spreadsheet how many pieces you mailed and what it cost you and how many pieces came back and how much revenue you generated, those four vital numbers, you can calculate all those other numbers using an Excel spreadsheet.

You can look at what your net income is—in other words, how much money you have left over after your expenses are taken away. You can look at what your net income per thousand was or what your net income was per piece. You can work out your cost per thousand, cost to raise a dollar, and I would say that the success of your direct mail fundraising program will depend to a great deal on how you look at these numbers and make sense of them over the year.

Direct Mail Fundraising ROI Calculator

RENEWAL MAILINGS

Enter these numbers to automatically calculate results

	Pieces Mailed	Costs	Number of Gifts	Gross Income	Response Rate	Net Income	Average Gift	Net Income Per 1,000	Net Income Per Piece	Cost to Raise $1	Cost Per Piece	Cost Per Gift	ROI
Mailing 1	19,090	17,424.98	2,090	121,220.96	10.95%	103,795.98	58.00	5,437.19	5.44	0.14	0.91	8.34	595.67%
Mailing 2	23,656	17,656.49	3,102	119,325.23	13.11%	101,668.74	38.47	4,297.80	4.30	0.15	0.75	5.69	575.82%
Mailing 3	24,212	19,565.25	2,685	98,523.21	11.09%	78,957.96	36.69	3,261.11	3.26	0.20	0.81	7.29	403.56%
Mailing 4	24,958	16,365.92	3,017	163,254.24	12.09%	146,888.32	54.11	5,885.42	5.89	0.10	0.66	5.42	897.53%
Mailing 5	25,321	18,525.47	4,521	132,568.25	17.85%	114,042.78	29.32	4,503.88	4.50	0.14	0.73	4.10	615.60%
Mailing 6	26,012	21,525.31	3,956	121,525.38	15.21%	100,000.07	30.72	3,844.38	3.84	0.18	0.83	5.44	464.57%
Mailing 7	35,658	28,526.40	8,545	321,254.28	23.96%	292,727.88	37.60	8,209.32	8.21	0.09	0.80	3.34	1026.16%
Totals	178,907	$ 139,589.82	27,916	$ 1,077,671.55		$ 938,081.73							
Averages	25,558	$ 19,941.40	3,988	$ 153,953.08	14.90%	$ 134,011.68	$ 40.70	$ 5,062.73	$ 5.06	$ 0.14	$ 0.78	$ 5.66	654%

ACQUISITION MAILINGS

Enter these numbers to automatically calculate results

	Pieces Mailed	Costs	Number of Gifts	Gross Income	Response Rate	Net Income	Average Gift	Net Income Per 1,000	Net Income Per Piece	Cost to Raise $1	Cost Per Piece	Cost Per Gift	ROI	Cost to Raise Donor
Mailing 1	100,000	99,562.35	999	30,232.65	1.00%	(69,329.70)	30.26	(693.30)	-0.69	3.29	1.00	99.66	-69.63%	69.40
Mailing 2	100,000	101,323.29	754	31,254.67	0.75%	(70,068.62)	41.45	(700.69)	-0.70	3.24	1.01	134.38	-69.15%	92.93
Mailing 3	100,000	97,326.25	1,125	39,653.51	1.13%	(57,672.74)	35.25	(576.73)	-0.58	2.45	0.97	86.51	-59.26%	51.26
Mailing 4	100,000	68,523.21	685	32,652.64	0.69%	(35,870.57)	47.67	(358.71)	-0.36	2.10	0.69	100.03	-52.35%	52.37
Totals	400,000	$ 366,735.10	3,563	$ 133,793.47		$ (232,941.63)								
Averages	100,000	$ 91,683.78	891	$ 33,448.37	0.89%	$ (58,235.41)	$ 38.66	$ (582.35)	$ (0.58)	$ 2.77	$ 0.92	$ 105.15	-62.60%	$ 66.49

This is by way of example. We're looking at renewal mailings. If you just look at mailing number one, you'll see that the fifth column over says it had a response rate of 10.95 percent. And if you look down that column, you'll see the other mailings tht you did during the year. They were 13 percent, 11 percent, 12 percent and so on.

At the beginning of the year you had a 10 percent response rate, and at the end of the year, mailing number seven, which is likely at Christmas, you had a 23 percent response rate. So that's double mailing number one.

And if you take your finger and move it across those lines, you'll see that for mailing number one, your average gift was $58. But for mailing number seven, your average gift was only $37. So you had a higher response rate at the end of the year, but you had a lower average gift. More people participated, but they didn't participate at the same level.

But if you look at your net income per piece, your first mailing it was $5.44, and at the end of the year it was $8.21. And you also notice if you look at the very left hand side, for the mailing at the beginning of the year, you mailed 19,000 pieces. But at the end of the year, you mailed 35,000. That's usually the case with an end-of-year appeal. That usually goes to everybody and his cousin.

This just shows that you can make a great deal of sense of your program, and this helps you plan for the coming year. That mailing calendar that you looked at earlier, that had the renewal letters, the acquisition letters, the newsletters, and so on, and when you can mail them, when combined with this spreadsheet, which shows your results, helps you see which of your mailings are most profitable. You can compare these numbers here with last year, the year before, the year before, and you'll see trends.

You may see that the last mailing of the year, number seven, is always your best, and you may discover that mailing number four, which drops in August, always tanks. And so if you can prove that over a couple of years, you can either reduce the number of pieces that you mail in August, or reduce the cost, or you can just segment it so you only mail it to your most valuable, most promising, most loyal donors and don't mail it to as many people, if you get the idea. The secret to success in direct mail fundraising is to know your numbers.

21

Response Rates to Expect in Direct Mail Fundraising

What kind of response rates do your direct mail fundraising letters generate? That's the most common question I'm asked by potential clients. And it's a good question, since non-profit organizations need the highest response rates they can get in today's competitive environment. Direct mail is an expensive way to raise funds if your response rates are low and your average gift is small.

So what's an acceptable response rate? That depends on the kind of mailing we're talking about.

Acquisition mailings (designed to acquire new donors) typically generate low response rates. An acceptable response rate with an acquisition mailing is somewhere between 0.5 percent and 2.5 percent. A response rate of only half of one percent might not sound adequate to you, but it's acceptable if your costs are low or your average gift is high.

Remember that generating a high response rate in an acquisition mailing is more important than receiving a high average gift, since the whole point of an acquisition mailing is to acquire donors. The higher your response rate, the more donors you acquire. And the more donors you acquire, the more donors you can appeal to in coming months, leading to higher revenue over time.

Renewal mailings (designed to obtain gifts from existing donors) typically generate higher response rates. An acceptable response rate with a renewal mailing is somewhere between 5 percent and 35 percent. Response rates for renewal mailings are higher than rates for acquisition mailings because the recipients already know you, trust you and have given to you before.

Remember that your response rate does not tell you enough. It only tells you the percentage of people who responded to your mailing. Your response rate, even if it's remarkably high, can't tell you if you made money, lost money or broke even. It can't tell you how much you spent to raise a dollar (or pound or yen). It can't tell you how much you spent per donation. Or your return on investment.

Part 6
Planning
Your
Year

22

Ask Early, Ask Often, Ask the Right Way

I once got a question from an annual giving officer. She said, "I have an executive director, and this executive director says that we should take the names of all people who give us a donation during the year, who give us a donation by direct mail and we should remove them from our mailing list so that we don't pester them during the year for another gift." She asked, "What should I tell my executive director when he tells me to do this?"

I felt sorry for her. That's a predicament to be in. I'm not sure what I would tell her executive director, except to present the facts. I would recommend that she read *Revolution in the Mailbox* by Mal Warwick. She's welcome to read some stuff on my website too, but Mal Warwick is the expert. And Mal Warwick says that the key to getting money from willing donors is to ask them to give and ask early and ask often. Don't wait too long.

The executive director that this lady has over her is misguided because he thinks that the more we ask, the more we annoy our donors. Now, that would be true if you phoned them during supper every week for two months, but it's not true if you send them four or five or six direct mail solicitations over a year. People forget that they got your last appeal, and even if they gave a donation to it, many donors would be hard pressed to tell you, if you phoned them and asked them, "Do you remember getting our appeal two months ago? You responded to it." Many donors would not remember.

So you're not pestering them by asking them for a gift more than once. The key to success in direct mail fundraising is to ask early and to ask often, in the right way. And you need to ask often enough that you stay on the radar of your donors and they don't forget you and simply fall away.

I suspect that you would lose more donors by neglecting them than you would be over-soliciting them. In other words, I think you'll do more harm to your direct mail fundraising program by reducing the amount of mail you mail to your donors than by increasing it. Mal Warwick says there are few non-profits in North America that mail too many appeals every year. Most non-profits, he says, under-solicit as far as direct mail is concerned.

Let's just do a little bit of a review. It's important for us to remind ourselves about how a direct mail fundraising program works, and then we're going to look at what you mail to your donors during the year and when you mail it and why you mail it. You need to be able to look at least a couple of months down the road and know what you're going to mail and to whom and why.

It's a planned program, not a series of mailings

Direct mail fundraising is a program, it's not a series of mailings. It's not a direct mail fundraising campaign.

What you're running is a program, and it's a planned program. It's not a series of packages that you drop in the mail. As far as professional fundraisers are concerned, every letter that they drop in the mail is not a one-off campaign, but part of a year-long program. And it's usually one that starts on January 1 and it ends on December 31, even though their fiscal year might be different.

Raising money through the mail is complicated, it's expensive and it's time consuming. That's why professional direct mail fundraisers plan their mailings at least a couple of months in advance, often 12 months in advance. They might not know what they are going to write in six or eight or nine months, but they do know that they're going to put a letter in the mail on that date.

And they make sure that their direct mail integrates with the rest of their annual giving program. So the direct mail integrates with the website, integrates with the telephone, integrates with face to face, integrates with the special events that they have. The themes, the colors, the branding, it's all integrated.

You'll also remember some of the disadvantages of doing what I call *ad hoc* mailings, where you simply put something in the mail as quickly as you can, often at the last minute and where the direct mail program tends to get neglected. If you just do your mailings one off and don't plan them, you face a number of disadvantages.

One of them is that things get overlooked. You'll make a mistake in your postage or you'll make a mistake in your data and you'll end up addressing your letters to the wrong people. You'll make a mistake in what you put in the package or what you leave out. Things get overlooked. You'll have typos, grammatical mistakes in your letters, and those can be avoided if you take more time and plan.

Another disadvantage of doing things on the fly and not planning them is that you miss your deadlines. You'll miss your deadlines because you need to be planning at least two months ahead before you drop anything in the mail. You need quite a bit of lead time, especially if you're hiring writers, hiring designers and outsourcing all your letter shop and printing.

You need two or three months before a donor ever receives anything. And you don't want to miss your deadlines. If you miss your deadlines, then you push everything back for the whole year. If you miss your deadline for an appeal, then the next newsletter will probably be delayed and then the next appeal will be delayed and you may end up mailing your Christmas appeal letter on the 18th of December. I've seen it happen.

Another disadvantage of not planning and not having a program is that your mailings are often rushed and put together at the last minute. If you don't put anything on your calendar, if you don't block off weeks at a time to know when you're going to mail and what you're going to mail and to whom you're going to mail, you'll be caught by surprise and you'll kind of rush stuff at the last minute.

Another disadvantage of not having a program is that if you don't have a program, you're likely not mailing enough pieces during the year and you'll get to the end of your fiscal year or your calendar year and be in a deficit. And your executive director or your board chair might be leaning on you to raise money through the mail, and so your appeals will end up sounding shrill. They may have lots of exclamation marks in them and lots of underlining and bold, and they may talk about nothing but your dire straights, your predicament and not about the case for support because you're in this terrible situation.

These kinds of appeals tend to stress a need for immediate funds, rather than long-term donor support to fund the program that your non-profit is involved in. And they do that because there's a shortfall in funds that was produced by a lack of planning. Remember, direct mail fundraising is a program, not a series of mailings. So you need to have a calendar and a calculator at hand when you sit down to do your planning.

It runs for 12 months

Direct mail fundraising works because it's a program that runs for 12 months. You've got the whole year planned out, 12 months.

And one of the greatest obstacles that you face running a direct mail fundraising program is the idea that the annual fund means you get one gift annually from your donors. The annual fund is called the annual fund because it runs annually, for 12 months. It's not called the annual fund because you're supposed to solicit gifts only once annually.

In direct mail fundraising, the most important gift that you get is not the first gift. Someone who gives you one gift is not even a donor, really. They're a pre-donor. They're someone who's come out to one ballgame and they're not a fan yet.

The most important gift is the second one. That shows that they've actually got some commitment to your organization. The majority of people who respond to a direct mail appeal give once and never again, so your goal is to convert these one time donors into repeat donors. And I don't believe you can do that by only asking them to give once a year. You can't do that if you wait 12 months before you ask them for another gift, the way that executive director was recommending.

If you send just one direct mail appeal a year, you don't really have an annual fund. You have an expense fund, because the people that you're mailing to are not likely to respond if they only hear from you once a year. All you're going to do is lose money. I know a fundraiser in the United States who does a lot of fundraising for hospitals, and he says this is his greatest challenge with management, persuading them to abandon what he calls the annual fund mentality, where they think annual means one gift a year or one solicitation a year. If you only ask for one gift a year, you'll likely see your donors fall away at attrition rates of 60 percent or higher.

You need to mail to your donors more than once a year for a number of vital reasons. If I asked you to go back six months and tell me who you gave to, you probably wouldn't remember. And if I named a charity that you gave to six or eight months ago, you might not even remember giving them a gift.

At tax time, when my wife and I look at our charitable receipts and the organizations to which we gave, sometimes we're surprised at how little we gave to some charities. We thought we gave more. And other times we're surprised at how much we gave some charities when we thought we gave a lot less. If you want to stay in people's memory over the year, you need to stay in their mailbox. And so your program needs to run for 12 months, not just one mailing a year.

Another reason that you have a direct mail program that runs for 12 months is that friends stay in touch. Your goal in direct mail fundraising is to raise money, yes, it is to raise a dollar, but mainly it's to retain a donor. It's to keep the friends you have. Not just get money from them, but keep them on board, enthusiastic, inspired, informed and gladly and willingly giving you their gifts.

And if you have friends, you stay in touch with them. You write them, you phone them, you visit them, you get together for a *grande latte*. And the people you spend the most time with are generally the people that you like and have good friendships with. And the people that you see very seldom are the people that you don't have as strong a relationship with.

Friends stay in touch. If you had a really, really good friend, she would be upset if you only talked to her once a year or wrote her a letter once or twice a year. Friends stay in touch.

The other reason that you need to mail more than once and that you need to have a 12 month program is that donors give for all sorts of different reasons. Some people give because of altruism, some people give because of compassion. Others give out of sense of guilt, but all of them give because someone asked them for a gift.

And this is a point that Mal Warwick mentions in his book, *Revolution in the Mailbox*. The majority of people that give in response to a direct mail appeal are giving out of discretionary funds. Most people don't set aside an envelope every month with a certain amount of money in it that's for charitable giving and then wait for somebody to ask them for it. The majority of people that respond to a direct mail appeal respond to it because it came in the mailbox and they had money to spare at the time.

I was reading the results of a focus group recently that was conducted by a hospital in Manitoba, here in Canada. And the moderator of the focus group asked the donors that were sitting around the table, "What makes you respond to a direct mail appeal?" And quite a few of the people at the table said, "Well, they asked," or, "It came in the mail first." So if the donor had discretionary money in the bank account, out of that account went the donation. And so you can't afford to mail just once a year because you might catch your donor at a wrong time, when they don't have the discretionary funds, and then you've lost your opportunity for another 12 months.

Here are three characteristics of a direct mail fundraising program.

1. Donors are solicited many times during the year, not just once.

2. It relies heavily on past donors to repeat their gifts. This is worth emphasizing. So you need to ask many times and you need to rely on people that are your friends and not always be looking for new gifts. Donor retention is very important.

3. New donors are identified and acquired each year. In other words, you identify and you acquire new donors each year. You need to be always acquiring in order to replace the donors that are falling away if you're going to have a healthy direct mail fundraising program.

23
What Should You Mail?

One of the questions I'm asked all the time is this: "What should I mail? What should I send to my donors?" Here are my answers. I've arranged them not in order of priority, but in the order that you would mail them chronologically. On the following page is a sample direct fundraising calendar with the following kinds of mailings on it:

Acquisition letters

Obviously, to start with, if you're a brand new organization, you would mail acquisition letters. You mail acquisition letters designed to acquire new donors and find new friends.

If your organization is typical, you lose around 15 percent of your donors every year. They stop giving, they stop responding to your direct mail appeals for all sorts of reasons. Sometimes it might be your fault, in that you've upset them or you've neglected them or you haven't thanked them, but often it's the case that the person has lost their job or the family has moved and they haven't given you their new address or they've retired or they've died.

Either way, there are lots of reasons that donors stop giving, and it's around 15 percent a year. This is the main reason that you need to create and manage a well planned annual donor acquisition program that is on a calendar somewhere.

You can't afford to simply mail your existing donors only. You need to replace the donors who never renew, the ones that fall away. Without a steady influx of new donors, you're going to be moving backwards every year and not forwards.

Now, you'll see on the left hand side of the direct mail fundraising calendar, there's a column, and it says Acquisition. You'll see that this organization would mail one acquisition mailing in March. They would call that Acquisition One. And they would mail another one in October. They would call that Acquisition Two.

If you're just starting out, you would likely mail more than

A Simple Direct Mail Fundraising Calendar

	Acquisition	Newsletter	Renewal	Major Donor	Lapsed donor	Special Appeal
January			#1	Annual report		
February		#1				
March	#1		#2	Annual meeting invitation	#1	
April		#2		Appeal #1		
May			#3			
June						
July			#4		#2	
August		#3				
September			#5	Progress report		
October	#2	#4				
November			Year-end appeal	Appeal #2	#3	
December				Banquet invitation		

two acquisition mailings a year. You might mail four. You'd spread them out throughout the year. I would suggest that you should mail at least one mailing a year, no less than one, because you have to replace the donors who fall away. And if you mail two, you'll likely acquire more donors than if you just mailed one.

So this is just a sample that you're looking at here. I'm not saying you have to mail two acquisition mailings a year. You could mail more or you could mail just one, but you need to mail something.

And you don't have to mail one in March and you don't have to mail the other one in October. We'll look a little bit later at exactly when you mail. This is just for illustrative purposes, to show that it is important that somewhere on your calendar you block out a place where you mail an acquisition mailing. And you do it at least once and you do it every year.

What else should you mail? Chronologically speaking, you should mail thank-you letters, thanking your first-time donors for their gifts. These thank-you letters are not included on this chart. A thank-you letter is almost a given. Someone gives you a gift, you need to thank them.

Newsletters

But what else should you mail? Well, you should mail newsletters. I had a phone call just yesterday from a prospective client in the United States, and he wanted me to help him get some lists because he was going to do an acquisition mailing for his client. He's a fundraising consultant.

And all he wanted me to do was help him get the names of some lists so that he could mail one acquisition letter. And I asked him, "Are you willing to lose money on acquisition?" and he said no. I said, "Well, most non-profits don't make a profit on acquisition mailings. They usually lose money. They spend $1.10, $1.15, $1.25, even more to raise a dollar, but they get a donor." And he said, "Well, we're not willing to do that."

So he didn't understand direct mail fundraising. And I then asked him, "What are your plans once you get these donors? If you do a mailing and you acquire a few donors, what are you planning to do with them?" He said, "We're going to mail them once, maybe twice again within the next 12 months."

And I was probably a little blunt with him. My name is Sharpe, but I'm actually blunt sometimes. I said, "You're going to lose money." If you do a direct mail acquisition mailing, you will likely lose money on your mailing if all you do is mail those people twice over the next 12 months, and if all you do is mail two mailings that ask them for more money and you don't send them any newsletters or any updates or any bulletins or anything informational. If all you do is appeal to them to give you more money, they will fall away at a rapid rate.

It's absolutely vital in your direct mail fundraising program that you block off the months when you're going to mail informational pieces to your donors. I'm not talking about your annual report. I'm talking about a newsletter or a newsy letter or something that you mail them that has photographs and text, that inspires your donors to give again. It informs them, it involves them and it inspires them. It informs them particularly about what their donations are accomplishing.

A newsletter is a stewardship vehicle that you use to show your donors that you're being a good steward of the money they've given you. You're saying, "Look, this is what we are doing with the money you gave us," or, "This is what your money is doing today. Helping children, feeding the poor, slowing down climate change," whatever it is that your organization does. You need to mail a newsletter.

And I suggest, and you'll see this on the sample calendar, you mail at least four issues of your newsletter a year. You can mail one in each quarter. So you mail them every three months. Try to avoid the summer when many people are away, and try to avoid having your newsletter land in their mailbox right around Christmas. It should be your appeal that arrives then, not your newsletter.

Let me just cover a couple of tips for what your newsletter needs to accomplish. It should focus on the donor. You don't want to have lots of photos and stories about your board of directors and other things that are of no interest to your donors. It needs to be a donor-centered newsletter.

You need to have original, compelling, interesting photographs. Your donors need to be able to pick up your newsletter and say, "I'm going to read this because it's always interesting and the photographs catch my eye."

You'll notice this if you look at the cover of Time magazine or Newsweek. Just go to the news stand—actually, this is true of just about the cover of every magazine in the news stands now. If you go to Chapters, just look down the magazine racks. They always have provocative photographs on the cover that get your attention.

You need to have good photographs, human interest photographs, with people in them, that inspire your donors to pick up your newsletter and read it. You need to put captions under your photographs. A photograph is never worth a thousand words. You have to explain it a little bit.

You need to have opportunities for your donors to be involved. Here you see the value of mailing more than one newsletter a year, more than two. You need to mail at least four so that throughout the year you give your donors meaningful, intelligent ways to take part and get involved in your work.

You could have a quiz, you could include a petition that they sign. You could run a poll where you ask them for their opinion. A little survey. You can have an order form in the newsletter that they fill in and ask you to mail them something. You could feature a crossword puzzle.

You need to mail your donors at least four times a year with your newsletter because they are being bombarded with appeals from other organizations. Most donors in North America support more than 10 charities a year, and so your mail will arrive with other mail. And your donors will forget you if you don't mail them more than four times a year. And they will think that you really are pestering them if all you do is ask for money, ask for money, ask for money, ask for money.

So mail a newsletter at least four times a year. It can be simple. It can be an 11 x 17 sheet of paper folded twice, and it can be printed in black and white. And remember, your newsletter needs to be large enough that it informs and inspires. It can't have too little content. But it needs to be short enough that your donors will read it and not be intimidated by something that's too thick.

You have busy donors. You don't want your newsletter to look daunting. But you don't want it to look like it's inconsequential or insubstantial either. So it needs to be large enough to inform them and inspire them.

It should be cost effective. It should not be an expensive

newsletter. You can't afford to acquire a new donor and solicit gifts from them every year if your newsletter is so expensive to mail that you use your donor's entire gift on postage and four color printing. So you don't want your donor thinking you're not a good steward of their money, or that all their money is going towards this glossy four-color fancy newsletter that arrives in a poly bag every couple of months. And you don't want your newsletter to be so fancy that they think, "Oh, they don't need my gift. They're obviously well off enough without it."

You need to have plenty of language in the newsletter that says "you are making a difference as a donor." I call this make-a-difference language. You need to show in photographs and captions and stories and quotes from your field staff and from your clients that the donors' gifts are making a difference and that donors are meeting the donors' goals through you, and that you're grateful for the donors' support.

And you need to emphasize people and not programs in your newsletter. Show that the gift is helping people, rather than paying salary, overhead and helping programs. Programs are impersonal. People are personal.

So you need to mail acquisition letters and you need to mail newsletters. The acquisition letter acquires the donor, the newsletter informs and involves and inspires the donor. And then you mail renewal letters during the year that keep the friends you have. They persuade the donor to renew his support.

Renewal letters

Remember that 65 percent of donors acquired by direct mail give one gift and never give again. The conversion rate in most organizations is only 35 percent.

What's vital over the long term for the success of your direct mail fundraising program isn't the first mailing that you mail that acquires the donor, although that's obviously vital. Your acquisition mailings are absolutely vital. But what's important, what should be important to your executive director and your chief financial officer, is not the number of donors that you acquire every year. That number might be really high, but that's not as important as the number of donors that you acquire every year who give again and again and again.

A healthy annual direct mail fundraising program mails a

series of renewal letters that are designed to renew the support of donors and members year after year after year. The reason that you mail more than one renewal letter is that donors acquired through direct mail usually generate net income (in other words, they pay for the cost of their own acquisition) only after they've made a second donation.

James Greenfield, in his books, and Kent Dove as well, have pointed out that re-soliciting an existing donor—in other words, going back to somebody who has already given you a gift—is likely to perform five to eight times more profitably than going out into the world and acquiring that same number of donors who are equally as generous.

The other reason that you need to be mailing your donors regularly is that you need to be stewarding them and cultivating them and developing the relationship so that they gradually move up your donor pyramid. They go from being a direct mail donor to becoming a monthly donor to becoming a major donor to making a planned gift or even leaving you a bequest in their will.

Now, if you're a non-profit organization that has members, if you're like Amnesty International or Greenpeace and people actually carry a membership card in their wallet or purse, then this makes absolute sense to you that you would mail a renewal letter every year, because you would mail a letter that says "Your membership is about to expire. Renew now." And you would know that not everybody responds to the first renewal notice, and so you'd mail a second one.

Well, not all direct mail fundraising programs have members, but it helps you in your renewal series to think of them as though you're renewing members or as though you're renewing a magazine subscriber. If you pretend that your donors are magazine subscribers and that their subscription is going to run out, you need to think of the letters (plural) that you're going to mail to renew them over the year, rather than just one letter (singular). Not everybody will renew and give you a second gift after the first letter. So you need to have a series of them.

In the sample calendar illustration, you'll see that under the renewal column, which is the third one in, there's one renewal sent in January, another one sent two months later, and then another one sent two months later, and they basically come every two months. The last one mails in November. It's mailed in November and it arrives maybe the end of November, maybe the first week of December. So there are five in that renewal series.

You need to expect to ask several times in order to get a renewed gift from your donors. Even a renewal mailing that only breaks even can perform better than an acquisition mailing. And it will only work better if you mail more than once.

And remember what Mal Warwick says: you need to mail early and you need to mail often. So when he says early, he means from the time you get the first gift from somebody to the time they get a second appeal letter from you should not be too long. It should be sooner rather than later.

Don't be afraid of annoying your donors with too many solicitations. Tests have shown for decades that the longer you wait to renew a donor, the lower your renewal rate will be and the lower your average gift. You'll fall off their interest level.

You need to mail a series of renewal letters. I recommend that you mail at least four letters a year. If you're mailing four newsletters, then you should mail four appeal letters.

So your donors get an appeal letter that asks them for a gift, and they get a newsletter that informs them about how you're using that gift. And they get a thank-you letter. Then they get another appeal, then they get a newsletter. They should not get appeals one after the other, and they should not get newsletters one after the other.

Mail a series of renewal letters

You should mail a series of renewal letters. And the key to this is to mail your first in the series to everybody, asking everybody to renew their support. That would be the first mailing you see on the calendar, the one in January.

You mail everybody in January and you ask them to renew their support. And you can even use that language, "Renew your support." Then you mail a second letter during the year. You might mail it in March, and you'd mail that to everybody who did not respond to the first letter. So it would be to a smaller list.

Then you mail a third letter in that renewal series. Remember, you're pretending that your donors are members or you're pretending that they are magazine subscribers and they haven't renewed because of the first letter and they haven't renewed because of the second one, and so you send them a third letter during the year.

Your first letter would have said "Please renew your support." Your second letter would have said "This is a friendly reminder that we have not heard from you."

And your third letter might be just a little stronger, and it might say, "We miss you, we haven't heard from you. Please renew your support immediately. We need to hear from you. We need to carry on the good work that we do."

And obviously, as you work your way down mailing after mailing during the year, you'll be mailing to fewer and fewer people. You'll only be mailing to the people that have not yet renewed their support. With the exception of your year-end appeal. Your year-end appeal you mail to everybody again. You wouldn't want to leave anybody out. You should ask everybody for a year-end gift.

Now, if you get to the end of your year and you have people that have not responded to any of those renewal mailings, then you should take them out of your renewal series and flag them as lapsed donors. A lapsed donor for you might be 12 months lapsed, 18, 24 months, whatever it is, and you need to flag them as lapsed and just take them out of this regular renewal series and treat them as special people. And you'll see how we do this in a second.

Major donor letters

You should also be mailing your major donors during the year. It just depends how sophisticated your non-profit fundraising program is. If you're reasonably mature as an organization, you have an extensive database and you can mine it and discover that there's gold in your mine. You can can mail a certain segment of your database every year, the major donors, maybe once, twice, three times, and you can treat them in a special way and you can ask them for special gifts that are larger than normal.

And you can also invite them to special events and mail them things that you wouldn't mail to everybody. One example would be that you could mail your major donors an annual report at the beginning of the year. You could invite them to your annual meeting. You could send them a progress report on a particular project that they funded. You get the idea.

You can invite them to your banquet at the end of the year. If you have major donors or potential major donors in your file, you should be mailing them a series of mailings during the year and you should plan your year and decide what it is you're going to mail them so that you're not caught off guard and having to mail these people suddenly.

You can ask them for more money than you ask most of your donors, and you can ask for designated gifts. And you can also steward those donors with particular progress reports that your other donors don't get. Most donors do not get your annual report, but your major donors should, and your potential major donors, your prospective major donors, should get it, too.

Lapsed donor recovery letters

Another type of mailing that you should mail during the year is a lapsed donor recovery mailing, sometimes called a reactivation mailing. I have a column set aside for this in the sample mailing calendar. This does not have to be a separate, distinct letter.

If you look over on the third column, the renewal letters, there are six of them during the year. One or two or three of those renewal letters could also be tweaked a little bit so that they become lapsed donor reactivation letters. The difference between a renewal letter and a lapsed donor recovery letter is that a renewal letter would say, "Alan, thank you for your gift last year. Please renew your support." Whereas a lapsed donor recovery letter would say, "Alan, thank you for your gift, which we received in 2005. We have not heard from you for three years. Please renew your support. It's absolutely vital to our work. We can use it today to do so and so and such and such."

A lapsed donor recovery letter might be exactly the same as your renewal letter, but it acknowledges the delay or the lapse. You have not heard from the donor for many years or many months, so you acknowledge that you have not heard from them and you tell them that you miss them. And you generally, in a lapsed donor recovery letter, stress how vital the person's support is. You have to work a little harder to re-sell the donor on your case for support, why they should give.

You may think this looks funny blocked off on your calendar like this, that you would have a series of mailings that you mail to people who have obviously fallen off the radar and have not given you a gift. But there are a couple of reasons that you should have lapsed donor recovery letters.

One of them is that you know for sure that these people support worthy causes, because they've supported you in the past.

You also know that these lapsed donors respond to direct mail appeals because they've responded to yours in the past. So they're not an unknown commodity.

You know that they know your organization, they know your mission and they know a little about your organization because they've supported you in the past. So you don't have as much selling to do or telling to do as you would do if you were mailing an acquisition letter to a stranger.

So they have some degree of interest in your cause. They gave before. You obviously won their hearts and minds to some degree in the past. And now you need to do that again.

Another interesting thing about lapsed donors is that they tend to give a higher average gift than a stranger does. And they tend to respond in larger numbers than strangers do. If you mailed 100 letters to complete strangers, you might get a one percent response rate. In other words, you'd get one donor. But if you mail 100 letters to lapsed donors, you may get a five percent response rate, and a larger average gift. So those are just a couple of the reasons that you should mail to your lapsed donors. You literally can't afford to just leave them in your file.

Repeated mailings to reactivate your lapsed donors will pay off if you do them properly. One thing you can do is to continue mailing to your lapsed donors until their average gift and their response rate and their cost to raise a dollar falls below what you would be spending if you were mailing acquisition letters. You don't want your cost of reactivation to be more than your cost of acquisition, if at all possible.

If you have long-lapsed donors, you should mail them at least one letter a year. When you keep in touch, you keep their address current, and they hear from you. You will likely find that one mailing like that will perform better than an acquisition mailing.

I also recommend that you make lapsed donor reactivation a higher priority than acquiring brand new donors for all the reasons that I've just given. These people know you, they've supported you, they understand your mission, and they've been fans of yours in the past. It's much easier to win them back than it is to win brand new people. So you should make it a high priority during your year to recover your lapsed donors. Keep track of them and recover them.

Special appeals

Some time during the year you can also mail a special appeal. I'm not going to arbitrarily tell you that in June of this year you should have an emergency, or that in October there will be a hurricane and you should send out an appeal letter in October. You can't block off in your calendar some of the events that you're going to mail for during the year.

But you can send special appeal letters for particular projects. Special appeals are particularly effective for raising money for a particular thing or a particular cause or a particular program. You can block those off during the year. You can decide that you're going to mail one in April and you're going to mail one in October, for example.

Special appeals are almost always used for emergencies, like floods and hurricanes and tsunamis. They're also used in political fundraising, where an organization like Hillary Clinton's campaign might suddenly run out of money and she has to put $5 million of her own money into the kitty. You can be pretty sure that the Hillary Clinton campaign has mailed an emergency appeal to raise money for her bid.

So you don't have to wait for an emergency to send a special appeal. You may have a special occasion coming up this year, too. You may be commemorating your anniversary. Doctors Without Borders one year won the Nobel Peace Prize, and so that became a special appeal.

You can mail a special appeal for a particular project where you designate the funds. You can have a special appeal for an urgent issue. It might be a natural disaster or a political issue, or it might be a petition, some lobbying or advocacy that you need to do during the year, or it might be a special event that you know for sure is coming up because of some kind of commemoration that you're doing.

24

How to Plan a Typical Mailing

You may be asking yourself, "If I'm going to mail acquisition letters, newsletters, renewal letters, major gift letters, lapsed donor letters and special appeals, and if I'm going to mail something in January and February and March, if I'm putting something in the mail just about every month except for maybe the summer, when do I need to start planning?"

Working backwards from your drop date

Based on my experience of working with graphic designers and letter shops and printers, I suggest that you give yourself enough time to meet your deadline by deciding what your deadline is and then working backwards from there.

In the direct mail fundraising business, we call it the drop date. It's the date that your letter drops into the mail stream, as it's called. The day that the postal service starts processing your letter, that's your drop date. You need to put that date on your calendar and work backwards from there.

The drop date is day zero, or D Day. And one day before the drop date, the letter shop would deliver all of your letters to the post office. They'd be sealed, they'd be stamped, they would all be ready to go. They'd be sorted, they'd be bundled with rubber bands around them and they'd be delivered to the post office. That would happen one day before your drop date.

Fourteen days before then, depending on the size of your mailing (if you have a small mailing, this might only be seven days before), you're going to give the components of your package—your letter, your envelope, your reply device, everything that's going to go into the package—to the letter shop. They are usually all separate pieces. You'll deliver a box of outer envelopes, a box of letterhead, a box of reply devices and a box of reply envelopes to the letter shop two weeks before the drop date, and they will take the letterhead, laser the text onto it, fold it, insert it into the outer envelope, laser the reply device, insert that into the outer envelope along with the reply envelope, seal the envelope and apply postage.

Task	Days before you mail
You dream up a compelling package theme	60
You write and design the package components	52
You get approvals from management	38
You run a query and export your list segments	32
You deliver artwork to printer	30
Printer prints pieces, delivers to lettershop	28
Lettershop folds, inserts, seals, applies postage	14
Lettershop delivers packages to post office	1

Give yourself enough time to create, write, approve, design, print and mail your pieces. The key is to start with your drop date and work backwards. For acquisition mailings, you must give yourself even more time, to source and secure lists, conduct a merge/purge, and to test.

Around two weeks before that date, you would give your final artwork to the printer and your printer would be printing. So at least a month before your drop date, you should be getting your artwork to the printer so your printer can print your letterhead, and print the static parts of your letter that are not going to be lasered at the lettershop, print your envelopes, print everything that's going to go into the package. Most printers like two weeks, and depending on the size of your mailing, most letter shops like at least a week or two, especially if there are going to be some holidays in there where they're going to take days off.

So, as you're working your way up the list, a month and two days before the drop date, you're going to run a query on your database. You're going to choose all the people that you're going to mail to. You might run some segmentation queries so that you have a segment that is existing donors, another segment that is new donors, another segment that is lapsed donors and so on.

You would save those as different files and send them to the letter shop. The letter shop would make sure that your addresses are correct. They would compare them against the national change of address register, and update any records that have moved and given a forwarding address, and so on.

And a couple of days before you did that, you would likely be getting the final approvals from your management, your board of directors, your chair, the executive director, any clients or volunteers that you've used in your fundraising letter if you've quoted anybody. You'd be getting all your final signoffs on those things. And two weeks or three weeks before you got the final signoffs, you would have started the whole process.

So in my case, I'm saying two months before you drop anything in the mail, you would sit down and decide, "We're going to write a letter. It's going to be two pages, and it's going to discuss such-and-such a topic and feature such-and-such a case for support. The theme we are using for the package is going to be such-and-such."

And then you would spend a couple of weeks writing, and a week or two designing. You need at least a week for reviews, where you pass the letter around and everything is done by committee these days. Everybody signs off on it and gives their blessing. And then you give it to the printer and the printer gives it to the letter shop and the letter shop gives it to the post office. You need to give yourself at least 60 days, depending on the size of your mailing and how complicated it is.

This is a renewal mailing that we're talking about. If you're talking about an acquisition mailing, you need to add a couple of weeks to this timetable, because you're going to have to talk to your list broker and find a couple of lists.

And then you're going to have to mail a couple of test packages or a test package to those lists, wait for the results, and then when you get your results, then you're going to roll out. And so you're going to need at least a couple of months, maybe three months on top of this. So you may need more like six months of lead time, from the time that you get the idea to the time you actually drop something in the mail to the full list.

When you look at this calendar, you'll see that there's a renewal mailing going out in January. You need to be starting on that mailing in October. So in October of one year, you're already thinking of January in the next year. You don't want to get left behind.

Part 7
Keys
to
Your
Success

25

Divide and Conquer

Let's look at a couple of keys to success when it comes to direct mail fundraising and running a successful program. One of the keys to success is not how many pieces you mail during the year but who you mail them to. The most important determinant of your success in direct mail fundraising is your list.

Segmentation

There are many, many times when you should not mail the same letter to everybody in your database. You may have a time of year when everybody gets a letter. It might be your Christmas appeal, for example, and it might be your first renewal mailing of the year. Everybody gets a letter, but not everybody should get the same letter.

You have people in your file, for example, that have not given you a gift for a year or two, and if they did give you a gift, they might have given only $20. They should not get the same letter as a more recent donor who gives you a couple of gifts a year and each one of those gifts is $500. They should not get the same appeal. They may get a letter at the same time of the year, but they should not get the same letter, and that's what I mean by segmenting your database.

You need to look at all your donors in your database and carve them up into meaningful segments so that you treat each segment differently based on the relationship you have with them and based on their value to you as an organization.

One reason that you do this is that segmenting saves you money. When you divide your database into categories or segments such as new donors, major donors, one-time donors and monthly donors, this helps you reduce your production costs and your mailing costs because you only mail to the people that you want to reach with a certain message.

Some donors will get a longer letter than others. They'll get first class postage rather than non-profit postage. They'll get a real stamp rather than a postal indicia. By segmenting your database, you save money, and segmenting increases your revenue by mailing a slightly different letter to your donors, or only mailing some of your donors.

By dividing your database into segments, you make your mailings more specific, you make them more customized for each of your audiences, and when you personalize a message and customize a message, you increase your chances of getting gifts, because your letters are by definition more personal, more effective. They're less generic. They sound less like boiler plate.

Just imagine if you wrote a letter to your major donors, just as a way of example, and you asked for a gift of $5,000 or more. You would likely see a higher response rate and a higher average gift than you would if you mailed that same letter to everybody in your house file. So it pays to segment. You save money, you save revenue and you generate more net income.

So how do you segment exactly? Some organizations call these flags. There's a way that you can set up your database so you flag individual records. But somehow you need to go through your database and create a field in each of the records that allows you to flag that record and show that this donor is of a particular segment.

It could be that you flag the record based on their giving level. They might be above $10,000 a year, for example. Or you may flag the record based on what they give to. You can also flag or segment your list as donor versus non-donor.

You may segment your list according to how you acquired the donor. Did you get them by direct mail? Did you get them by a special event that they came to, or did they come on board from a telephone campaign? You can segment them that way; how they were acquired.

You can segment your list according to their giving frequency, or their giving preference. They might prefer to give by credit card, by check, by monthly giving program. That's not as valuable as some other ways of segmenting.

If they give monthly, you should treat them in a slightly different way than you would do if they give annually. For example, if you have donors that give every month out of their credit card or bank account, you would not send them a series of six renewal notices because they renew every month automatically. So you need to treat them differently and segment them accordingly.

You might have one-time givers. You might have lapsed donors. You may flag your records based on what stimulates a gift, generally speaking. You may have some donors that always respond to your year end appeal or that always respond to a request for a particular project. For example, let's say you do relief and development work in India. You may find some donors who always support work or an appeal letter that is for urban women or that is for orphans or AIDS/HIV patients, that type of thing.

And you can also flag your list based on the donor's affinity with your organization. They might be a board member, for example. You can segment your list and have all the board members get a particular tweaked letter. Or they might be employees, they might be volunteers, they might be long term donors or major donors. You can flag them that way too.

You get the idea. If you segment your database not just based on how much money people give you, but in other intelligent ways, you can write one letter and then just adjust it a little bit, segment it 2, 3, 12, 14, 24 ways. And your response rates will improve and your gift income will improve, because you'll be speaking to people individually, or more personally than sending the same letter to everybody. That's one of the keys to success in direct mail fundraising, is to segment your letters, segment your database.

Concentrate on your best donors

Another key to success in your program is to concentrate on your best donors. And this is one of the advantages of having a comprehensive donor database—you can spot these trends over time. Instead of keeping records using index cards or an Excel spreadsheet, if you have a comprehensive donor database—a database designed for processing gifts and managing donors and managing the relationships—you notice these trends over time. You notice how often people give. That's their recency, or how frequently they give, and you notice how much they give.

A supporter or member of your organization who responds to your direct mail appeals many times a year—in other words, frequently—is much more likely to respond to your next appeal than a donor who mails you a gift maybe just once a year. You've got some donors that are more important to your organization than others. For example, if you have donors that give very often, they're more valuable than donors who give less often. If you have donors that give you lots of money, they're of more value to your organization strategically than donors who give you very little money. So I recommend that you conduct an RFM analysis: the recency of gifts, the frequency of gifts, and the monetary value of gifts.

You can then start a cultivation process. You can start cultivating your donors so that at the right time and in the right way, you gradually move them up the giving pyramid. You're familiar with this, I'm sure. Most organizations have a broad base of support of people who either attend events or donate by direct mail. Maybe they give online and there are many, many of those donors who give to an organization. Then you have slightly fewer donors who are regular donors, repeat donors, monthly donors.

And then there are even fewer of them, and they tend to be donors who have given over time and been with you longer. They would be your major donors. And then you have people who take out a planned giving instrument, a charitable remainder trust or they leave you a bequest in their will. They are the people that are at the top of your pyramid, and they're the ones that give you more money than anybody else.

So at the bottom of the pyramid, you have people that give you gifts of $20, $30, $40, $50, $100 a year. And then further up you have people who give you maybe somewhere between that and $500 a year. Then you have major givers who give you tens of thousands, maybe even hundreds of thousands of dollars. And then at the very top, you have people who leave bequests in their will of large amounts.

The reason you concentrate on your best donors is so that you can, excuse the term, maximize their potential. In other words, get the most from them, but also they get the most from your organization. They want to give and you help them give to the organization and the causes that they care about. So you're not just milking them. You're working with them because they care about where their money goes, and you work with them as a partner.

By concentrating on your best donors, you can be far more purposeful when you look at that calendar that we looked at. You can be far more purposeful about who you write to and what you ask them for. And you're looking long term, months ahead.

26

Build Your List Three Ways

Your success as a direct mail fundraiser depends on the quality of your list. A mediocre letter mailed to the right list will outperform a terrific letter mailed to the wrong list. How you build that list is up to you. Here are three ways.

Method #1: Build Your List Yourself

Host a special event, offer a free newsletter, ask your members to recruit new members, put a sign-up form on your website. In other words, use every method you can to get the names and addresses of potential donors.

Advantages:

1. Every name you gain is yours to keep and use as many times as you want.
2. You control the quality of the names you acquire.
3. You build a highly targeted list of people who want to receive your fundraising letters and newsletters.

Disadvantages:

1. Time consuming
2. Labor intensive

Method #2: Rent A List From Someone Else

The mailing list you want to build might already exist. Simply call the owner of the list and ask if you can rent it. There are tens of thousands of lists available. If you want to reach Jewish donors, for example, you can mail to a list of Compassionate Jewish Contributors (192,377 names), Hi-Dollar Jewish Women Donors (109,527 names), Jewish Book Buyers (14,289 names) and Committed Jewish Educators (4,877 names).

You can also borrow names from another organization in exchange for them borrowing names from your list. This is called a list exchange.

Advantages:

1. You can reach tens of thousands, even hundreds of thousands, of potential donors immediately.
2. Someone else does all the work of collecting the names and addresses.

Disadvantages:

1. Renting names costs roughly $100 per 1,000 names.
2. You can only mail to these lists once. To mail them again, you must rent the names again.
3. Only the names who respond to your mailing are yours to keep.

Method #3: Use A List Broker To Create A Custom List

A list broker is a specialist who helps not-for-profit organizations rent lists from list owners (usually businesses or other not-for-profits). Their services include research, selection and recommendation of lists. Look in your local Yellow Pages under "Mailing Lists and Services." List brokers can create a custom list for you (usually by combining other lists), one based on your needs and campaign goals.

Advantages:

1. List brokers save you time and money because they know the lists that are available. They can recommend the lists that will likely work best for you.
2. You can reach tens of thousands, even hundreds of thousands, of potential donors immediately.
3. Someone else does all the work of collecting the names and addresses.

Disadvantages:

1. Renting names costs roughly $100 per 1,000 names.
2. You can only mail to these lists once. To mail them again, you must rent the names again.
3. Only the names who respond to your mailing are yours to keep.

27

How List Brokers Can Help Your Appeal

Last time I checked, there were 25,000 response lists and 50,000 compiled lists currently on the market. Among all of these lists, you'll find hundreds that work for fundraising appeals. Actually, you likely won't find them. Locating the best names for your mailing is complicated and best left to an experienced list broker. A list broker is a specialist who researches and recommends lists for you, and manages all the paperwork and other details of renting the list.

An experienced list broker:

- helps you find new lists
- identifies profitable segments on unlikely lists
- helps you create a matrix for testing your mailing against other lists
- negotiates the best prices for you with the list owner
- recommends other media (such as email) to consider testing
- makes sure the list gets to your lettershop on time
- helps you evaluate your response rates, gift income and other results
- manages invoicing for lists you rent

A typical list rental transaction

1. You phone a list broker that specializes in the non-profit sector
2. You describe your organization's mission, including what you do and who you help
3. You describe your ideal donor (such as "female, 55 years old, married, owns home, $150,000 household income, cares about animal welfare, lives in the United States and responds to direct mail fundraising appeals from animal rights organizations")
4. You email the list broker a PDF sample of the direct mail package that you are going to mail to the list, and the list broker

forwards it to the list owner

5. The list owner reviews and approves your package
6. You tell the list broker the following:
   a. the selects you want, if any*
   b. how many names you want to order
   c. when you will mail your piece
   d. when you need to receive the names
   e. where you want names sent (lettershop, usually)
7. The list broker prepares your list and sends it to your lettershop or service bureau
8. Your lettershop keys your reply device and other components so you can track the results of this mailing back to this list
9. You mail your package to the names on the list
10. You process each donation you receive, adding the names to your database (they are yours to keep), and flagging each new donor record to note the package and list used to acquire the donor

Mailing list brokers know the industry. The firms they work for have researched and tested thousands of lists. So working with a qualified mailing list broker is vital.

* A select is a process that the list broker conducts on your behalf to choose only some names from the entire list. You might ask the broker to select names from a particular zip code, for example, and only rent you those names.

28

How to Upgrade Your Donors Over Time

In direct mail fundraising, your goal is to move your donors up the giving ladder so they eventually give you larger gifts than the gifts they gave you at the beginning of their relationship.

You also should nurture them and cultivate them so that they join your monthly giving program, if you have one. Donors that give every month through an electronic funds transfer system (directly from their bank account or directly from their credit card automatically), are hard donors to get. Most monthly donors convert from being an annual donor to becoming a monthly donor. Few monthly donors start out that way from day one. So one of your goals, if you have a monthly giving program, is to upgrade your donors from annual, one-time gifts to monthly gifts.

A third way of upgrading your donors is to have them join a membership program, where they become members of your organization rather than simply donors or advocates. Becoming a member is an upgrade. You're getting them to increase their commitment to your organization by becoming a member and not simply a donor.

Another way that you can upgrade your donors is by having them join a giving club. Perhaps you have a President's Circle or a Founder's Circle. Or, if you're a hospital or a university or a museum or an orchestra, or a performing arts center, you likely have different levels of giving. You have a Platinum Club, a Gold Club, and so on. These are giving clubs, and when donors join a giving club like that they receive certain benefits that others do not receive. So one of your goals as an organization is to move your donors up the ladder from ordinary, everyday donors to people that join your giving club.

Another way to upgrade your donors is to have them give you major gifts, not just a larger gift than what they gave in the beginning, but a major gift. Your definition of a major gift may be anything over $1,000. Or it may be anything over $10,000. One of your goals as part of your direct mail fundraising program is to move your donors up the ladder so they begin to give major gifts. That will take time. That will take effort and planning.

Finally, another way to upgrade your donors is to have them leave you a bequest in their will. You don't get that kind of gift easily. People will only put you into their will or write a codicil that goes into their will if they really believe in and admire your organization. And trust you. And that takes time.

One of your goals as an organization that uses direct mail is to upgrade your donors over time so they go from being a donor to becoming an advocate to becoming a supporter to becoming a fan and eventually leaving you a bequest in their will. Or, if they don't do that, perhaps they will take out a planned giving instrument like a gift annuity—something along those lines.

29

Increase Your Average Fundraising Gift By Segmenting Your File

How many of your current donors would give you a larger gift if you only knew how to ask them? Quite a few, quite likely. The secret to upgrading your supporters to larger levels of giving is to discover what they want and then to give it to them. Here's one way to do it.

Let's say you launch a direct mail fundraising letter campaign to raise funds for people in India who have been displaced by an earthquake. After most of your donations are in, tally the results and flag everyone in your database who gave to this appeal.

Now the next time you mail an appeal letter, send a special letter asking these same donors to consider the following:

- giving another gift at the same level to help the same people in India
- giving another gift to help earthquake victims in Honduras
- giving to the victims in India and to the ones in Honduras
- joining your monthly giving program for India
- joining your monthly giving program for earthquake relief

You could include all of these options on the donor reply card (not recommended; there are too many), or you could simply choose one of these options and make that your only ask in the letter. Once your donations are in, you would do some analysis of the results. Your data from this second campaign would help you identify:

- donors who are interested in earthquake relief
- donors who are interested in India
- donors who support emergency appeals in general

What you are doing with this exercise is segmenting your

house mailing list into groups of donors who share interests. This knowledge is valuable to your organization because it helps you to customize your appeals to donors based on what they like to support.

Another advantage of segmenting your database is that it helps you increase revenues. Donors who are asked to support only those projects or initiatives that interest them are likely to give you a larger gift than donors who are asked to support your general fund.

You can slice and dice your database as many ways as you want. Using the above example, you could flag all donors who support your work in India, further segment this group into those who support your earthquake relief work in India, and further segment this group into donors who support your medical aid to victims of earthquakes in India.

As long as you have a robust donor tracking software system, competent staff, and time to do this kind of segmenting, you will be in a good position to increase the number and dollar amount of the donations you receive from donors in your house list.

30

Improve Donor Tenure and You'll Boost Revenue

How long do most of your donors contribute to your organization before they walk away? One year? Five? Ten? You should know.

Direct mail fundraising, like all effective fundraising, is about raising friends rather than raising funds. Raising a friend is always more important in the long term (the only term worth considering in fundraising) than raising a dollar. And losing a donor is always worse than losing a dollar.

Which means you must pay as much attention to your donor numbers as you do to your donation numbers. Response rate, average gift and cost-to-raise-a-dollar are donation numbers. They tell you how you are doing as far as funds are concerned. But donor attrition rate, renewal rate and average tenure are donor numbers. They tell you how well you are doing as far as your friendships are concerned.

Average donor tenure is a vital number to watch. Simply put, your average donor tenure is the length of time, measured in years or months, that your average donor gives to your organization before stopping. The for-profit world watches this number. You should, too.

Learn from the for-profit world

A lady at my church described to me her work as an insurance sales agent. She explained that most agents make a commission when they sell an insurance policy and make another commission when their customer renews that policy, usually a year later. "Clients, on average, buy a policy and renew it six times," she said, "which means one sale delivers seven years of residual income."

This lady knows her average tenure. Most of her customers stay with her firm for seven years and then go elsewhere. What about your not-for-profit organization? How long do most of your donors stay with you before going elsewhere? Find out today. And watch that number every year.

Naturally, you want to attract donors who stay with you for a lifetime. For many organizations, the lifetime value of a donor is about five years. That's not a very large number. But at least you can start improving it once you know what it is.

You are in trouble if your donor base is shrinking each year. You are also in danger if most of the donors you acquire give you one gift and never give again. But remember that average donor tenure is just one button on your calculator. You also need to watch how much your donors give each year. Some may stay with you for decades but contribute little. Others may stay with you for a few years but donate enough to build a new wing on your facility.

You'd be disappointed if you lost all the friends you made each year, or if they hung around but showed no sustained interest in you. So measure and watch your average donor tenure. Then take whatever remedial action you think is necessary to keep your friendships with your donors healthy—and lengthy.

31

Answers to Common Questions

Let me just answer a couple of commonly asked questions about direct mail fundraising programs. I've just picked the top three that people ask me all the time.

Q. How many times a year should I mail my donors? My board wants to save money. How many times should I write to donors without pestering them and bothering them?

A. I recommend you mail at least eight times a year. Mail at least four appeal letters and mail at least four newsletters (or donor cultivation, donor information type pieces). Your appeal letters ask for money and your newsletters simply inform and involve and inspire. Your donors should hear from you eight times a year.

Q. We've got all these people on our list that don't give us any money. When should we drop them from our mailing list?

A. Never drop anybody from your mailing list. When you're looking at an individual donor, someone who regularly repeats her gifts, think of her as an individual and treat her as an individual and talk to her as an individual. Don't treat her like a number. She'll just walk away.

But with lapsed donors, donors that you haven't heard from for awhile, don't treat them as individuals. Treat them as a list. If you had a list of 100 strangers that had never given you a gift and you mailed them an acquisition letter, you might get a one percent response rate. But if you took 100 people that used to give to you before and no longer do, and you mailed them an appeal letter, you'd likely get a better response rate than one percent.

So I advise that you don't go through your database line by line by line, looking at every single donor and asking yourself, "When did they last give us a gift? If it hasn't been for three years, we'll drop them." Don't do that. Instead, look at all the people in your database that have not given you a gift for two, three, four, five years or more and treat them as a list. Don't look at them as individuals.

Don't let your executive director arbitrarily say, "If they haven't given us a gift in five years, they're never going to. Let's drop them." Instead, look at all those people as a list and mail to them as a list. If your response rate is lower than it would be for an acquisition mailing, and if your average gift is also lower, and if your cost to acquire a donor is higher than mailing to strangers, then by all means go through that list and start culling people, starting with the people that haven't given you a gift in a donkey's age.

But look at your lapsed donors as a list rather than as individuals. And don't just arbitrarily decide that you're going to drop people if you don't hear from them.

Now, if you send your current donors your newsletter, and if the newsletter is a privilege of being a member of your organization, and if your newsletter is expensive, then obviously you should not send that newsletter to lapsed donors indefinitely if they never give you a penny.

With donors who haven't given for some time, ask them if they still want to receive your newsletter. And send them an appeal letter once a year at Christmas, at the least. But don't drop them altogether if their response rates and average gift are higher than you would achieve by mailing to a list of strangers, because you're still making money from them.

Q. How can we save money with donors who rarely give?

A. One of the easiest ways to boost your revenue in direct mail fundraising is to stop sending every single appeal to every single donor. We looked at that just a minute ago.

In every donor database, you've got donors or members who are either unresponsive or they're less responsive than you'd like them to be. These donors should receive fewer mailings than your most responsive donors. If you reduce the number of letters that you drop in the mail every year, it's going to lower your cost right away. Your printing costs go down, your letter shop costs go down, your postage goes down, and so you'll boost your net revenue as a result.

The most valuable donors you have are the ones that gave recently, give frequently, and give you a lot of money. And your least valuable donors are the ones who have not given recently and give infrequently and don't give you very much money. Segment your database according to those who give often and have given recently and have given you a lot of money, and give them lots of fertilizer. Spend lots of time and energy and money nurturing them, inspiring them, encouraging them to give again.

And those donors who have not given you much money recently and rarely do, don't spend as much money on them. Don't send them as many appeals. The easiest way to save money on them is to stop writing them as often. Don't spend as much time and energy and money and effort on donors who give little.

32

41 Things You Can Mail to Your Donors

Want to learn a lesson in direct mail fundraising from Winston Churchill? He once observed that a fanatic is "someone who can't change his mind and won't change the subject."

A fundraising letter fanatic, of course, is someone who thinks the only thing you can mail a donor is a fundraising letter. But that's just one of more than 40 things you can mail to make friends and raise funds using paper and postage. Here are some more:

1. **Acquisition package**: Designed to attract new donors.
2. **Welcome kit**: An assortment of informational pieces and a cover letter, mailed to first-time donors, welcoming them to your organization and your cause.
3. **Thank-you letter**: The most important letter in direct mail fundraising, and it should never ask for a gift.
4. **Renewal letter**: Designed to persuade last year's donors to renew their support again this year.
5. **Member renewal letter**: Mailed by member-based organizations to members whose membership is about to expire and must be renewed.
6. **Reminder letter**: Mailed a few weeks after your appeal letter, encouraging donors who have not responded to give. Popular at year-end.
7. **Lapsed donor recovery letter**: Mailed to donors who have not given a gift in 12 months or more, inviting them back on the train.
8. **Monthly donor conversion letter**: Mailed to annual donors (those who respond to your annual appeals), inviting them to join

(convert to) your monthly giving program.

9. **Special appeal**: Mailed during the year to raise funds for a special cause, often an emergency, such as a natural disaster.
10. **Year-end appeal**: Letter that capitalizes on the year-end tax advantages and "spirit of the season" of Christmas.
11. **Upgrade letter**: Appeal inviting donors to increase the dollar amount (and sometimes frequency) of their gifts.
12. **Donor club invitation**: Letter inviting high-dollar donors to join a President's Circle or other exclusive donor group.
13. **Legacy gift prospecting letter**: Mailed to a select group in your house file, asking if they are interested in making a planned gift (bequest, charitable remainder trust, and so on).
14. **Special event invitation**: A card or letter inviting donors and potential donors to a golf tournament, banquet, concert or other fundraising event.
15. **Newsletter**: Sent to current donors to inform them of how your organization is using their donations to change the world.
16. **Annual report**: Usually mailed to major donors, loyal donors and donors with influence.
17. **Survey**: Designed to solicit the opinions of donors and prospective donors.
18. **Petition**: Mailed by advocacy organizations (Amnesty International and Mother Against Drunk Driving, for example) to members, inviting them to complete and mail the petitions, usually to a decision-maker in federal government.
19. **Member-get-a-member letter**: Mailed by member-based organizations, inviting members to recruit new members to the organization.
20. **Pledge appeal**: Usually sent during capital campaigns, these appeals ask recipients to pledge a larger-than-normal gift (for the donor, that is) towards the campaign, a pledge that is usually honored by the donor by making a number of gifts over a period of a year or two.

21. **Congratulatory card**: Mailed to donors on the occasion of the donors' wedding anniversary, birthday or other special event.

22. **Testimonial**: Written endorsements from clients or donors or others affected by the work of your organization, usually accompanying an appeal letter.

23. **Plaque**: Sent to faithful or particularly generous donors as a sign of your gratitude for their extraordinary support.

24. **Gift catalog**: Describes through pictures and text the items that donors can buy from your organization to support your work (a goat for a family in India, for example).

25. **Resource catalog**: Describes the books, DVDs and other educational materials that donors can order to educate themselves and others about your cause and the people you help.

26. **Matching gift appeal**: Invites donors to give gifts that, collectively, match a large gift made by another donor.

27. **Newspaper clipping**: Has your charity received favorable press recently? Mail a copy of the article to your donors (with the newspaper's permission).

28. **Quiz**: Do you want to stir the imaginations of your donors, particularly if they are under the age of 12? Mail them a quiz that gets them thinking about a vital subject (climate change, poverty, nuclear war, homelessness, for example).

29. **Factsheet**: Sometimes you need to give your donors statistics and facts and figures, maybe even a history of your organization. Put these into a factsheet.

30. **Special report**: Dealing with a hot and timely topic that will galvanize your constituents.

31. **Calendar**: Special calendar that highlights special events of yours and days during the year that are of interest to you and your donors.

32. **Special event teaser**: Postcards or other short notices that pique the curiosity of your supporters about upcoming events.

33. **Photographs**: Mailed to donors to show the before-and-after

results of their generosity.

34. **Premium**: Return address labels, notepads and other incentives designed to persuade the recipients to donate.

35. **Freemium**: Items enclosed with a direct mail appeal that have no intrinsic value, but help you communicate your appeal in a tangible, memorable way. A hospital, for example, might enclose a facsimile of a patient bracelet once worn by a young cancer survivor.

36. **Involvement device**: Scratch-off cards, checkboxes and other devices that involve the donor in meaningful ways and encourage a donation.

37. **Brochure**: Shows in pictures and words what you cannot discuss in the body of your letter.

38. **Reprint**: Has your CEO just given a speech to the United Nations? Transcribe the speech and mail it to your donors (assuming your CEO is a dynamic speaker, of course!).

39. **Progress report**: Mailed to donors, usually major donors, who have designated their gifts to a particular project, and who need to be kept informed about your progress with their money.

40. **Follow-up note**: Mailed after you've phoned your donor or made a personal visit, usually to thank the donor.

41. **Income tax receipt**: The more of these you have to mail each year, the better, right?

33

A Helpful List of Direct Mail Fundraising List Brokers and Managers

Nothing is more important in direct mail fundraising than who you mail to. A terrific letter mailed to the wrong list of people will flop. I have a client who mailed a donor acquisition package to people who had not supported his organization but had supported another. The response to his appeal was zero.

The reason is simple. He mailed to a terrible list. His organization helps offenders leave prison and integrate back into society. But he mailed his donor acquisition letter to a list of people who support a non- profit organization that tries to throw offenders in prison and keep them there.

With over 75,000 lists currently on the market, choosing one is no simple task. To find a good list you need a good list broker. Since my agency is asked all the time to where to find good list brokers, we have drawn up a list of some of the best list brokers and list managers in North America that specialize to one degree or another in non-profit fundraising lists.

Atlantic List Company, Inc.
Specializes in non-profits. Arlington, VA. www.atlanticlist.com

Cornerstone
Donor database managers and list brokers. Canada's largest.
Toronto, ON. www.cstonecanada.com

Dunhill International List Company, Inc.
Largest compiler of specialized mailing, telemarketing and email lists.
Boca Raton, FL. www.dunhills.com

Mal Dunn Associates, Inc.
Represents mostly businesses, but works with non-profits as well.
Brewster, NY. www.maldunn.com

Mary Elizabeth Granger & Associates, Inc.
List broker and manager. Baltimore, MD. www.maryegranger.com

Millard Group
Works with major fundraising and membership mailers.
Peterborough NH. www.millard.com

Names in the News
List broker and manager for national charitable, environmental, animal protection and cultural organizations.
Oakland, CA. www.namesinthenews.com

RMI Direct Marketing Inc.
List broker and manager. Danbury, CT. www.rmidirect.com

Specialized Fundraising Services, Inc.
List broker and manager exclusively to non-profits.
Spartanburg, SC. www.specializedfundraising.com

True North List Marketing
Represents mostly businesses, but works with non-profits as well. Monroe, CT. www.truenorthlist.com

21st Century Marketing
List broker and manager. One of the largest in North America. Farmingdale, NY. www.21stcm.com

Glossary of Direct Mail Fundraising Terms

Accordion fold: Two or more parallel folds in a letter so it opens like an accordion.

Acquisition mailing: A fundraising package mailed to prospects to acquire them as new members or donors.

Active donor: A donor whose last gift was received within the last 12 months. Some organizations stretch that time period out to 18 or 24 months.

Address accuracy: The percentage of matches that a database attains when compared with a national address database.

Address block: The format in which name and address are printed on top of letters.

Addressed Admail: Canada Post Corporation's category for bulk or third-class postage that applies to large quantities of identical pieces that are prepared for mailing before being delivered to the post office.

Address service requested: A message appearing on mailing envelopes that authorizes the post office to charge the sender a fee for providing a new address (where known) of a donor or member no longer at the address on the mailing piece.

Annual fund: Gifts received by a non-profit organization to support (in whole or in part) yearly budgets and general operations.

Ask: The request or appeal being made in a fundraising letter. Often called "The ask."

Ask string: In a fundraising letter, the sequence of values found on the reply card that lets donors chose the amount they wish to donate, usually expressed in a currency. For example: $25 [ ] $35 [ ] $50 [ ] Other ______

Attrition: Loss of donors because they die, move, lose their job, change their giving priorities or for other reasons can no longer donate.

Attrition rate: The rate at which donors do not renew their gifts, usually expressed as a percentage of active donors.

Average gift: In a direct mail fundraising campaign, the total money received divided by the total number of gifts received.

Back end: All the activities necessary to receive, process and receipt a gift once it has been received.

Back-end premium: A free gift offered to donors in exchange for a donation.

Bangtail: Promotional return envelope featuring a perforated slip of paper beneath the flap. Readers tear off, complete and include this slip in the return envelope.

Bind-in: A promotional reply device or order form that is stitched into the gutter of a print publication, such as a donor newsletter or annual report.

Bingo card: A reply card inserted in a magazine and used by readers to request free samples and literature from organizations who advertised in the issue. Many advertisers are listed on the reply card. Readers circle the advertisers they are interested in (much as bingo players circle winning numbers on their bingo card).

Bleed: In printing, the extension of colour to the edge of the page, accomplished by printing on oversized paper and trimming the excess.

Blow in: A promotional card inserted into a magazine during assembly (which falls onto the floor as you read the magazine).

Bounce: An email message returned to the sender with a notice indicating why the transmission failed (messages commonly bounce because the email address of the addressee is incorrect or is no longer active).

Bounce rate: In email fundraising, the percentage of visitors to a website who leave (bounce away) without getting any deeper into the site. Each page has its own bounce rate.

Broadside: A single sheet of paper, printed on one side or both, folded for mailing or direct distribution, and opening (much as a broadside daily newspaper does) into a single, large advertisement.

Buckslip: Slip of paper the size of a dollar bill, inserted into a direct mail fundraising package, reiterating the main points of the letter, or describing something else, such as planned giving or monthly giving opportunities.

Business Reply Card (BRC): A card included in a mailing to simplify reader response. One side contains a response form that the donor completes, the other side features the return address and pre-paid postage.

Business Reply Envelope (BRE): A self-addressed envelope whose postage is paid for by the organization that prints it.

Caging: The process of recording gift amount, date of gift, donor name and other data from a direct mail fundraising campaign. Taken from the 19th Century post office practice of placing sorted mail into small wire enclosures, called cages.

Call to action: Copy that encourages the reader to respond, and describes how (by mailing in a reply card or phoning a toll-free number, for example).

Call out: A short section of copy, usually rendered in bold or larger typeface, and often set off from the main text, that emphasizes key points about the case for support, benefits of donating, or other key messages.

Carrier: The envelope that contains the letter and other contents of your direct mail message. Also called a *carrier envelope* or *outer envelope*.

Carrier Route Presort: In Canada, mail that is sorted before delivery to Canada Post, arriving at the post office in bundles assigned to the routes that each letter carrier walks, and qualifying the mailer for discounts on postage.

Cheshire labels: Address labels printed on specially prepared paper and mechanically affixed to mailing envelopes one at a time.

Cleaning: The process of correcting or removing names from a mailing list.

Clickthroughs: Readers who have clicked on a tracked link in an HTML email message.

Closed-face envelope: An envelope that does not have a window.

Cluster selection: A list selection technique in which groups of names (clusters) are taken from a list in a series. A cluster selection on an nth name basis, for example, might select the first 10 names out of every 100 names.

Compiled list: Names and addresses that are compiled into a list from directories, newspapers, trade show registrations and other sources, to group prospects who share something in common.

Continuation mailing: Mailing a package to the remaining portion of a mailing list after having tested the package on a smaller portion of that list. See *Rollout.*

Control package: A direct mail package (usually a donor acquisition package) that is the best performing so far, and against which all new packages are tested.

Controlled circulation: Distribution at no charge of a publication (such as a trade journal) to individuals or businesses based on their job title or industry. Readers qualify to receive the publication based on their ability to purchase or influence the purchase of products and services advertised in the publication. (See Paid Circulation.)

Copy: The written portion—the words—of your direct mail fundraising package.

Cost Per Piece: Cost to produce each package (carrier envelope, letter, reply device, reply envelope) in a mailing. Usually includes writing, design, printing, list rental and postage. Calculated by dividing total mailing costs by the number of pieces mailed.

Cost to raise a dollar: Popular measurement used by fundraisers to gauge the cost effectiveness of their fundraising methods. Measures the amount that must be spent to raise one dollar of income. Calculated by dividing fundraising campaign costs by gross income.

CPM (Cost Per Thousand): One of the most common measurements in advertising and direct marketing. Tells you how much you must spend to communicate your sales message to one thousand people. The M in CPM stands for *Mille,* the Roman numeral used to represent 1,000.

Coupon: Slip of paper included in a direct mail fundraising package, which the donor completes and returns to the sender with a donation, usually in a postage-paid business reply envelope. Also called a *reply device.*

Data card: Detailed description of a mailing list, supplied by list brokers and list owners.

Decoy: A unique name inserted into a mailing list so that the list owner can verify that the mailing list is used according to the terms of the list rental agreement. If a non-profit organization mails letters to a rented list more times than it is allowed to, the list owner will know because the decoy names in the list will receive each mailing, and notify the list owner of what is going on.

Donor acknowledgement: The act of responding to gifts from donors, usually with a receipt or thank-you letter.

Donor acquisition cost: The cost of a mailing after gross income has been subtracted, divided by the number of donors acquired, and expressed in dollars and cents per donor acquired.

Donor conversion: The process of encouraging one-time donors (usually acquired through an acquisition mailing) to give again and become regular supporters of the organization.

Donor cultivation: The long-term process of nurturing donors towards higher levels of understanding, commitment and giving.

Donor file: A computer database containing the names, addresses and donation history of a non-profit organization's donors.

Donor renewal: The process of approaching individuals who have given donations before, inviting them to renew their support with another gift.

Donor retention: The process of encouraging donors to remain active and continuing supporters of an organization.

Double Opt-In: The process of requiring subscribers to an email list to confirm their membership before being added to the list. Subscribers opt-in once by subscribing to the list, and opt-in the second time by confirming their subscription.

Drop date: The calendar date when a direct mail campaign is to be delivered to the post office for mailing.

Dupe: Short for duplicate. Identical or almost identical names that appear more than once in a mailing list.

Dupe rate: The amount of names in a mailing list identified as duplicates, expressed as a percentage.

Duplex lasering: Laser printing on the front and back of a letter or promotional piece, usually performed at the lettershop.

Electronic Funds Transfer (EFT): The means by which a donor's bank transfers a donation (usually monthly) from the donor's bank account to the bank account of a non-profit organization that the donor designates.

Exchange: A transaction where two mailers exchange equal quantities of mailing list names.

File: A structured collection of customer records.

Flash count: Report that summarizes the results of a mailing over a given period of time, usually by response rate and average gift.

Frequency: The number of times a donor has given a donation within a given time frame.

Front end: All the activities (writing, designing, printing, mailing) necessary to generate a gift by mail.

Front-End Premium: An item (such as return address labels) offered to a donor in a direct mail package, usually at no charge, to encourage them to make a donation.

Fulfillment rate: The percentage of people who give a donation after pledging to do so, usually following a telephone solicitation that requests pledges instead of immediate cash gifts.

Fundraising ratio: The ratio used to gauge the cost-effectiveness of fundraising campaigns and programs, usually expressed as the ratio of cost to revenue or cost to raise a dollar.

Hand-match insert: The process of hand inserting personalized package elements, such as certificates of appreciation, into closed-face mailing envelopes.

Hard bounce: An email message that permanently fails to reach its intended recipient but instead returns to the sender. Causes include non-existent domains and the recipient being unknown.

Hotline list: The most recent names available on a list, typically names added within the last three months.

House list: A list of names and addresses that a non-profit has compiled from inquiries, donations or acquisition, used to request donations.

Independent Sector: The part of the economy consisting of non-profit organizations. Also called the Non-profit Sector.

Indicia: A unique printed artwork box in the top right corner of an envelope, authorized by the post office, indicating that postage has been paid by the mailer.

Involvement device: An element in a direct mail fundraising package that donors peel off, sign, cut out or handle with their hands in others ways. Involvement devices can boost response, and include surveys, petitions, stamps and stickers.

John Samples: Sample direct mail packages addressed to a fictitious

John Sample of Any Street, Any City, and kept by the mailer as a record of the look and contents of each mailing.

Johnson Box: Copy placed at the top of an appeal letter and surrounded by a box or other graphic element, usually highlighting member benefits or the need, to persuade donors to read on. Named after Frank Johnson, American direct mail pioneer, who invented the device to promote magazine subscriptions in the 1970s.

Key code: A group of letters or numbers (or combination of letters and numbers), colours or other marks, usually placed on donation forms or reply cards, to help mailers measure the effectiveness of their mailing lists, asks, creative, timing and other variables.

Landing page: A web page where people go once they click on an online advertisement or search listing. In online fundraising, the landing page is usually the page where the donor makes a donation, having arrived there by clicking a link in an email appeal letter.

Lapsed donor: A donor who has not sent a gift during the last 12 months, or longer.

Lettershop: A business that addresses, folds, inserts, sorts and applies postage to direct mail fundraising packages, and delivers them to the post office for mailing.

Lifetime value: The long-term value of a donor or member, such as the total revenue received during the time a donor or member is active. Useful when calculating how much to spend to acquire a new donor.

Lift note: Also called a *lift letter*. A second letter included in a fundraising package to reiterate the main points of the letter, or to give other reasons for making a donation. Often signed by a celebrity or person of influence.

List: Also called a mailing list. Names and addresses of individuals who share a common characteristic (such as all being women, or all being people who donate to organizations that protect the environment).

List broker: A specialist who helps a not-for-profit organization rent or borrow a list from a list owner (usually a business or another not-for-profit). Services include research, selection and recommendation of lists.

List compiler: An individual, service bureau or business that assembles mailing lists from directories, government records and other public sources.

List exchange: A transaction in which two organizations swap donor, member or subscriber lists, usually one for one, so that each organization can mail to the other organization's list.

List maintenance: The never-ending process of updating and correcting donor records in a house list.

List manager: The organization or individual, often a list broker, that manages the promotion of a mailing list for rental or exchange.

List owner: The individual or organization that owns the right to rent or lend a mailing list.

List rental: The process of renting a mailing list for a one-time mailing.

List test: A mailing sent to a small, random sampling of a list (perhaps 10,000 names) to determine if mailing to the entire list will be profitable.

Live stamp: An ordinary postage stamp, sometimes affixed to a carrier envelope or reply device to boost response.

Mail-responsive: Term used to describe individuals who are known to respond to direct mail offers or appeals for funds.

Membership renewal: A direct mail package sent to members of a non-profit organization, inviting them to renew their membership by paying their annual dues.

Merge dupes: Donors, members or subscribers whose names are found on two or more lists of prospective donors.

Merge/purge: The act of combining (merging) two or more lists into one list while removing (purging) duplicate names.

Multi-Donors: Donors, members or subscribers whose names are found on two or more lists of prospective donors.

Negative option: A direct mail buying option in which the donor agrees to receive and pay for products or services at regular intervals (such as receiving a book a month) unless the donor tells the not-for-profit in advance not to ship the product. (See Positive Option, below).

Nixie: A mailing piece returned to the sender by the post office because of an incorrect or undeliverable name or address.

Nth name: The method of testing the pulling power of a list by selecting and mailing to a representative sampling of the list. The list owner or broker selects every 5th name, 20th name or other variable (Nth name) that provides a valid representation.

Open rate: Number of emails opened by recipients, expressed as a percentage of total emails sent.

Overline: The headline in a letter, usually placed on a line over the salutation.

Offer: In traditional direct mail, the incentive that you give prospects to motivate them to respond to your mailing, either by placing an order or by taking the next step in the sales process.

One-time usage: The stipulation in a list rental agreement that the advertiser will mail to the names on the list once only. The stipulation in a list rental agreement that the advertiser will mail to the names on the list once only.

Package: Everything contained in a direct mail fundraising appeal, such as the carrier envelope, letter, insert, reply device, return envelope and premium.

Package test: Test in which two or more direct mail packages are mailed to statistically equivalent groups of individuals from the same list or lists to determine which package performs best (often measured in response rate and average gift).

Package insert: Any promotional piece included in a product shipment. It may be for refills and replacements from the same company, or for products and services from other companies.

Paid circulation: Distribution of a magazine, newsletter or other publication to individuals or organizations who have paid for a subscription. (See Controlled Circulation.)

Pass along: The readership of a newspaper, magazine or direct mail letter other than the addressee. In publishing, the pass along readership is always higher than the readership.

Peel-off label: A self-adhesive label enclosed in a mailing package, intended to be removed and attached to an order card.

Personalization: The process of customizing each package in a mailing so that each package contains information that is unique and personal for each recipient. Areas of personalization include name and address, salutation, and date and amount of last gift.

Piggy back: An offer that accompanies another offer, free of charge.

Pledge card: A printed notice mailed to individuals who pledge to donate to an organization, usually in response to a telephone appeal.

Poly bag: Transparent polyethylene (plastic) bag used instead of envelopes for mailing.

Positive option: A method of selling products and services using the same technique as Negative Option (see above) but requiring the customer to place an order each time.

Postage-paid envelope: A self-addressed envelope whose postage is paid for by the organization that prints it. Also called a Business Reply Envelope, or BRE.

Premium: An item offered to a donor, usually at no charge, to encourage them to make a donation. Premiums that are included in the mail package are called front-end premiums. Premiums that the donor must request are called back-end premiums.

Presort: Discount offered by post office to mailers who transport letters directly to the post office sorted in the order that they will be delivered by the letter carrier (usually sorted by postal code or zip code). Also called Letter Carrier Presort.

Pressure-Sensitive Labels: Mailing labels that do not require moistening before being affixed to an envelope. Also called peel-off or peel-and-stick labels.

Prospect: A person on a list who is considered to be a potential donor but who has not made a donation yet.

Prospect mailing: A direct mail appeal sent to prospective donors or members. Also called an acquisition mailing.

Purge: To remove duplicates or unwanted names from a mailing list.

Recency: The latest donation or activity recorded for an individual.

RFM: Recency, Frequency, Monetary Value, a formula used by direct mailers to calculate the income potential of names on a mailing list.

Renewal mailing: A direct mail fundraising package mailed to donors or members who have supported the organization's work, inviting the donor or member to renew support with a donation.

Reply card: A card included in a mailing, which the donor completes and returns to the sender in response to the ask. Often postage-paid.

Response count: The number of responses received from a mailing, expressed as a total number rather than a percentage.

Response device: The coupon, order form or reply card that a donor completes and returns to the sender to complete a donation.

Response rate: The number of responses received from a mailing, expressed as a percentage of the total number mailed.

Return Postage Guaranteed: An endorsement printed on the face of envelopes stating the sender will pay the post office to return undeliverable standard (third-class) bulk mail.

Rollout: Mailing a package to the remaining portion of a mailing list after having tested the package on a smaller portion of that list. See *Continuation mailing.*

Salutation: The way in which the donor is addressed at the start of a letter ("Dear Tom" or "Dear Friend," for example).

Seeding lists: The practice of adding (seeding) unique names to a mailing list so that the list owner can verify that the list is used according to the terms of the list rental agreement. If a non-profit organization mails letters to a rented list more times than it is allowed to, the list owner will know because the seeded names in the list will receive each mailing, and notify the list owner of what is going on. Also called "salting lists."

Segmentation: The practice of dividing mailing lists into segments (such as major donors, monthly donors, lapsed members) so that each segment receives a customized appeal letter.

Self mailer: A direct mail piece that mails without an envelope.

Sorting: Process of arranging envelopes in zip code or postal code order before mailing to improve delivery and, for large mailings, reduce postage costs.

Source code: A group of letters or numbers (or combination of letters and numbers), usually placed on donation forms or reply cards, and stored afterwards in donor database records, to help mailers determine the list or segment of a list from which the donor's name and address originated. Also called a key code.

Source code report: An analysis of source keys (key codes indicating the source of a list) that shows the profitability of each list used in a donor acquisition mailing.

Special appeal: A direct mail fundraising package, mailed to existing donors or members, inviting them to support a particular program, project or fund. Often mailed several times a year.

Split test: A test in which a direct marketer takes two or more samples from a list, each sample considered to be representative of the entire list, and mails a different package to each sample to test the effectiveness of each package.

Statement stuffer: A slip of paper, printed on one or both sides, and inserted into the envelope that contains a customer's bank statement. Also called a *bill stuffer*.

Swatching: Attaching samples of fabric (swatches) or material to a printed piece.

Sustainer Program: A program through which supporters of a non-profit organization give a regular donation automatically, usually by direct withdrawal from their bank account or credit card once a month. Also called a Monthly Giving Program.

Tap test: The process of tapping the ends and the top and bottom of a stuffed, sealed window envelope to make sure the name and address appear through the window.

Teaser: A phrase, or an image, or a phrase and an image, on a carrier envelope that arouses curiosity and motivates the recipient to open the envelope. Also called an *envelope teaser*.

Test mailing: The first appeal that a non-profit organization mails to potential donors, to discover if direct mail is a cost-effective way for the organization to acquire donors and raise funds.

Throwaway: A promotional piece, usually printed on inexpensive stock, intended for widespread, free distribution to houses, businesses or to passersby.

Tip On: An item, such as a promotional piece or reply card, glued to a printed piece.

Token: A device that involves the reader in some way, often consisting of a perforated label that the reader removes from a sheet and sticks to a designated place on the order card, signifying a desire to buy.

Unique names: The names and addresses that remain after two or more mailing lists are merged and then purged of duplicate names and invalid addresses.

Universe: Total number of individuals that might be included in a mailing list, or all those who meet a set of specifications.

Upgrade: The process of persuading donors to increase the size or frequency of their gifts.

Window envelope: An envelope with a die cut hole on the face, covered with clear acetate, that reveals the mailing address, return address or special messages written on the enclosed materials.

Index

Acquisition, eight steps for acquiring donors 44
develop your case for support 44
clone your best donors 45
find the names of potential donors 47
create a package 52
test the package against your lists 53
rollout 56
follow up with new donors 56
measure your results 58

Acquisition, general tips
avoid donors who never renew 115
acquisition letters 196
how donor acquisition mailings differ from donor renewal mailings 66
how it integrates with your annual campaign 63
mistakes to avoid 61
why donor acquisition letters are longer 107

Acquisition, how direct mail donor acquisition works 37
loses money initially 37
needs a popular cause to succeed 39
needs other mailings to succeed 40
needs volume to succeed 40

Acquisition packages, anatomy of one 70
brochure 89
letter 75
outer envelope 72
reply device 97
reply envelope 105
survey 103

Attrition, donor
easy ways to reduce donor attrition rates 63
improve donor tenure and you'll boost revenue 226

Calendar
direct mail fundraising program repeat every 12 months 14
direct mail fundraising programs run for 12 months 12

how many times a year should I mail my donors? 228

Case for support
direct mail works by building broad base of support 16

Costs
how can we save money with donors who rarely give? 229

Goals of direct mail fundraising
acquire new donors each year 6
renew your donors each year 7
upgrade your donors 9

Individual donors
most start with a small gift 5
source of 80% of income 4

Involvement, donor
essential to donor renewal 132

Lapsed donors
easy ways to reduce donor attrition rates 63
lapsed donor recovery letters 205
save money on acquisition mailings through testing 64
when should we drop people them from our mailing list? 228
why donors stop responding to direct mail appeals 62

Lists
build your list three ways 218
list brokers 219
list brokers, how they help your appeal 220
list of list brokers and managers 235
list rental 218
typical list rental transaction 220

Major donor letters
part of every direct mail program 204

Newsletters, donor
boost donor loyalty 136
common mistakes to avoid 137
essential to donor renewal 133
vital to your program 198

Planning
ask early, ask of ten, ask the right way 190
forty-one things you can mail to your donors 231
how to plan a typical mailing 208
planning your year 188
work backwards from your drop date 208

Renewal, donor
avoid donors who never renew 115
before you ask again , W-I-N them 129
four goals of renewal letters 143
how donor acquisition differs from donor renewal 66
how to craft fundraising letters that renew donors 141
how to renew your donors with direct mail 110
mail a series of renewal appeals 145
renewal letters 201
spend time and money on your most promising donors 147
think friends, not funds 146
think recency, frequency and monetary value 147
three things donors demand before they give again 117
treat donor groups differently 147
treat high, medium and low donors differently 147
why you must renew your donors 112

Response rates
rates to expect in direct mail fundraising 185

Response, why people respond to direct mail appeals
achieve immortality 33
achieve status 32
altruism 32
anger 32
fear 34
find meaning in life 31
guilt 34
idealism 32
join others in a worthy cause 32
meet an immediate need 31
receive a personal benefit 31
religious reasons 33
save on taxes 33
solve a problem 33

Results, tracking
attrition rate 179
average cost per gift 175
average gift 174
cost per piece 170
cost per thousand 170
cost to acquire a donor 177
cost to raise a dollar 176
donor loyalty 181
gross income 173
net income per thousand pieces 178
net income 174
renewal rate 178
response count 171
response rate 172
return on investment 175

Revenue
improve donor tenure and you'll boost revenue 226

Segmentation
increase average gift size by segmenting your file 224
spend time and money on your most promising donors 147
think recency, frequency and monetary value 147
treat donor groups differently 147
treat high, medium and low donors differently 147

Special appeals
part of every direct mail program 207

Success, what you need for
case for support with broad appeal 18
commitment that lasts for decades 28
commitment to brand differentiation 26
commitment to donor-centered fundraising 23
commitment to segmentation 27
concentration on your best donors 216
dedicated fundraising software 20
dedicated team 22
frequency and volume 27
new donors you can reach cost-effectively 19
obsession with your data 21

Testing, acquisition packages 156
acquire as many donors as possible 156
choose lists to test 158
create your test package 157
discover if direct mail is cost for your organization 157
discover which acquisition package performs best 157
how to budget for a typical mailing 160
recover your costs 157
test as many lists as possible 156

Testing, general
acquire as many donors as possible 156
acquisition, testing reveals which package performs best 157
budget, how to budget for a typical mailing 160
data never lies (but it misleads if you let it) 152
direct mail characterized by incremental improvements 15
discover if direct mail is cost effective for your organization 157
four tests to see if DM donor acquisition is right for you 41
lists, choose lists to test 158
lists, test as many as possible 156
mistakes to avoid 169
recover your costs 157
save money on acquisition mailings through testing 64
test package, creating 157
testing, tracking and analyzing with confidence 170

Testing, rules for
acquire loyal donors in greatest numbers at lowest cost 166
don't let large gifts skew your results 166
if starting out, acquire as many donors as possible 166
make your test large enough to be significant 165
test one thing at a time 165
test things that are significant 165
test things you can control 165

Testing, what to test
every time you mail 166
involvement devices 167
length of your letters 168
new packages 168
outer envelopes 168
personalization 168
premiums, front and back end 167

prospect lists 167
size of the initial gift in your ask string 167

Thank-you letters, cards and notes 118
anatomy of an effective thank-you letter 126
four reasons you must mail thank-you letters, cards and notes 118
thank your donors using the four P's 120

Timing
how many times a year should I mail my donors? 228

Upgrading donors
how to upgrade your donors over time 222
increase your average gift by segmenting your file 224

Welcome kits 129

What should you mail?
acquisition letters 196
newsletters 198
renewal letters 201
major donor letters 204
lapsed donor recovery letters 205
special appeals 207

About the author

Alan Sharpe didn't discover that he wanted to write fundraising letters for a living until he had first fought in the Falklands War, travelled with the circus, lived in a snowhole, taught children with disabilities how to downhill ski and lived in Jane Fonda's old house in Paris.

Today, Alan is a direct mail fundraising copywriter, consultant and coach. He helps non-profit organizations worldwide to raise funds, build relationships and retain loyal donors using cost-effective, compelling, creative fundraising letters.

As a seminar leader and speaker, Alan coaches executive directors and directors of development to craft engaging, warm appeal letters that win the hearts and minds of their donors. Alan's popular email newsletter, "Direct Mail Fundraising Today," is read weekly by professional fundraisers worldwide. Alan is also a contributing editor to *Canadian FundRaiser*.

Alan is the author of *Breakthrough Fundraising Letters* and 25 handbooks on direct mail fundraising.

Alan served as Director of Development and Communications for two international non-profits, where he was responsible for strategic planning, annual direct mail fundraising campaigns, major giving, planned giving, major events, publicity and other enjoyable headaches. He lives and works in the other London (the one in Ontario, Canada).

www.raisersharpe.com

Subscribe to *Direct Mail Fundraising Today*

Sign up for the only weekly email newsletter that covers nothing but the art and science of raising money through the mail. Each Friday you receive a short, practical, free tip on using direct mail fundraising to raise funds, build relationships and retain loyal donors.

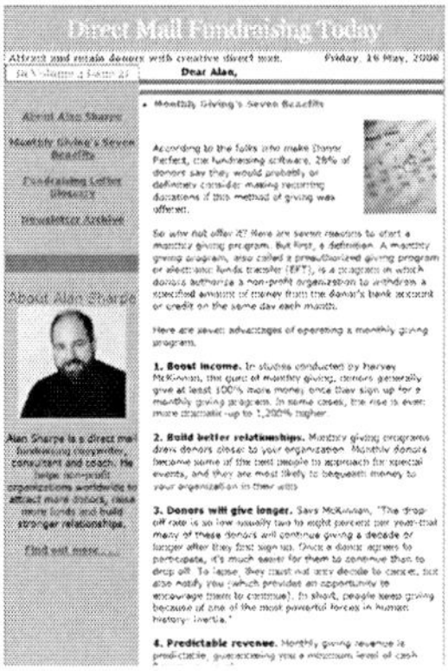

Visit www.raisersharpe.com